Wild Therapy

Undomesticating inner and outer worlds

Nick Totton

PCCS BOOKS
Ross-on-Wye

PCCS BOOKS
2 Cropper Row
Alton Road
Ross-on-Wye
HR9 5LA
UK
Tel +44 (0)1989 763900
www.pccs-books.co.uk

First published 2011

Wild Therapy: Undomesticating inner and outer worlds

ISBN 978-1-906254-36-0

Cover artwork: *Spiderwoman* (acrylic) by Hélène Fletcher, www.ecopsych.org.uk
Cover design in the UK by Old Dog Graphics
Typeset in the UK by The Old Dog's Missus in 'Univers'
Printed in the UK by ImprintDigital, Exeter

Contents

For Spider, Bear and all the Others;
and in memory of Alison Tyas

ACKNOWLEDGEMENTS

As well as sources cited in the text, some portions of this book have appeared in earlier and often rather different versions in the following journals and at the following events: 'Can psychotherapy help make a better future?' in *Psychotherapy and Politics International, 3*(2), 2005. 'Wild at heart: Another side of ecopsychology' in *Therapy Today*, December 2005. 'Living on Earth' in *Self and Society, 35*(5), 2007, and previously as a keynote speech at the Association for Humanistic Psychology Gathering, 2007. Keynote talks at the European Transpersonal Association Conference in Canterbury, 2008, and at the International Adventure Therapy Association Conference in Edinburgh, 2009. 'Wild Therapy': talk given at the 'Confer' event *The Big Idea* on March 5th 2010. Editorial in *Psychotherapy and Politics International, 8*(2), 2010. 'Boundaries and boundlessness' in *Therapy Today*, October 2010. My thanks to all the editors and organisers involved, and to any others I may have missed, for giving me these opportunities to develop my ideas.

Introduction

> Talk of mysteries! – Think of our life in nature, – daily to be shown matter, to come in contact with it, – rocks, trees, wind on our cheeks! The solid earth! the actual world! the common sense! Contact! Contact! Who are we? where are we?
>
> (Thoreau, 1864)

Therapy is by nature wild; but a lot of it at the moment is rather tame. This book is intended to help shift the balance.

'Wild Therapy' is a way of naming the intersection point of several trends in psychotherapy and counselling. Most crucially, it is a response to how human connectedness to the other-than-human and more-than-human, to all the beings with whom we share this universe, has been largely severed, with the result that we no longer take care of the world in which and through which we live, and which is increasingly damaged and destroyed. As Kim Stanley Robinson writes, 'The world is not a machine we can use and then replace; it is our extended body. If we try to cut it away then we will die' (Robinson, 1994: 10).

Most therapy takes place in an imaginary world where none of this is happening: a world where politicians can boast that growth is their first priority, where flying to Australia is simply a splendid adventure not (also) an insult to the earth's atmosphere, where animals and plants and rivers and mountains exist not for themselves but to hold *our* projections and serve *our* material and psychological needs, where we can plan for and imagine a future in which consumption continues to grow indefinitely rather than reaching the limit point of the planet's carrying capacity. This is very strange. How and why has therapy bought into the bubble of unreality in which most human activity now takes place?

Well, therapists are of course human, and it is very frightening for any of us to face the reality of the collapsing biosphere; it fills us with grief and anger and despair, and we don't know whether we could function in the everyday world if we fully admitted it. Ecopsychology and ecotherapy (e.g. Roszak et al, 1996; Fisher, 2002; Buzzell & Chalquist, 2009) are the parts of the therapeutic field which address these issues, including ways in which we may be able to face our despair and other feelings about environmental catastrophe; and this is one of the trends I mentioned above which contributes to Wild Therapy.

But facing unpopular realities is also frightening because it excludes us from the social consensus: it puts us in the position of the crazy person, the freak, the unpopular and misunderstood. And I think there is a struggle going on for the soul of psychotherapy and counselling, between our wish for status and social normality on the one hand, and on the other hand our identification – which is part of our historical roots, our therapeutic family story – with the margins, the unconscious, the path less travelled. We can treat this marginality as belonging to our clients, and try to adjust them to the demands of society. Or we can recognise that *we too are clients*, and look for ways to support our own marginal perceptions and understandings.

CONTEXTS

One of the contexts for Wild Therapy is the history of psychotherapy and counselling, and their roots in radical social theory and practice (Totton, 2000; see Chapter 1, below). Another context is the history of humanity, and the fork in the road which confronted us during the Neolithic era when we began to farm and to build cities (Chapter 5, below). And thirdly, Wild Therapy links very directly with the current battle over the regulation of our field (e.g. Postle, 2007), which raises big questions of what therapy is and should be, what values inform it and who should control its practice.

These three contexts are linked by the theme of control and its impossibility. In the move from hunter-gatherer society to agriculture, human beings tried to gain control over the world, over each other, and over the other-than-human and more-than-human. In doing this we split ourselves off from the world – it became, in fact, our 'environment', rather than the whole of which we are an integral part. In Ursula Le Guin's resonant phrase, we learnt to live 'outside the world' (Le Guin, 1988: 153). By trying to control the world we have made it *other*, and therefore dangerous and frightening. The more we seek control, the closer we seem to get to it, the further our goal recedes.

Therapy has generally stood against the dominant cultural message, 'Be in control of yourself and your environment': it has tried to help people tolerate the anxiety of not being in control – of our feelings, our thoughts, our body, our future. There has always been a struggle over this issue, however: new forms of therapy constantly arise which claim 'You can be in control after all'. And now the dominant social structure has started saying that therapy itself must be controlled, brought within the field of surveillance, monitoring, regulation, safety. As the world becomes increasingly frightening, it becomes increasingly necessary to pretend that security can be achieved, through ever-greater monitoring, surveillance and censorship – and this process in turn ratchets up our fear and insecurity. This is the path our society seems to be taking; but equally, of course, it is an internal psychological process, embodying exactly the anxieties which therapy arose to address.

Although the path of control is becoming increasingly emphasised in society, it has been with us since the Neolithic development of domestication. This was not just about humans domesticating other species; we also and above all domesticated *ourselves.* Hence the subtitle of this book, 'Undomesticating Inner and Outer Worlds'. How far can we reasonably hope to go in moving away from domestication, given that the sustainable forager population of the earth in the Palaeolithic era was perhaps around one person per square mile (McClellan & Dorn, 2006: 12), compared with an average of nearly 130 per square mile today?

In a literal sense, we clearly cannot go very far at all. A reduction of humanity to Palaeolithic population levels – which a few people are desperate enough to hope for – will only happen through catastrophe, and only in this way could surviving humans live wild in the literal sense. In what follows, though, I want to explore the possibility of developing a wildness which is less literal, but perhaps none the less real and important: a reconnection with what I will describe as 'Wild Mind', which is necessarily at the same time a reconnection with the world and with the other beings which inhabit it – and this will involve living, as well as thinking and feeling, in very different ways. Wild Mind refers to a state of awareness in which humans will not *want* or be prepared to damage the world for our own short-term comfort and convenience.

A shift of consciousness and practice like this is perhaps only slightly less hard to imagine than a return to hunter-gatherer lifestyle. However, it is necessary. Without it, a literal return to hunter-gatherer life (and population levels) may be the *best* we can hope for. I believe that psychotherapy and counselling, which I will usually refer to together as simply 'therapy', have a potentially important role to play in promoting and facilitating Wild Mind, or ecological consciousness, and this is what the book is about. In one sense, I am offering therapy a new, or renewed, set of metaphors around wildness and domestication; and metaphor can be a powerful engine for therapeutic change (Cox & Theilgard, 1987). But these metaphors are powerful because they reflect a reality beyond therapy, and I believe that therapy needs to respond to that reality while it still can. When psychoanalysts were considering in the 1980s whether they could ethically take a stance against nuclear weapons, it was pointed out that, without civilisation, there would be no psychoanalysis. We are in a similar situation today as regards environmental crisis.

'Who are we? where are we?' asks Thoreau in the epigraph to this Introduction; and in many ways we have to come up with some sort of response to these questions in order to address the more specific question posed above. The best response I can find is that we are creatures – so far as we know, uniquely on this planet – who ask such questions: creatures who experience the astonishment Thoreau articulates at finding ourselves 'in nature, – daily to be shown matter, to come in contact with it, – rocks, trees, wind on our cheeks! The solid earth! the actual world! the common sense!' This response-ability both enables and requires us to act consciously in support and defence of wildness, inner and outer; in which, as Thoreau also famously states, 'is the preservation of the world' (Thoreau, 1862: para 18).

THIS BOOK

Although I mean everything I say in what follows, there is of course more than one way to 'mean' things; and I have made frequent use of what I want to call the Trickster mode of discourse (following Samuels, 1993: 81–8). The Trickster appears in many cultures, but I am thinking particularly of the native North American figure of Coyote. Tricksters use paradox and absurdity to undermine dualism by turning it against itself. Of course it is easy to use the Trickster as a cover for intellectual laziness, airily dismissing criticism as a failure to get the joke; but when I use dualistic pairs like 'true/false self', 'conscious/unconscious', or indeed 'wild/domesticated', it is not because I haven't noticed that I am doing so, but because turning dualism against dualism is often the best way forward. To a degree, my whole use of scientific research also has a Tricksterish, cherry-picking edge to it; and at times I accept without demur models like attachment theory, about which I have many reservations, in order to press on with my main argument.

I frequently use the terms 'other-than-human' and 'more-than-human'. These terms, which may seem awkward at first sight, are increasingly widely used as a way of recognising and constantly reminding ourselves that we as humans are not 'higher' or more central than other species, and have no right to define them reactively as 'nonhuman' or 'animal': we ourselves are animal, and forgetting that fact is part of our problem (see Chapter 7). I first encountered 'more-than-human' in David Abram's book *The Spell of the Sensuous* (Abram,

1997): I use it to refer to the world as a complex of ecosystems, towards which the appropriate response is love and awe.

In his book *The Origins of Agriculture*, to which I will refer several times, Graeme Barker writes of hunter-gatherer ('forager') culture:

> Land needed for living is appropriated not by fences and boundaries, in the way of farmers, but by moving through it along paths. Thus a forager's territory is something to be *related to* and *associated with*, not *owned*, and tracks and paths are symbolic of the process of life itself.
>
> (Barker, 2006: 58–9, original italics)

This is the methodology of this book, in at least two ways. Firstly, it roams around freely in a large space covering many fields of knowledge and practice, rather than following a straight line of argumentation. Some of this space I know pretty well, some less well; some areas of it I have studied only for the purposes of writing the book, and it is not unlikely that I have made mistakes and misinterpretations. I apologise for these, but not unduly – I think that it is worth that risk to try to synthesise material from many specialist fields; besides which, 'misunderstandings' from outside a specialisation can sometimes actually be useful to the specialist. Because of this wandering path, however, it may not be obvious at every point what the current subject has to do with therapy; but I hope it will become apparent by the end of the journey. Clearly many other paths could be taken through this space, with many different points of arrival.

The second way that Barker's statement is relevant is that I don't assert *ownership* of what I am saying here, but instead seek to *relate and associate with it*. I see the book as a chorus of voices, past and present, all speaking to the same themes and issues, each in their own way. Hence I have included many quotations: not from the academic motivation of justifying everything I assert, but more because I don't want to pretend to reinvent the wheel, or to paraphrase inadequately what has already been expressed superbly. I have drawn on poetry and literature as well as academic material; especially useful have been writers of visionary fiction like Ursula Le Guin, Doris Lessing, and Kim Stanley Robinson. They provide a striking contrast to the dissociated mainstream of contemporary science fiction, where one fashionable theme (e.g. Stross, 2006) is the demolition of the entire solar system in order to power virtual realities for disembodied human consciousness to inhabit.

In particular I want to acknowledge the crucial role which Mary-Jayne Rust has played in the creation of this book. Originally, we planned to write it together. In the end, this was not possible; but by the point when this became clear, Mary-Jayne's thinking and feeling had become so deeply embedded in the text (especially in the first three chapters) that there was no possibility of fully identifying it, and no desire on my part to remove it. So far as I can I have acknowledged her specific contributions or turned them into direct quotations; but she has given much more than that to the project – including finding several of the authors I have quoted – and I am deeply grateful. She is of course in no way responsible for the final book and its eccentricities.

I am most grateful to the School of Health at the University of Leeds, and later the School of Health in Social Science at the University of Edinburgh, for giving me access to library resources. I also want to thank all the other people who have contributed to my thinking through conversations and interactions and through sharing material; in particular, the other members besides Mary-Jayne of my ecopsychology peer group, Zita Cox, Tania Dolley, Adrian Harris, Martin Jordan, Paul Maiteny, Viola Sampson, and Sandra White; Allison Priestman; my father, Michael Totton; and, above all, Hélène Fletcher (who first introduced me to ecopsychology). I also want to thank Hélène Fletcher, Kamalamani, David Key, Margaret Kerr, Paul Maiteny, Allison Priestman, Andrew Samuels, Viola Sampson and Michael Soth for reading and commenting on some or all of the book in draft form; errors remaining are of course my responsibility, not theirs. Thanks also to Hélène Fletcher for the cover illustration; to my copy-editor Sandy Green for her commitment, accuracy and enthusiasm; and to Maggie and Pete at PCCS Books for agreeing to take on this rather awkwardly interdisciplinary work.

As well as the acknowledgements above, and the dedications preceding the book, I want to acknowledge the presence of my indirect ancestor, Anthony Knyvett (Hitchcock, 1996, found by my sister Julia Pither). Anthony, whose surname is my middle name, sailed with Thomas Cavendish in 1591 on what was intended to be a voyage to the Far East. After a series of setbacks to the expedition, he was put ashore along with other sick members of the crew on the coast of Brazil, where they were attacked by Portuguese. Most of his comrades were killed, but Anthony survived by claiming (perhaps truthfully) to be Catholic, and was enslaved by the Portuguese.

There followed a series of almost unbelievable adventures, including a period of some months during which he lived with an indigenous tribe called the Tamoio, was appointed their war leader, and led them in a disastrous campaign against the Portuguese. I have recently discovered that in 2007 a disused Museum of Indians in Rio de Janeiro was occupied by twenty indigenous Indian members of the 'Tamoio Movement', named after this the earliest resistance to the colonisation of Brazil (Frayssinet, 2007). Recaptured, Anthony escaped to Portuguese West Africa, was recaptured again, ended up in Portugal, and after twelve years was able to return to England where he eventually became a Teller of the Royal Mint. As it survives in garbled form, and as it unfolds in my imagination, my ancestor's story encapsulates many of the tensions and conflicts between wildness and domestication which are the subject of this book.

1

Wild Roots

> In the course of the millennia, we have succeeded not only in conquering the wild nature all around us, but in subduing our own wildness, at least temporarily and up to a point.
> (Jung, 1938/1969: para 87)

In this chapter I am going to talk about the sources of what I am calling 'wild therapy' in psychotherapeutic tradition, tracing it from Freud and Jung through to contemporary ecotherapy and ecopsychology, and pointing out the struggle and ambivalence that often develop around this theme. First, though, we need to establish some basic orientations about the multiple meanings of 'wild' and the role which it plays in relation to other terms and concepts.

THE ECOLOGY OF LANGUAGE

> 'Nature,' as Raymond Williams has remarked, is one of the most complex words in the language. Yet, as with many other problematic terms, its complexity is concealed by the ease and regularity with which we put it to use in a wide variety of contexts. It is at once both very familiar and extremely elusive: an idea which we employ with such ease and regularity that it seems as though we ourselves are privileged with some 'natural' access to its intelligibility; but also an idea which most of us know, in some sense, to be so various and comprehensive in its use as to defy our powers of definition.
> (Soper, 1995: 1)

What Kate Soper and Raymond Williams say about 'nature' is almost equally the case about 'wild'. Powerful words have power through their complexity, which is to say, through their links with other words, their function as nodal points in a complex network of language, a web of subtle and shifting contrasts and affinities which gives rise to meaning as an emergent property. 'Wild' is such a word, and as we shall see, this distinction between the thing-on-its-own and the web-of-relationships is a crucial part of understanding wildness. An important feature of complexity is the way in which patterns are mirrored and repeated on different nested levels, and what I have just written is an example of this – the method of enquiry into wildness matches a key feature of wildness itself, that it is a network of relationships rather than an ensemble of distinct units.

For example, 'wild' can be opposed to 'tame', each dependent on the other for its sense, so that 'wild/tame' is a sort of unit of meaning constellated around the role of domestication in organising human perception and disposition of the world. But there are several other complementary polarities (Benjamin, 1998; see also Wilden, 1987a, b) which help to constitute the meaning-field of 'wild': for example, 'wild/civilised', 'wild/cultivated', 'wild/peaceful', 'wild/restrained' – all related, but all importantly different. Among the thirty-six different senses which the OED lists for the adjective 'wild', it begins by stressing the relationship to 'natural', 'in a state of nature', moves on to a number of meanings which imply inferiority to human cultivation and civilisation, and thence to ideas of an ambiguous freedom from constraint, seen sometimes as positive and sometimes as negative. Further senses have an increasing emphasis on energy, passion – but then also confusion, distraction, abandonment. 'Wild', the dictionary tells us, can be used positively by the cultured as a signifier of refreshing artlessness; but in other milieux or at other times it can represent savagery and crudity. Finally, 'wild' can indicate a freedom from control that goes to the extent of randomness, the 'wild card' whose meaning is arbitrary, and whose arrival defeats all assumptions.

This whole range of meanings is significant in what follows. But to call it simply a 'range' is to adopt a metaphor of domestication, 'a row, line or series of things' as the Oxford English Dictionary puts it, which exists only under human discipline or interpretation; alternatively, a grazing area ('home on the range'), or the distribution area of one particular species. The notion that an area can belong to one species alone is of course false: in 'a state of nature', a given area is an *ecosystem*, a web of species existing in dynamic relationship with each other. Every niche in that ecosystem must be occupied for the whole to function with full richness and complexity. The grazing range is a monoculture imposed by humans, who tend to shorten and simplify every food chain by eliminating competitors (De Landa, 2000: 108, 153; Simmons, 1979: 192–3): the complex, multiply connected 'food web' of a full ecology is transformed into a 'food pyramid' where every path leads to human mouths.

> The main characteristic of an urban ecosystem is its homogeneity: human beings shorten all food chains in the web, eliminate most intermediaries and focus all biomass flows on themselves. Whenever an outside species tries to insert itself into one of these chains, to start the process of complexification again, it is ruthlessly expunged as a 'weed'. ... Together, humans and their 'extended family of domesticates' ... transformed a heterogeneous meshwork of species (a temperate forest) into a homogeneous hierarchy, since all biomass now flowed towards a single point at the top. In a sense, a complex food web was replaced by a simplified food pyramid.
> (De Landa, 2000: 108)

This is not what a 'food pyramid' technically means to ecologists, where the term refers to the decreasing number of individuals at each level of consumption, with large predators having the smallest populations. For humans, in fact, the opposite applies; in this sense we are operating a 'food mushroom' rather than a pyramid, using the stored solar energy of fossil fuel (Paul Maiteny, personal communication). But what is pyramidal about this situation is the decreasing number of *species* at each level, the simplified flow towards humanity at the apex. The more an environment tends to simplicity, the more it tends to end up, literally, as dust on the wind – as happened in the Oklahoma Dustbowl, or happens in the Amazon jungle when it is cleared for cattle leaving a thin unstable soil.

This all relates to a more modern sense of 'wild' which has not yet made it into the dictionary, a sense which will be crucial to what follows: wild as *complex*. For previous eras, 'wild' often signified something simple, elemental, refreshingly straightforward compared with the subtleties of civilisation. To our contemporary sensibility, now that wilderness is profoundly scarce, 'wild' is more likely to signify the irreplaceable richness and depth of the climax forest, threatened by the crude slash of the bulldozers and the geometric grid of cities. A garden is *visually* more ordered and complex than wild land; but wild land – as I will try to show in Chapters 2 and 3 – has far greater depth of organisation and complex order than a garden.

Yet despite this developing sense of complexity, it has been confirmed for me in telling people about this book that 'wild' still carries for most a strong suggestion of danger, ranging from exotic excitement – 'walk on the wild side' – to something crude, brutal and out of control. The tension of these two significations is barely contained in David Lynch's film *Wild at Heart* (1990), a film about passion and its violent consequences. To let either gardens or feelings 'run wild' is seldom understood as unambiguously positive. I suggest that there is both a fear and a longing contained within the idea of 'running wild'.

THE LIST

Wildness and its various opposites, in fact, form a key component in a system of oppositions which structures our thinking at a very deep level. We can call these oppositions 'The List', because they can be most simply portrayed as a very long list of matched binary oppositions (Totton, 1998: 25–7). It is arguable though not certain that the starting point, the seed, for the whole list is a binary opposition between male and female. What then happens is that male|female is matched up with light|dark, with sky|earth, with culture|nature, and so on indefinitely – and crucially, each pair is seen as parallel with all the rest, '*a* is to *b* as *x* is to *y*'; so that 'male, light, sky, culture' make part of one set, and 'female, dark, earth, nature' make part of an opposing set. And, of course, the List is essentially patriarchal, with the first set privileged over and valued above the second.

male|female
light|dark
sky|earth
culture|nature

Actually these paired oppositions are of many different kinds, and only in appearance are the different kinds parallel to each other, let alone equivalent. For example, while 'sky|earth' are paired opposites with nothing in between them, nothing that is 'a bit sky and a bit earth', 'light|dark' form a continuum, with infinite gradations of 'more dark', 'more light'. 'Nature' and 'culture', however, are part of a nested hierarchy of concepts – culture is one *part* or *aspect* of nature. We can see that the destruction of nature would entail the destruction of culture, but the opposite is not true: nature can exist without culture. This vertical relationship between the two concepts – one more fundamental than the other – is wrongly portrayed as a *horizontal* one, making the relationship appear symmetrical when it is actually nothing of the kind (Wilden, 1987a: 31–4, 1987b: 79–82). Simultaneously, the horizontal, symmetrical relationship between other pairs like male|female is portrayed as *vertical*, setting up a supposed hierarchy of being which I will discuss later.

By having the List installed deep in our psyches, we are inducted into Western culture. It is a very long list, and no one in our society, I suggest, could *accidentally* reverse one of the pairs and, for example, align male with earth and female with sky as the Ancient Egyptians did – although we might choose to do so for subversive effect. The most relevant extract from the List for our immediate purposes runs like this:

mind | body
conscious | unconscious
thought | feeling
civilised | wild

Western culture sees the first set of terms as essentially better, 'higher', more advanced, than the second set; so that mind, thought, civilisation and consciousness are to be privileged over body, feeling, wildness, the unconscious. But simply reversing the values of the List, privileging the second set over the first as some radicals do, does little to change its nature. This reversal is the equivalent of the old festival of Saturnalia, when for one day the poor and powerless ruled over the rich and powerful – a day which actually reinforced the existence of hierarchies of power and privilege. The dualistic structure of the List, the way in which it forces pluralistic experience into a binary framework, remains unchallenged. I prefer to think in terms of the open network of language with which I began this chapter.

In what follows, I will be endeavouring to resist this simple reversal of privilege, which exalts the wild over the domesticated while simultaneously reinforcing the hegemony of the List. Instead, I want to argue that wildness and domestication are an example, like nature and culture, of a true vertical pair: the domesticated depends on and is rooted in the wild, whereas the same is not true in reverse (Wilden, 1987a: 16; see Chapter 6, this volume). At the same time, the two categories are *different in kind*: domestication is a continual process of simplification (simple is safe) whereas wildness is a continual tendency towards complexity. As I have indicated, domestication shortens every food chain, always inserting human beings and their food animals and excluding as many other species – wild 'pests', 'vermin' and 'weeds' – as possible.

Both domestication and wildness are essential aspects of human culture; but when domestication becomes predominant, as it is in our modern society, this creates a world out of balance. Many indigenous societies have been doing their best to warn us of the consequences of this imbalance, consequences which we now see all around us. I am arguing for the redressing of the balance by recognising the value and the fundamental character of wildness. Wildness is the First Nation of human culture; it is the ground of our being. Denying and suppressing it can only be disastrous.

THE WILD ROOTS OF THERAPY

This view was at the heart of psychoanalysis: in the works of Freud and Jung and the post-Freudians, primitives were equated

> with children and the mentally disturbed ... Thus the myth of the Wild Man, which had become a fiction, again became a myth, a projection of repressed desires and anxieties.
>
> (Pieterse, 1992: 37)

The network of words and ideas involving wildness has many resonances for psychotherapy and counselling (I will generally use 'therapy' as shorthand for both of these). A part of what clients encounter in therapy is precisely their own wildness: the spontaneous complexity and creative/destructive energy of their unconscious process, as it manifests, for example, in dreams, in body experiences, and in relationships. This can be intensely frightening: the realisation that most of our self is happening *of its own accord,* while in some ways exhilarating, is not easily tolerable to the ego which believes and hopes that it is in control, and gives rise to all sorts of anxious fantasies of annihilation and transgression – the savage and violent connotations of wildness.

Many of us as clients feel, at one point or another, that to let our feelings run wild would be to risk serious harm to ourselves and others. Therapy, therefore, can often confront us with a sort of gamble or wager: can we take the chance of letting things happen of their own accord, letting ourselves run wild, in the hope of finding a deeper meaning and order? Similar things happen in therapy groups: there is often a need for the group to descend into chaos before it can find its creativity, but the onset of chaos produces panic and escalating attempts to take control of the process – generally just adding to the confusion.

These issues are already represented in the language and imagery of Freud's original formulations, where he identifies wildness with the unconscious in very ambivalent ways. Freud many times describes the relationship between conscious and unconscious as a struggle for power between control and the out-of-control: 'the unconscious has no other endeavour than to break through the pressure weighing down on it and force its way to consciousness or action' (1920: 19); it is 'a chaos, a cauldron full of seething excitations' which 'has no organisation, produces no collective will' (1933: 73). In all his writings Freud draws very heavily on the List. He frequently presents the unconscious as primeval: an earlier phase of life (1916–17: 211–12), an earlier geological stratum (1920: 19; 1923: 21–2), an aboriginal and primitive race (1915a: 195), an earlier species:

> Behind this childhood of the individual we are promised a picture of a phylogenetic childhood – a picture of the development of the human race, of which the individual's development is in fact an abbreviated recapitulation.
>
> (Freud, 1900: 548)

The unconscious described by Freud is, in many senses, primitive. 'All ... which is old and infantile and was once dominant, and alone dominant, must today be ascribed to the unconscious' (1916–17: 211–12). In line with the usual value judgement that Western culture puts on height/depth polarities, he characterises this primitive, 'archaic', 'primeval' quality as 'lower' and the ego as 'higher' (e.g. 1920: 19).

Some of the metaphors Freud uses to describe this are explicitly colonial, drawing on the 'wild/primitive/uncivilised' section of the List. Regions, provinces, realms, he points out, may have a mixed population of different ethnic groups (1933: 72–3). He compares unconscious contents to 'an aboriginal population in the mind' (1915a: 195); and describes certain repressed phantasies as like:

> individuals of mixed race who, taken all round, resemble white men, but who betray their coloured descent by some striking feature or other, and on that account are excluded from society and enjoy none of the privileges of white people.
> (1915a: 191)

Quite beyond the pale, in fact (a concept to which I will return). Here Freud contributes to a whole picture of repression as the White Man's Burden which was rather fashionable in the earlier part of the 20th century. As the novelist John Buchan has one of his characters say:

> The civilised is far simpler than the primeval. All history has been an effort to make definitions, clear rules of thought, clear rules of conduct, solid sanctions, by which we can conduct our life. These are the work of the conscious self. The unconscious is an elementary and lawless thing. If it intrudes on life two things must follow. There will be a weakening of the power of reasoning ... And there will be a failure of nerve.
> (Buchan, 1924/2001: 9)

Buchan at least realises here that the wild, 'primeval' unconscious is *complex*, rather than simple and childlike as the colonial analogy commonly suggests. Far more unambiguously than Freud, Jung aligns himself with this classic colonialist view of simple, childlike natives/unconscious, which is amplified in his descriptions of the trips he made to Africa and to the United States (see Hill, 1997). 'The different strata of the mind correspond to the history of the races,' he writes; and although 'in the collective unconscious, you are the same as a man of another race ... he probably has a whole layer less than you [the assumed white reader]' (Jung, 1935/1976a: 46). This layer which he suggests people of colour lack is the layer of civilised consciousness;

non-whites are identified by Jung with the wild, archaic, unconscious aspects of the psyche.

The wildness in Jung's vision of black people is brought out vividly in his account (1963: 253–4) of an incident while travelling from Kenya to the Sudan, when some African men – 'the blackest Negroes I had ever seen' – began singing in the firelight and dancing fiercely with their weapons. At first Jung and his friend joined in, Jung swinging his rhinoceros whip (!) above his head. The Africans 'beamed', but as the dancing and drumming became more energetic and 'their excitement got out of bounds', Jung, frightened that 'the dancers were being transformed into a wild horde', tried to persuade them to go to bed. When this failed, 'I swung my rhinoceros whip threateningly, but at the same time laughing, and for lack of a better language, I swore at them loudly in Swiss German. ... General laughter arose; capering, they scattered in all directions and vanished into the night.'

As Michael Ortiz Hill points out (1997), the Africans showed a highly 'civilised' tolerance of an interfering, blustering colonialist. Jung's anxiety at their 'wildness', which he links with animality, simplicity and childlikeness ('beaming', 'capering', 'roaring'), was founded on his belief or fear that it was contagious: 'Even today the European, however highly developed, cannot live with impunity among the Negroes in Africa; their psychology gets into him unnoticed and unconsciously he becomes a Negro' (Jung, 1927/1970a: 121). Jung believed that this fate had befallen white Americans, who 'present a strange picture: a European with Negro behavior and an Indian [i.e. Native American] soul' (Jung, 1930/1970b: 507). Hill sums it up with great clarity:

> In 1925 Jung hallucinated a whole continent of instinctual 'others' and called it 'Africa.' The African 'other' whom Jung did not know accompanied him to his deathbed. Like the rest of us, it seems he was wedded to what fascinated him and what he least understood.
>
> (Hill, 1997: 31)

Our understanding both of colonialism and of the relationship between wildness and the unconscious has hopefully clarified since Freud and Jung; and in this book I intend to show how a developed concept of wildness can help therapy to understand both itself and its clients. Paradoxically, both Jung and Freud, simultaneously with their racist and speciesist assumptions about wildness, were also profoundly aware of its value as an inherent quality of the psyche. We can see this in Freud's case through considering one of the central images he used for the unconscious, that of a mycelium, the underground mass of a mushroom or other fungus. In his first great work, *The Interpretation of Dreams,* Freud says that:

> The dream-thoughts to which we are led by interpretation cannot, from the nature of things, have any definite endings; they are bound to branch out in every direction into the intricate network of our world of thought. It is at some point where this meshwork is particularly close that the dream wish grows up, like a mushroom out of its mycelium.
>
> (Freud, 1900: 525)

A mushroom not only 'emerges' out of mycelium, it is *made* out of mycelium, is literally a condensed and tight woven 'expression' of that underground mass of threads (the 'tangle' of dream-thoughts – Freud, 1900: 282, 442, 525), which springs up overnight into the surprised daylight world – a phallic, sexual-smelling, mysterious mushroom, yet also an umbilicus joining us to the mycelium, the placental dream which twins and feeds us. At the same time, Freud's use of this analogy connects us to his actual outdoor life, which was intensely important to him. Many of his central ideas emerged on long country and mountain walks, first with his friend Wilhelm Fliess, and later with Ferenczi and other analytic colleagues. 'In Aussee,' Freud writes to Fliess in 1897, 'I know a wonderful wood full of ferns and mushrooms where you must reveal to me the secrets of the world of lower animals and the world of children' (Masson, 1985: 254).

Freud's and Fliess's interest in mushrooms was part of a 19th-century trend, following on from the quite recent realisation that fungi are not in fact spontaneously generated, perhaps through thunder or some sort of fermentation of the earth, but that they appear lawfully, so to speak, as a minor adjunct, an occasional fruiting body, of the 'real' but hidden organism. The mycelium has many parallel properties to the unconscious: it is enormous, hidden, ancient – arguably the largest known organism on the planet is a honey mushroom or *Armillaria ostoyae* covering 2,200 acres of eastern Oregon and believed to be 2,400 years old (Barnard, 2000) – and composed of a network of branching and interwoven threads. A modern mushroom writer spontaneously echoes Freud's language in the *Interpretation:* 'what we call toadstools are ... the tip of an immense and intricate network of threads' (Mabey, 1993). In Chapter 4 I will develop an ecological picture of the human psyche which closely parallels Freud's image of the mycelium and of consciousness as the visible tip of 'the intricate network of our world of thought'.

With his very different personality, Jung is as alive as Freud to this wild and tangled aspect of the psyche. When a scholarly colleague wrote to him about a psychological crisis, and shared a dream of a dark forest where a single bright star shone, Jung responded 'There is the star. You must go in quest of yourself and you will find yourself again only in the simple and forgotten things. Why not go into the forest for a time, literally? Sometimes a tree tells you more than can be read in books' (Jung, 1992: 479). Later in life he lamented that:

> No voices now speak to man from stones, plants and animals, nor does he speak to them believing they can hear. His contact with nature has gone, and with it has gone the profound emotional energy that this symbolic connection supplied.
> (Jung, 1964: 95)

Jung saw individuation as a natural process that could proceed just as well without consciousness as with it (Sabini, 2002: 10), and claimed at times that consciousness was overvalued, a 'Promethean conquest' (ibid). This image of Prometheus – 'Forethought', who stole fire from the Gods and was eternally punished for it – in some ways sums up Jung's ambivalence in this whole area, partly a product of his inability to see beyond the 'primitive/civilised', 'nature/culture' dichotomies which permeate his work. Although deeply drawn to and valuing both the other-than-human and the other-than-rational, Jung's attraction always seems mixed with wariness, a fear of the collapse of 'civilised' values. However, he emphasises over and over again that reason and civilisation need to be rebalanced, reconnected with something unreasonable and undomesticated, and that a part of what we have lost touch with is *connectedness,* between humans and humans and between humans and the rest of the world. 'There is nothing ... with which I am not linked' (Jung, 1963: 225).

The tensions in Jung's thinking and feeling come out very clearly in his essay on 'Archaic Man' (Jung, 1930/1970c): a constant effort to stand up for and give an even-handed account of what Jung terms 'primitive' ways of thinking is equally constantly undermined by a sense of patronising superiority – not least in the use of 'primitive' and 'archaic' as descriptions of what he is trying to talk about. It is hard, for example, to argue convincingly for the validity of non-Western ideas of causality if you continually refer to what they are theorising as 'chance'.

What I am trying to establish here is that both Freud and Jung realised that the unconscious – that central force in human affairs – was deeply bound up with other-than-rational, wild modes of thinking, feeling and perception, and that both of them felt an extreme ambivalence about this situation. In what follows I will trace out the development in psychotherapy over the last century of both that realisation and that ambivalence.

WILD ANALYSTS

Freud himself suggested, and critiqued, a category which he called 'wild psychoanalysis' (Freud, 1910), by which he primarily meant the use of educative persuasion as a method of curing neurotic symptoms. Freud pointed out that what he called 'analytic technique' was also required – primarily, a specific sort of relationship between analyst and patient. As Adam Phillips says, 'it is not clear what the opposite of wild analysis is: tame analysis? Civilised analysis?' (Phillips, 2002: xvii). These might actually be more appropriate names for the approach which Freud is criticising, which makes a distinctly 'civilised' appeal to the patient's better judgement, rather than – like Freud's kind of analysis – recognising the unconscious and nonrational forces which determine the course and outcome of treatment.

The unorthodox early analyst Georg Groddeck referred to himself with some relish, and in a rather different sense, as a 'wild analyst'. Honouring Groddeck's sixtieth birthday, Ernst Simmel wrote:

> We remember the day when he first appeared in our midst in person during the conference at The Hague. He went up to the platform and announced: 'I am a wild analyst.' He was right. Yet one should understand the word 'wild' in a way that is different from the usual meaning ... Groddeck may call himself wild – as a member of our movement who owes his training to nobody except himself.

This description of course applies equally to Freud. Simmel continues, of Groddeck:

> His nature is the source of that 'wildness' which has enabled him, a fanatic of the art of healing, thanks to his unique gifts, to apply successfully Freud's discoveries about the unconscious psyche in the fight against organic illnesses. ... We believe that a wildness of this kind should not be criticised, particularly when it is accompanied by such blessed innate artistic gifts as in the case of Groddeck.
>
> (quoted in Schacht, 1977: 7–8)

This sort of exceptionalist rhetoric is often used to isolate and contain a charismatic nonconformist who might otherwise be dangerous. But there is something more than that going on. Freud himself wrote to Groddeck at the start of the latter's relationship with psychoanalysis, arguing against Groddeck's own ambivalence about that relationship:

> I have to claim you, I have to assert that you are a splendid analyst who has understood for ever the essential aspects of the matter. The discovery that transference and resistance are the most important aspects of treatment turns a person irretrievably into a member of the wild army.
>
> (Groddeck, 1977: 36)

The fascinating phrase 'wild army' (*wildes Heer*), is alternatively translated (Roazen, 1976: 336) as the 'Wild Hunt' said to be led across the sky by Woden or other mythical figures, which dovetails very well with Simmel's portrayal of Groddeck as some sort of archaic, 'passionate', natural being, very like the medieval Wild Man whom we shall be meeting in Chapter 7; Freud's biographer Peter Gay calls Groddeck 'the wild man of analysis' (Gay, 1995: 408). It is also rendered as the 'mad horde' (Grossman & Grossman, 1967: 72), or the 'savage army' (Rudnytsky, 2002: 145). In Jung's narrative of his African encounter quoted above, he is afraid that the Africans are turning into a 'wild horde' (Jung, 1963: 254).

With the image of someone 'irretrievably' assimilated into the wild, mad, savage horde of analysts, Freud is speaking from one side of his own double image of analysis – from the side of the wild, mad, savage unconscious. Freud used Groddeck to speak for his own partially suppressed wildness. He writes to Oskar Pfister in 1921, 'I energetically defend Groddeck against your respectability' (E. Freud & Meng, 1963: 81). But Freud's own drive for respectability has been a powerful influence in the development of psychoanalysis, and as we will see below, affected his relationship with Groddeck's ideas.

We can begin to see why psychoanalysts have always been fascinated by the phrase 'wild analysis', never more so than at present (with the psychoanalytic division of the APA organising a conference in 2010 on 'Wild analysis then and now'). Speaking at a 2006 conference in Baden-Baden which explored the relationship between Groddeck (on the site of whose sanatorium it was held) and another great analytic nonconformist, Sandor Ferenczi, Emanuel Berman seeks to rehabilitate the wild analyst:

> The image of the wild analyst can serve us ... as the image of the deeply involved, personally motivated analyst, whose work is intense and emotionally risky. This is the opposite of the 'civilized' analyst who uses well-defined existing paths, takes no personal risks, and therefore stays at an emotional distance from his/her patients.
>
> (Berman, 2007: 212)

Berman quotes a letter from Groddeck to Ferenczi:

> It seems to me that science stops at the very point it becomes codified into a rule or a law. The process of making laws is, in my view, so far advanced in our field of expertise that essential matters can no longer be discovered by convinced analysts, but only by the doubters, among whom I count Freud, you and myself.
>
> (Groddeck to Ferenczi, 1922, in Fortune, 2002: 35)

Interestingly, perhaps tactfully, Berman omits the final phrase of this quotation, 'among whom ...', which enlists Freud into the 'wild army' of those who question his own codified theory. In this Groddeck was right about the Freud who so enthusiastically welcomed him to psychoanalysis and took up his concept of the It (known in Strachey's translation as the Id); but sadly, wrong about the other Freud who equally enthusiastically stripped out the wilder aspects of Groddeck's concept from his own version, telling Groddeck with his habitual complex irony 'I do not of course recognize my civilized, bourgeois, demystified It in your It. Yet you know that mine derived from yours' (Freud to Groddeck, 1925, in Groddeck, 1977: 93).

Berman identifies this conflict as between 'wild Freud and respectable Freud' (Berman, 2007: 215). Elsewhere in his paper he says:

> Moreover, every analyst's capacity to develop a unique analytic self, based on his/her genuine life experience and worldview, is endangered if stepping out of line is slandered as 'wild analysis' or as insanity. Such threats pave the way to developing a false analytic self.
>
> (Berman, 2007: 214)

I suggest that this applies not only to the clinical situation, but also to the theoretical stance and the social role of psychoanalysis, and of therapy in general: therapy's domesticated false self.

WILD DEVELOPMENTS

The later history of psychotherapy and counselling is full of elements of wildness contesting the rule of this false self. A part of my purpose in this book is to bring some of these ideas together so that they form an explicit point of view (and can also be seen to be some of the currents that flowed into the formation of ecopsychology). However we need to be aware of an ongoing struggle within the field of therapy between what we may call wild and domesticated interpretations of what we are all doing. A good example is a passage from W.R. Bion, one of the most explicit analytic writers on the topic of the wild and unpredictable elements of the psyche. In a book produced after his death and transcribed directly from tape recordings he made in his study, Bion says:

> If a thought without a thinker comes along, it may be a 'stray thought'. Or it could be a thought with the owner's name and address upon it, or it could be a 'wild thought'. The problem, should such a thought come along, is what to do with it. Of course, if it is wild, you might try to domesticate it.
> (Bion, 1997: 27)

Like much of Bion's writing, this is rich with implications that are not directly drawn out in the text itself. Bion is performing what he describes, and following his mind where it flows, practising the fundamental analytic technique of free association through dictation into a tape recorder. Free association, the attempt to verbalise whatever passes through our awareness, is portrayed by Freud precisely as a method of accessing the wild ecology of mind, the 'intricate network' which he compares to mycelium. What is very clear, it seems to me, is Bion's essentially welcoming, exploratory and accepting attitude towards 'wild thoughts'. And what is therefore extraordinary is that, on the basis of this passage – and again, performing what is described – the book was entitled by his executors *Taming Wild Thoughts* (Bion, 1997).

This mistitling sums up very well the history of wildness in psychotherapy and counselling: a series of spontaneously creative innovations later tidied up by the conscious and anxious mind. As is of course common in human history, therapy has experienced a number of renewals, when reformers have pointed out the stagnant and vacant state of the field, and put forward schemes of innovation (often cast as or combined with a return to the true original state). The largest of these happened in the 1950s and 1960s, in parallel with a ferment of social innovation and renewal (Totton, 2000: 25–9).

Perhaps the most explicit attention to issues of spontaneity and control has been in the body psychotherapy tradition initiated by Wilhelm Reich, initially within psychoanalysis until, for a number of mainly political reasons, Reich was forced out of psychoanalytic organisations in the 1930s. As a result his work became very influential in the humanistic/ growth movement of the 1950s, 1960s and 1970s, when spontaneity and control were also central cultural and political issues. In the 1950s Reich was also one of the very first to point out and try to address the effects of pollution on the atmosphere and vegetation (Sharaf, 1984: 377ff). The prominent bodywork theorist Don Hanlon Johnson sums up the common project of the many and various styles of body psychotherapy which have developed since Reich:

> Underlying the various techniques and schools, one finds a desire to regain an intimate connection with bodily processes: breath, movement impulses, balance and sensibility. In that shared impulse, this community is best understood within a much broader movement of resistance to the West's long history of denigrating the value of the human body and the natural environment.
> (Johnson, 1997: xvi)

To take a well-known example, Gestalt is very much a body-oriented psychotherapy, and right from the start spontaneity has been one of its core values. Perls and his colleagues, in their foundational book *Gestalt Therapy* (subtitled *Excitement and Growth in the Human Personality*), identify 'an epidemic fear of spontaneity; it is the "infantile" par excellence, for it does not take into account the so-called "reality"; it is irresponsible' (Perls et al: 1951/1973: 449), and counter this with the assertion that 'what seems spontaneously important does *in fact* marshal the most energy of behaviour; self-regulating action is brighter, stronger and shrewder' (ibid: 324, original italics).

> The relaxation of deliberateness and the vanishing of boundaries is the reason for the extra brightness and vigour – e.g. the 'flash of insight' or the 'shock of recognition' – for the energy that went into withholding oneself or aggressively putting connections into the environment is now suddenly added to the final spontaneous experience.
> (Ibid: 474)

These are profound insights that deserve a lot of unpacking, and in Chapter 4 I will try to connect them up with other kinds of thinking, including indigenous thinking, relating to what I call 'Wild Mind'. Perls and his colleagues are suggesting that Western humans use a lot of our energy in what amount to strategies of *defence* and *attack*: either separating ourselves from the world around us, or forcing our own concerns onto it. Either way, we are putting ourselves out of community with the world, and hence lessening our ability to react spontaneously and creatively with it, for example through a 'flash of insight', a creative dream, falling in love or hate. (These ideas are greatly developed and extended in another Gestalt text by Stevens, 1977.)

The radical psychoanalytic thinker Norman O. Brown makes a similar point, though rather more obscurely: 'The split of self from environment, and of self into both self and environment, is also the split of self or soul from body' (Brown, 1959/1968: 51). And many psychotherapy theorists – by no means only body psychotherapists – have for decades now been chipping away at the dualism of mind/body which is such a crucial element of the List (Totton, 1998), and at the more subtle but related and equally crucial dualism of self and environment. In the 1960s and 1970s many schools of therapy took a similar position to Gestalt, emphasising what I am calling the wild side of therapy (Totton, 2000: 25–9). For example, Eric Berne, the founder of Transactional Analysis (TA), foregrounded what he called 'autonomy'. This was made up of three elements (all the following quotations are from Berne, 1968: 158–60): awareness ('living in the here and now, not the elsewhere, the past or the future ... the aware person is alive because he [*sic*] knows how he feels, where he is and when it is'; spontaneity ('the freedom to choose and express one's feelings ... liberation'); and intimacy ('spontaneous, game-free candidness'). Another important TA teacher, Claude Steiner, used TA concepts and techniques to help people in the project of 'rebelling against obedience, hierarchies, respect for authority, the leader-follower relationship' (Steiner, 1981: 172).

Carl Rogers, founder of Person-Centred Therapy (PCT), published a book in 1978 called *Carl Rogers on Personal Power: Inner Strength and Its Revolutionary Impact*, where he makes explicit connections between his therapeutic approach and the wider world. He states that PCT 'is based on a premise which at first seemed risky and uncertain: a view of man [*sic*] as at core a trustworthy organism [with] an underlying flow of movement towards constructive fulfilment of its inherent possibilities' (Rogers, 1978: 7). All practitioners of PCT would no doubt subscribe to this statement, but not all of them would follow Rogers in the sociopolitical consequences which he draws from it. 'Simply describing the fundamental premise ... is to make a challenging political statement', Rogers suggests (1978: 9), and in the book he traces out the implications of this on the levels of personal relationships, community, and national politics.

All of these writers and many others (e.g. Fromm, 1973, 1980; Marcuse, 1955/1966; Parry, 1989; Polster & Polster, 1974; Wyckoff, 1976) are plainly responding to and speaking out of their historical moment; at the same time, though, they are enabled by that moment to recognise and articulate authentic core elements of psychotherapy, elements which go back to the work of Freud and Jung. Psychotherapy has in a sense always been about the mystery of the mind/body relationship – not the supposed mystery of how they come together, but the mystery of how they appear to be split apart! It offers an alternative to the alienation of mind from body, and as this chorus of voices from the 1960s and 1970s makes clear, that alternative has radical implications. The splitting apart of mind and body is closely related to the splitting apart of self and environment, civilised and wild.

ECOPSYCHOLOGY AND ECOTHERAPY

On the one hand, the project of psychotherapy is to support us in retrieving lost pieces of ourselves. It welcomes us back into our emotional bodies, helping us experience our connectedness to self and other humans. On the other hand, psychotherapy has grown up in urban Western culture and is inevitably formed by it. Our development is supposedly shaped by human relationship alone, as the pioneering analyst Harold Searles wrote in 1960:

> The nonhuman environment ... is ... considered as irrelevant to human personality development ... as though human life were lived out in a vacuum – as though the human race were alone in the universe, pursuing individual and collective destinies in a homogenous matrix of nothingness, a background devoid of form, colour, and substance.
>
> (Searles, 1960: 3)

In line with this, many therapists have difficulty in seeing the links between psychotherapy and our environmental crisis. (For some clear arguments about the relevance of the connection, see Maiteny, 2008.) However there is now a burgeoning field of ecopsychology, wilderness therapy and ecotherapy, in the USA, Australia, and more recently in the UK, in which therapists of many backgrounds are articulating these links. An enormously influential book was Roszak, Gomez and Kanner's *Ecopsychology: Restoring the Earth, Healing the Mind* (1996); this assembles some of the many different forms of ecologically oriented work that were already taking place, but in the following decade and a half these have multiplied many times.

There are two complementary aspects to the rise of ecologically oriented therapy, which can only really be separated on an abstract level – in practice they are inextricable from each other. One is the steadily increasing realisation of the immense environmental crisis which we are facing. The other, partly intensified by the knowledge of our loss, is an increasing realisation of the value and preciousness of the other-than-human and more-than-human (see my explanation of these terms in the Introduction), of the huge role they play in all our lives and the huge role which the impact of their damage and destruction can play in individual lives and in leading individuals into therapy. A corollary of this realisation is the bringing into the therapy room of the other-than-human and more-than-human, and the taking of therapy out to meet them in the wider world. In Chapter 8 I will describe some of the many forms, both literal and symbolic, that these processes take.

More and more frequently – and no doubt partly because therapists are giving them greater implicit permission to do so – clients are bringing issues of environmental damage and loss, and of the central role of connection with the land and with other species, into the therapy room. Jungian analyst Jerome Bernstein describes how a patient in his thirties was talking about his struggles to get his life together, and stopped mid-sentence, with a long silence. Then he said:

> I feel a Great Grief. I feel it inside (points to his heart). It's never not there. It is never far from me. In Montana I felt connected. (He had just returned from a trip there). Here I am disconnected – in my car, living on top of the land. I'm part of the land; that's my home. But I'm a product of my culture and therefore cut off from my home. I felt expanded there; I feel contracted here.

Bernstein describes how:

> The challenge in this instance is not to interpret at all – certainly not in the moment – to hold an experience that can feel between language, that can leave one with the tension of holding one's rational breath for far longer than any of us can imagine doing. To not seek the comfort of rational understanding, but to come to some kind of knowing through a holding and wonderment.
>
> (Bernstein, 2005: 73)

It can be hard for ecologically aware therapists to know how much to bring these issues into the work with clients – how much, for example, to interpret dreams and associations in terms of the environmental crisis. Kleinian analyst Hannah Segal writes about similar dilemmas regarding the danger of nuclear weapons during the 1980s:

> Even when patients do refer to nuclear issues, psychoanalysts remain faced with an ethical and technical dilemma. On the one hand ... we must not collude with the patient's denial of any external situation that we may guess at from the material and that the patient does not bring out in the open.
>
> On the other hand, we must also be very wary of imposing on the patient our own preoccupations and convictions ... If we do our job properly in dealing with the patient's basic defences, the relevant material will appear, because, in fact, below the surface, patients are anxious, even terrified.
>
> (Segal, 1988: 56)

This terror is rapidly rising towards the surface, in individuals and in the social collective. It may well be that helping people process their environmental fear and grief is becoming an increasingly central part of our work as therapists. In doing so, we are also helping people to contact their love of the other-than-human and more-than-human world, and to draw on this as an inner resource in facing what comes. Fear of environmental disaster has both a subjective and an objective connection with general fear of loss of control, which therapy is tasked with addressing. Like nuclear war, environmental crisis often appears in therapy as a symbolic expression of feelings of being overwhelmed and out of control; at the same time, and again like nuclear war, it is an objectively very real danger, and one which is in many ways the result of our civilisation's obsession with the impossible project of total control. Hence, therapy cannot avoid addressing the issue. Making these connections will be the purpose of this book.

2

Wild Complexity

> Things do not produce each other or make each other happen ... they *help* each other happen by providing locus or occasion or context, and in so doing, they in turn are affected. There is a mutuality here, a reciprocal dynamic. Power inheres not in any entity, but in the relationship between entities.
>
> (Macy, 1991: 58)

> *We say there is no end to any act. The rock thrown in the water is followed by waves of water, and these waves of water make waves in the air, and these waves travel outwards infinitely, setting particles in motion, leading to other motion and motion upon motion endlessly. We say the water has noticed this stone falling and has not forgotten. And in every particle every act lives, and the stars do not frighten us, we say, starlight is familiar to us.*
>
> (Griffin, 1984: 172, original italics)

I stated in Chapter 1 that *wild is complex*. Now I want to flesh out that statement and its implications, and to explore how Western culture maintains an elaborate denial of wild complexity.

What immediately follows is inevitably quite dense and difficult. In this book I am attempting to break with the long-established habits of Western culture and think *ecosystemically*, which means seeing each species, each being, each person, not as an isolated monad, a sort of old-fashioned billiard ball atom interacting with other billiard balls by knocking into them – but as inherently and profoundly linked with every other species, being, person, in a way that Buddhism terms *paticca samuppada*, 'dependent co-arising' (Macy, 1991, 1995). Joanna Macy writes that she has come to use 'deep ecology' as a 'functional equivalent' for dependent co-arising because both concepts refer to 'the interdependence of all life forms' (Macy, 1991: 64). As she points out (pp. 63–4), what is essentially the same concept of interdependent, self-organising open systems appears in general systems theory, which is the philosophical basis of ecology; the close relationship between systems thinking and ecology emerges very clearly in the work of Gregory Bateson (1973, 1980; see also Harries-Jones, 1995).

Dependent co-arising is both a metaphysical concept and a very physical reality. In an ecosystem, which can be defined as 'a community ... of organisms and their physical and chemical environment ... in which there are continuous fluxes of matter and energy in an interactive open system' (Willis, 1997: 270), each member affects and is affected by every other member. Usually, the whole system is closely linked together, with an average of only two degrees of separation – that is, indirectness of contact – between any two species (Williams et al, 2002): 'almost everything is connected to everything else' (ibid: 12916). The greater the connectedness and complexity of an ecosystem, the better its chances of maintaining long-term stability, as interactions dampen each other out and return to a settled state (Buchanan, 2003: 152–5). When one population expands, for example, it sets off cascades of change in the other species of whose environment it is part, and which are part of its environment, but this has the eventual effect of limiting its numbers – most simply, it runs out of food. Real ecosystem interactions are vastly more complex than this, but the more complex, the more stable; hence the positive *practical* value of biodiversity (as opposed to its spiritual or aesthetic value).

The web of life is only a subset of the web of all existence: dependent co-arising applies not only to the living elements of ecosystems, but equally to the soil, water, and atmosphere (all of which are of course saturated with living organisms). The contemporary picture is that species don't just passively fit into available ecological niches: they *create* their own niche, or more precisely co-create it, through effecting change in their environment (Odling-Smee et al, 2003). For example, earthworms have the anatomy and physiology of freshwater animals, yet are able to live in soil because they modify the soil to suit their physiology, through activities such as choosing the optimal soil horizon, tunnelling, exuding mucus, eliminating calcite, and dragging leaf litter below ground (Turner, 2000). They have created a niche for themselves as creatures which 'swim' through soil. The environment shapes the species, and simultaneously the species shapes the environment – at the same time forming a part of every other species' environment.

Dependent co-arising is also close to contemporary ways of thinking about genetics and 'nature/nurture': that just as important as how genes are coded is the environmental context which supports the 'expression' of specific genes in specific ways at specific times (Ridley, 2004). This takes us beyond the either/or question, 'is it nature or is it nurture?': always and everywhere, the answer is 'both'. This model, by the way, also applies to how we *perceive* the world. Perception used to be understood as essentially a one-way process, whereby things 'out there' made themselves known 'in here'. James and Eleanor Gibson (J.J. Gibson, 1979; E.J. Gibson, 1969) and others have shown that perception is actually an *ecological* process, a mutual interaction between the subject and their environment in which both are changed (Sewall, 1999). Related ideas, though very differently expressed, were articulated by Maurice Merleau-Ponty (1968; see Totton, 2009). I briefly discuss James Gibson's work again in Chapter 4.

Ecosystems themselves are dependent for survival on the other ecosystems which form their own environment – this is what it means to be an *open* system. The world consists of a network of nested open systems on every scale of size and level of organisation. (There is an excellent account of all this in Maiteny, 2005.) All of these open systems are *adaptive*: that is, they respond to changes in the other systems which constitute their environment, in such a way as to best survive. There is no need to attribute intention to this process: it happens of its own accord, just as a flock of birds or school of fish precisely coordinates its flight in a way which looks like evidence of a 'group mind', but which can be generated from a few simple hard-wired rules followed by each individual – avoid crowding neighbours, steer towards average heading of neighbours, steer towards average position of neighbours (Spector et al, 2003). These three rules alone create the heart-lifting beauty of flying geese. The universe is a clean machine.

Change in ecosystems is a complex non-linear process, best modelled through the mathematics of complexity. It is not accidental that this mathematics also offers the best model for a number of other processes – for example, weather, the brain, and societies. Complexity theory describes open systems, systems 'on the edge of chaos' as it is sometimes put (e.g. Kauffman, 1995), balancing stability with constant flux, order with unpredictability, as all living organisms do. As Wolf Singer puts it in a well-known article (Singer, 2005), the brain is like an orchestra without a conductor; and this is an excellent image for all open systems. The best mathematical simulation of an ecosystem on the edge of chaos is one based on *coevolution* – a spontaneously self-organising interdependent community without any central direction (Kauffman, 1995, 2000).

This is both a new idea, and a very old one: as well as dependent co-arising, its Buddhist conceptualisation, it is strongly articulated in Taoism, the ancient Chinese teaching which can be viewed as the philosophical arm of shamanism (Wong, 1997: 11–19; Pratt, 2007: 103). Lao Tse said: 'The Tao principle is what happens of itself' (Watts, 1979: 38). *Tzu-chan*, the Taoist term usually translated as 'nature', more precisely means the spontaneous, what happens of its own accord (Watts, 1979: 42).

Self-Organizing Complexity in Psychological Systems (Piers, Muller & Brent, 2007) demonstrates some of the ways in which complexity theory can be applied to psychotherapy. Particularly relevant is the concept of 'emergence', the appearance of new levels of organisation in systems which could not be predicted from preceding conditions. This can be applied for example in relation to symptoms:

> Symptoms are emergent in at least two respects. First, symptoms represent a rupture or qualitative shift in the individual's experience of volitional self-direction or agency. ... [Second,] they arise from a psychological content that does not at first glance contain the necessary ingredients to explain their arrival.
> (Piers, 2007: 101)

Complexity theory accounts for these qualities of mystery and alienness which we experience in symptoms, and shows how they develop unpredictably from initial conditions. In the context of this book, what is being described is the *wildness* of symptoms, their function of challenging and breaking open existing attitudes and habits.

SYSTEMIC WISDOM AND UNWISDOM

> Our industrial culture has traditionally depended on an 'ethic of disposability' for which natural resources, other people's ecosystems, 'other' human beings in general, and the disposable beercan have roughly the same (exchange) value. Having taught that all that it defines as environment is disposable, modern industrial society has only just begun to learn that THE SYSTEM WHICH DISPOSES OF ITS ENVIRONMENT DISPOSES OF ITSELF.
> (Wilden, 1972: 207, original upper case)

Drawing on both Taoist and Buddhist perspectives, in *Steps to an Ecology of Mind* (1973) Gregory Bateson draws parallels between an ecosystem, an organism, and a society or social group (which might nowadays be called a human ecosystem). Each is a balance of competition and mutuality, where the balance is achieved through feedback loops – as with a thermostat, each shift away from homeostasis is corrected by changes elsewhere in the system. Hence all these open systems tend towards a steady state, unless external input pushes them so far out of equilibrium that amplifying positive feedback loops develop, and they jump to a new balance, what complexity theory calls a new attractor. (This is also what symptoms – an internal input that *feels* external – can accomplish.)

Bateson points out (1973: 402–14) that human consciousness has difficulty in grasping this steady-state, homeostatic reality. Consciousness is an arrow moving forwards, rather than a homeostatic loop. Since consciousness has the function of choosing and achieving specific goals, it selects from our experience only the information which is relevant to those goals; hence the systemic nature of internal and external reality is necessarily obscure to it.

> On the one hand, we have the systemic nature of the individual human being, the systemic nature of the culture in which he [masculine *sic* throughout] lives, and the systemic nature of the biological, ecological system around him; and, on the other hand, the curious twist in the systemic nature of the individual man whereby consciousness is, almost of necessity, blinded to the systemic nature of the man himself. Purposive consciousness pulls out from the total mind, sequences which do not have the loop structure which is characteristic of the whole systemic structure.
> (Bateson, 1973: 410)

'Lack of systemic wisdom,' Bateson continues, 'is always punished.' On an individual level, we can see this punishment – inflicted, of course, not by any deity but as an automatic consequence of denying reality – in what the Buddha identified as suffering derived from craving, aversion and delusion. On a societal level, we are experiencing punishment in the form of a multitude of out-of-order crises and catastrophes, including the financial crash and culminating in climate change. Both levels are perfectly summed up in the Buddha's description of 'the doom of the waste, the woeful way, the constant faring on' (*Digha Nikaya* II.91, quoted in Macy, 1991: 63): constant faring on along the woeful way of waste is exactly what our society is doing, and also what individual consciousness does so long as it is unable to let go and rest in a steady state.

I have said that complex self-organising processes happen of their own accord, without external control. We can go further: complex self-organising processes *cannot* be controlled in a hierarchical sense, because trying to do so pushes them further and further out of balance. The *Tao Te Ching* gives firm warning of what will happen if one tries to control the spontaneous:

> Do you think you can take over the universe and improve it?
> I do not think it can be done.
>
> The universe is sacred,
> You cannot improve it.

> If you try to change it, you will ruin it.
> If you try to hold it, you will lose it.
> (Feng & English, 1973: Section 29)

And as Bateson indicates, an example of such a process – one which is crucial for my argument – is the human psyche. Just as domestication is simpler than wildness, consciousness is simpler than the unconscious. 'Of course, the whole of the mind could not be reported in a part of the mind. ... We therefore have to settle for very limited consciousness' (Bateson, 1973: 408). For the conscious mind to try to control the unconscious is like the individual trying to 'take over the universe and improve it'. This has huge implications for therapy, as we shall see.

CONQUERING NATURE: THE MYTH OF PROGRESS

> The art of selective breeding had enabled humans to realize the 'telos' inherent within them and to transcend gloriously the primal struggle for survival. Animals by contrast were consigned to remain for ever lodged in that struggle. They were stuck, not only in their own nature but also in the space called nature that was somehow left over and behind after humans, or at least Man – as Thought, Culture (and later on, Progress) – had heroically detached himself.
> (Anderson, 1997: 472)

I have favoured one side of the therapy narrative, the side which is about supporting and fostering the wild, the spontaneous and the unconscious, and more recently about moving into conscious connection with the more-than-human environment. But there is of course another side, equally important in both historical and current contexts, a side which is wedded to cure, to regulation, to evidence-based practice, to replacing the unconscious with the conscious: in Freud's words, 'Where Id was, there shall Ego be' (Freud, 1933: 80). One current consequence of this approach is the move to regulation of psychotherapy and counselling in the UK through a government-created body, the Health Professions Council (Postle, 2007). This side of therapy, I suggest, is caught up in the myth of Progress (see Rust, 2008a: 159ff, and Rust, 2009a; the following discussion is in constant dialogue with Mary-Jayne Rust).

The myth of Progress is a deeply familiar story about how we have achieved – and will continue indefinitely to achieve – satisfaction of all our needs and freedom from want through our fight against nature, made possible by reason and technology. If we continue to gain material wealth, and fight towards the top of the hierarchy of life, we will live happily ever after. But this story leaves out the shadow of

Progress, the damage that it has created: what began as an understandable struggle to increase our freedom within nature has turned into an attempt to escape nature itself – to tame the wild, to gain security through total control (see Chapter 6).

The side of Freud which sympathised with this attempt wrote: 'The principle task of civilisation, its actual raison d'être, is to defend us against nature. We all know that in many ways civilisation does this fairly well already, and clearly as time goes on it will do it much better.' He goes on in the same passage, however, to say:

> There are the elements which seem to mock at all human control; the earth which quakes and is torn apart and buries all human life and its works; water, which deluges and drowns everything in turmoil ... With these forces nature rises up against us, majestic, cruel and inexorable; she brings to our mind once more our weakness and helplessness, which we thought to escape through the work of civilisation.
>
> (Freud, 1927: 15–16)

Is this simply pessimistic, or is it more deeply ambivalent? I have just mentioned Freud's famous colonialist statement: 'Where Id was, there shall Ego be'. But again, when one looks at the full passage (and improves the translation, replacing Latin terms with English ones that match Freud's original use of German) the picture is more complex. Freud is discussing the intention of psychoanalysis to strengthen the ego, 'so that it can appropriate fresh portions of the It. Where It was, there shall I be. It is a work of culture – not unlike the draining of the Zuider Zee' (Freud, 1933: 80).

As Bettelheim (1982) and others have discussed, the Zuider Zee in Holland was just a small fragment of the North Sea – and a name which, at the time Freud wrote, would have brought to mind repeated and disastrous floods. The passage was published in 1933, the year after the completion of a massive dam which was clearly in Freud's thoughts, and which domesticated the Zuider Zee into useable land. However, 1933 was the same year that Hitler came to power and Freud's sons left Germany with their families, as over the next few years did most Jewish analysts: the dykes, one might say, had well and truly failed. But this is again to identify the unconscious solely with the barbaric and destructive aspects of wildness. Perhaps, as many people have argued, the unconscious only takes on this destructive form when it is suppressed, rejected, shut out from our awareness. Is this suppression the appropriate 'work of culture'?

Freud's image further refers (perhaps unconsciously) to his favourite poet, Goethe, and his portrayal of Faust's final vision of reclaiming land from the destructive forces of the ocean (Goethe, 1838/2003). The hundred-year-old Faust, stricken with blindness by Care, mistakes 'the clattering of shovels' (line 11539), which is Mephisto and the Lemures (the spirits of the restless dead) digging his grave, for the sound of work on his vast project to create 'Free earth: where a free race, in freedom, stand' (line 11580):

> The crews still labouring on,
> Till earth is reconciled to man,
> The waves accept their boundaries,
> And ocean's bound with iron bands.
> (Goethe, 1838/2003: lines 11540–3)

Like the Chinese Three Gorges project and many other dams worldwide, the work of control is not merely hopeless, but deathly.

Many stories of the myth of Progress are 'about young male heroes who slay dragons on a journey towards the light. Darkness, insecurity, depression, are seen as failure and killed off. The earth has been "reclaimed", made into a collection of objects for our use' (Rust, 2009a: 9). The traditional shadow side of the Myth of Progress is the Myth of the Fall, the original sin that excludes us from the Garden, and of course there is an environmentalist version of Original Sin – 'we humans are a plague and the earth would be better off without us'. The stories of Faust and Prometheus, which as we have seen were important for Freud and Jung, also represent the shadow side of progress: Prometheus, who steals fire for humanity and is eternally punished by having his liver torn out by eagles, then renewed and torn out again; Faust, who sells his soul for knowledge and reaps death and damnation.

These stories both involve a tension between heaven and hell. Jung offers his own powerful mythic account of the primal split between higher and lower, heaven and hell, which develops out of human domestication:

> Man [*sic*] became split into a conscious and an unconscious personality. Thus we became highly disciplined, organized, and rational on one side, but the other side remained a suppressed primitive, cut off from education and civilization. ... Think of the great triumph of the human mind, the power to fly: we have accomplished the age-old dream of humanity! And think of the bombing raids of modern warfare! Is it not a rather convincing demonstration of the fact that, when our mind went up to conquer the skies, our other man, that suppressed barbarous individual, went down to hell?
> (Jung, 1939/1970d: 527)

SPIDERS AND WEBS

The tension between conscious and unconscious, heaven and hell, can also be cast as a tension between individual and collective. The Myth of Progress prizes individual freedom very highly: we are taught that indigenous cultures have no sense of individual identity, and that part of our long struggle towards Western modernity has been to realise ourselves as separate individuals. Our individual development is also seen in this light: part of the goal of growing up is to become separate from the maternal matrix in order to achieve adult maturity.

Many of the stories of our culture reflect this struggle; they are about young male heroes cutting their way out of webs (Rust, 2008a:162). The kind of freedom that is achieved is rather like an adolescent dream of escaping the parents. With webs of relationship dissolving in our society, we see more and more people living and struggling alone; and now the very web of life is unravelling. By cutting ourselves (quite literally) out of the forests, and then continuing with the same mindset into the present, we have attacked the ecological networks on which survival rests. Think of Bilbo Baggins and the dwarves in the forest of Mirkwood, cutting the webs and escaping from the dreadful giant spiders; now, accounts of giant spiders discovered in distant forests thrill us and give hope for the survival of biodiversity!

For Southwestern Native Americans, Spider Woman, Grandmother Spider, is the creator of the universe: she spins existence out of herself, and weaves all beings together (Hazen-Hammond, 1999). She embodies the ecological self, in other words – the experience of interdependence, of mutual co-arising. In Chapter 1 I mentioned Western culture's story of Prometheus, who stole fire from the gods and is eternally tortured for it. In some Native American stories, it is Grandmother Spider who steals fire, able to succeed after other animals have failed through her inconspicuousness and cleverness (she carries the fire back in a clay pot); and she is not punished at all (Kearns, 1992; Arneach, 2008).

As we shall see in Chapter 5, human phobias about spiders and other 'creepy-crawlies', as we call them, can be related to our fear of wildness: we generally find the shallow order of domestication more comfortable than the deep order of the wild. Domesticated wildness tends to be managed in a top-down, dominance-based fashion, complexity's constant tendency to reassert itself kept under control with bleach, weedkiller, concrete and ideology; the greatest of these is ideology, which splits the world into us and them, subjects and objects.

Until we can see beyond the subject/object split, where some beings are the objects of others' will, then Faust's dream of freedom

– achieved by putting the ocean in 'iron bands' – is meaningless. *Individual* freedom, it turns out, is an illusion: freedom is collective or it is nothing (see Bookchin, 2005; Hardt & Negri, 2006). We are interdependent and interconnected. Our struggle for individual consciousness is always in relation to the rest of life; we are challenged to bear that tension between individual and collective, rather than cut our way like young Alexanders out of the knotted net of relatedness.

An ancient model of relatedness is known as 'Indra's Net': an infinite net with a jewel at every intersection of strands, and every jewel, together with all its internal reflections, reflected in every other jewel (Cook, 1977). In fact Alan Watts uses the image of a spider's web to illustrate Indra's Net:

> Imagine a multidimensional spider's web in the early morning covered with dew drops. And every dew drop contains the reflection of all the other dew drops. And, in each reflected dew drop, the reflections of all the other dew drops in that reflection. And so on, ad infinitum. That is the Buddhist conception of the universe in an image.
>
> (Watts, 1999: 28)

In his novel *Moonchild* (1929/1972), Aleister Crowley explores the ambivalence of this image of the web of life. One of his characters has a vision of the web which turns drastically towards the negative: a vast network of triangles, each made up of a god and two worshippers, 'and upon each thread of the web, from knot to knot, danced incredible insects, and strange animals, and hideous reptiles'.

> Now she noticed that each pair of worshipers had newborn children in their arms; and they offered these to their god, who threw them instantly towards the centre of the web. Following up those cruel meshes, she beheld the spider itself ... Its head and body formed one black sphere, covered with moving eyes that darted rays of darkness in every direction, and mouths that sucked up its prey without remorse or cessation, and cast it out once more in the form of fresh strands of that vibrating web.
>
> (Crowley, 1929/1972: 253)

Later another character shows her (with the help of some unfortunately rather poor poetry) that she was projecting her own fears onto a vision of the interconnectedness and constant renewal and transformation of all being, and turning Grandmother Spider into a horror rather than a wonder. Ultimately, both of these valuations are our projections onto something which just is.

FORESTS, WEBS AND PYRAMIDS

The Myth of Progress also means conquering the wildness of *inner* nature. As European empires expanded, 'civilised peoples' projected their own instinctuality onto indigenous others. Rinda West writes in *Out of the Shadow: Ecopsychology, Story and Encounters with the Land*:

> The conquerors felt alienated from their own 'natural' selves. Because they identified nature, women, and native people with instinct, passion, violence, idleness, and dreaming, they had to deny these parts of themselves and assert the primacy of commerce and practical reason. ... Most people today who live in western countries have inherited this disconnect. ... Gradually both instinct and fantasizing, dreaming, and intuitive parts of the mind have taken on negative associations, assumed to be female, and devalued.
>
> (West, 2007: 10–11)

The end result is the white man's pyramid of life – the exact social equivalent of the 'food pyramid' I mentioned in Chapter 1, where the web of life is simplified and redirected towards human sustenance:

> When a piece of forest was cleared to create arable land, an assemblage of plants in its climax state was driven back to its very first stage of succession, its species composition homogenized and its energy and nutrients redirected towards a single centre.
>
> (De Landa, 2000: 108)

At the top of this food/rank pyramid sits white Western middle-class urban intellectual man (myself included) and his values. All other humans – women, working-class people, people of colour, those who work on the land – and their values are cast below in descending ranks, with indigenous people usually at the bottom. Underneath humans altogether, on the other side of a firm dividing line, and often simply left out of the picture entirely, is the whole earth community in descending order of animals, plants, and finally the earth, soil, rock: the ground on which we all depend.

In the rank pyramid, those seen as 'lower down' and 'closer to nature' have carried the projections of those on the top, filtered through the List described in Chapter 1. The abolition of slavery, the banning of apartheid, women's fight for equal rights, are all examples of ways in which oppressed peoples have challenged those at the top to take back their projections. The emotional work of the oppressor involves facing guilt, anger, and grief about what has happened, and is still happening, to these peoples – taking a share of responsibility for it.

But while we – some of us – are in the midst of retrieving what has been projected out onto other peoples, we remain widely unconscious of those same projections onto the other-than-human and more-than-human aspects of the world. There is still a hard line separating human subjects from the other-than-human as objects (with a partial exception for pets, charismatic megafauna, 'beauty spots', etc); and this split between humans and the rest lies at the heart of our ecological crisis. We may know this intellectually, but we often do not feel how it operates in our lives.

The difficult psychological work of seeing the perpetrator in ourselves and retrieving our projections is very painful, and yet therapy has shown us that it brings enormous gains. While it may be a relief, and even at times necessary, to project outwards, there is great relief in reclaiming that lost part of the self, reclaiming the energy previously bound in denial and repression. As Mary-Jayne Rust sums it up:

> When the white man projects his wild instinctual self onto black people, all the colour is taken out of him, he is left like a monochrome print, cut off from his colour and creativity.
>
> When a man projects his vulnerability, intuition and emotional side onto women, he is left in a cut-off autistic world, unable to relate.
>
> When a woman projects out her wild animal self, she becomes afraid of the fur on her face, the hair and flesh on her body, afraid of her instincts and intuition.
>
> When we idealise wilderness, we feel cut off from our own divinity and beauty, and we fly to unspoilt places in hordes, in search of peace and tranquillity, inevitably spoiling the places we visit.
>
> (Rust, 2009a: 12)

The social pyramid, with its simplification and redirection of energy flows, suffers from an exactly equivalent problem to the food pyramid which distorts ecosystems. Leaving out or denigrating much of what exists, turning forest web into homogeneous hierarchy, denying its own roots in the soil, it is *thin*; and this thinness makes it ultimately unsustainable. In time it will turn to dust and blow away on the wind. Meanwhile, it leaves us cheated and unsatisfied, like hungry ghosts trying to fill the hole left in our reality by consuming more and more *things*.

CAGED WILDNESS

Splitting off our animal selves, we also split ourselves off from other animals; in particular, from the huge numbers of feeling animals who are caged and abused for the benefit of humans – for medical science, for cosmetics testing, and for food in factory farms (about 10 *billion* animals per year in the USA alone (US Department of Agriculture, 2006a, b). Every day most of us use or eat products which have something to do with abused animals. In the original introduction to his novel *The Naked Lunch*, William Burroughs defines the Naked Lunch as 'a frozen moment when everyone sees what is on the end of every fork' (Burroughs, 1959/1968: 7). But this moment, for most people, is indefinitely postponed.

It is through turning 'the other' into an unfeeling object that atrocities are made possible. How else do we allow chickens to live knee deep in their own shit, having lost most of their feathers, never seeing the light of day or able even to stand up – and then eat them? Anthony Weston observes: '[As] far as I know, there are no worked-out ethical defences of factory farming; it is hard to escape the conclusion that it is a practice sustained by silent collusion, by the "wish not to know"' (Weston, 1999: 189). The implicit or explicit assumption behind this wish not to know is that animals are 'lower' than humans, and that this 'lowness' entitles us to use them as objects. Hence people argue about whether the use of animals in experiments is or is not necessary *for human benefit* – without asking why and how human benefit justifies animal suffering.

Often these ideas are expressed in moderate and civilised tones; but sometimes they come out very rawly indeed. In the comments blog for an American PBS programme about the laboratory use of chimps, *Chimpanzees: An Unnatural History*, one blogger interrupts a chorus of shock and horror to say:

> I am confused by the controversy. Human life takes preference [*sic*] over the life of a chimpanzee. If chimpanzees are required for medical research, then so be it. I suffer from an illness that at one time was 100% fatal. But due to research done on chimpanzees, I will live a normal life span which at one time was not possible. God put animals on the earth to serve man. The money spent on these chimps once research is no longer needed is money that could be better spent on children starving in the world. What is more important? The life of a child or the life of a chimpanzee? Once the animal is no longer needed for research they should be humanely euthenized [*sic*]. Then, there will be more money for starving children than keeping these animals alive

> who have a reputation of being brutal at times ....
> (Frank Guarino in PBS, 2006)

Chimps are not the only animals with 'a reputation for being brutal at times'. Another blogger later puts things even more brutally, making a revealing connection between 'lower' animals and women, and also between rights and (supposed) intelligence:

> Tell an AIDs patient that a stupid animal is more important than they are.
> ... If humans are so bad then make a difference by leaving the earth yourselves. But none of you will do that because you are lazy and a bunch of hypocrites.
> And what a shock that it's all women crying. Please stop living up to the stereotype of being oversensitive. ...
> The chimps didn't invent the internet or television. I am typing about a stupid chimp. The stupid chimp is not typing about me. Right now he is scratching his hairy butt. So the heck with them. If we can cure cancer and AIDs then bleep the animals.
> (Mark Danga in PBS, 2006)

We can perhaps be grateful to these bloggers for saying directly what is unspoken or muffled in more liberal discourse. I will return to the relationship between human and other-than-human animals – including chimpanzees – in Chapter 7.

RELAX, NOTHING IS UNDER CONTROL

In Chapter 1 I discussed units of meaning organised as oppositions, like 'wild|domesticated', 'human|nonhuman'. In the rest of the book I will try to detach the 'wild|domesticated' opposition from the 'human|nonhuman' one, and to show that wildness, in the senses of spontaneity and complexity with which I am primarily concerned, is also an attribute of humanity. However, humans are also deeply drawn to domestication – of ourselves and of other-than-human species. Domestication enriches our lives in countless ways; it is the fabric from which all civilisations so far have been woven. But without a living connection to underlying wildness, domestication is destructive of both human and other-than-human; it operates by *eliminating* complexity and substituting a crude and simplified replica of wild organisation. The ultimate form of domestication without wildness is the theme park.

Our human attraction to domestication clearly has much to do with security. Every organism seeks its own preservation, along with that of its offspring; this is both a biological necessity, and an experience of deep emotional significance. Humans are physically vulnerable creatures, without claws, strong muscles, powerful jaws, fast legs, shells, scales or wings; for us, the best hope of safety lies in our ability to control our environment through mental modelling. By bringing our environment as close to mental models as we can, we soothe our deep anxiety. At the same time we create new sources of stress, by eliminating from our environment the sorts of complexity which we evolved to inhabit.

Complete control of reality is impossible. This stark reality is hard to accept, and hard to endure. How can we relax in the face of this profound uncertainty about what the future will bring? This is the problem that different forms of psychotherapy and counselling address in different ways. Some therapies focus on strategies of micro-management; others, on acceptance of non-control. Body psychotherapy, at least in the Reichian stream, is centrally concerned with two intertwined states: *relaxation* and *spontaneity.* It investigates – for each individual and for people in general – how these states can be supported and strengthened, and what interferes with them, how people learn to live in chronic tension and alienation from their organismic need to relax and express their impulses. In doing so, it constantly comes up against important elements of our culture which *demand* tension and alienation. We can look at these from many points of view – political, developmental, sociological – and we shall touch on some of these as we go on; but thinking about them philosophically, they involve a particular attitude towards what we generally call 'nature'.

THE DOMESTICATION OF PEOPLE

What we call 'the rise of civilisation' can be understood as a process of human domestication: not only the creation of homes, but also – as we use the word in relation to other animals – making humans more pliant, biddable, and easily controlled. This domestication of human culture wrenches it out of communion with wild ecosystems, which are then in turn reshaped to satisfy the needs of domesticated humans.

The domestication of human beings – facilitating our domination and control by collective social systems – involves our *disembodiment*, our alienation from direct experience of bodily emotions and impulses. Many Western ethical and religious systems are essentially efforts to strengthen our domestication and weaken our embodiment. The reason for this, I suggest, is a *fear of spontaneity.* If spontaneity itself is perceived as dangerous, then spontaneous wisdom and kindness will never be given the chance to appear.

Body psychotherapy has deeply explored this fear of spontaneity as it manifests in individuals during therapy, and discovered that it rests on a fear of loss of control (Totton, 1998: 131ff). The ego, as it exists in Western culture at least, is functionally identical with a state of muscular tension which aims to control our bodily states and impulses. In fact we can't control our states and impulses, since in many ways we *are* our states and impulses; instead we control their *expression*. And we identify our selves with that state of expressive control, so that to relax and open up to spontaneity appears as a loss of selfhood.

In the List which I have suggested is a key element of Western culture, animals, organisms, dirt and messiness are all in the 'lower' set, alongside nature, spontaneity and wildness, and in opposition to the 'higher' set which includes humans, mentality, cleanliness, order, culture, control and civilisation. In Chapter 8 we shall see how in therapy clients frequently identify what is spontaneously emerging in their body experience with other-than-human creatures: apes, fishes, snakes, wolves, lions, mice, birds – all these beings and many more enter the therapeutic space once our fear of the spontaneous begins to relax and we can make room for 'mess'.

We fear the other-than-human because we identify it with spontaneity and therefore with danger. Hence we relate to the world from an instrumental position: we seek to control it, to make it do what we want, in much the same way that we try to make 'our' bodies do what 'we' want. We seek to domesticate the world as we ourselves are domesticated. From this point of view, the relationship which relatively 'wild' indigenous cultures have with their environment is incomprehensible to us.

WILD THERAPY

This book, then, explores and tries to support the 'wild side' of psychotherapy: the side which is concerned not to transmit the demands of culture to the nonconforming individual, but to support the individual's authentic and spontaneous self-organisation. However, it is not enough to take one side in this conflict (even though, if I did face this impossible choice, the wild side is where I would walk). Taking sides, as I have already indicated, simply underwrites the false horizontalisation of the issue: the idea that 'wild' and 'domesticated', for example, can be seen as paired concepts of equivalent status. It is true that 'individual' and 'culture' are mutually dependent and co-arising: a human individual can only organise herself authentically and spontaneously in and through culture, while at the same time there can be no culture without the individuals who carry and express it.

However, that aspect of individuality which is an organismic and energetic signature – the *impersonal* aspect of self – is part of nature, which precedes and grounds culture. For domestication to take place, there must already be wildness.

Just as the civilised is always already and simultaneously natural, the domesticated is always already and simultaneously wild. The destruction of wildness is also the destruction of civilisation. In Thoreau's famous words: 'In Wildness is the preservation of the world' (Thoreau, 1862: para 18). And in wildness, as well, is the preservation of individual wellbeing and growth: Thoreau also said 'It is in vain to dream of a wildness distant from ourselves' (Thoreau, 1856: 303).

So I will be looking at the currents of thought and practice in psychotherapy which flow towards this realisation, and at its implications for the future development of therapeutic work. Adam Phillips suggests that in his paper on the subject, 'Freud asks both what is wild psychoanalysis, and what is wild about psychoanalysis?' (Phillips, 2002: x). In what follows, I will be asking both what is wild therapy, and what is wild about therapy. But I will also be drawing on many other fields of investigation to inform and enrich the wildness of therapy, so that therapy can in turn enrich our general understanding of how humans can best live on this earth.

3

In and Out of the Wilderness

> There's no way to dismiss the wilderness. It demands that you imagine yourself in relation to something which by definition you know nothing about.
>
> (Thompson, 2008)

> People rarely perceive the irony inherent in the idea of preserving the wilderness.
>
> (Tuan, 1974: 112)

> Appreciation of wilderness began in the cities.
>
> (Nashe, 1967: 44)

Western civilisation has fallen in love with wilderness – just when, and perhaps just because, it is becoming unobtainable. Wild places have historically been seen as desolate places, comfortless and uncomfortable, far from home. However wild places are now and also, and increasingly, attractive, at least to Westerners: only a century or so ago to seek out wilderness was an exceptional and eccentric act, but now it seems to be the wish of many hearts.

This attraction to wilderness has of course grown as our technologies make it easier for us to access wilderness and survive there comfortably. It has also grown in proportion to the domestication of the ordinary Western environment. True wilderness appears to be the ultimate elsewhere, the opposite pole of existence to urban Western culture. But there is a deep paradox here: what makes it wild is the absence of humanity. To go to the wilderness is, in some measure, to destroy it. Mount Everest is littered with plastic and frozen human shit.

For centuries the primary Western response to what were seen as 'unused' areas of the planet was to shiver with distaste, and work out how they could be abolished by domesticating and exploiting them. Now, the mushrooming Western yearning for an experience of wilderness also tends to abolish what is being sought, in the act of seeking it: large numbers of people tramping, driving, boating or flying into wild areas drastically affect the ecology and ambience which form the object of desire. This what Hardin (1968, 1998) describes as 'the tragedy of the commons': whatever good resource exists in limited quantity, but freely available to all, will over time be degraded. To illustrate the paradox, here is Toni Frohoff writing in relation to dolphin viewing tours off the US North West coast:

> I was told of one professional boat operator who, when criticized by one of his passengers for running down and encircling the dolphins, justified his actions by saying, 'Well, there are so many boats out here that the dolphins don't come around as much any more, and people won't pay unless they get to spend time with the dolphins.'
>
> (Frohoff, 1998: 82)

This paradox rests at least partly, however, on a particular understanding of wilderness as *the place untouched by humanity*, and there is something impossibly abstract and romantic about this notion. It is also of course Romantic in the more precise sense, conforming to the aesthetic philosophy of the Romantic Movement, as expressed for example by Byron:

> There is a pleasure in the pathless woods,
> There is a rapture on the lonely shore.
> There is society where none intrudes,
> By the deep sea, and music in its roar:
> I love not man the less, but nature more
> From these our interviews, in which I steal
> From all I may be, or have been before,
> To mingle with the universe, and feel
> What I can ne'er express, yet cannot all conceal.
>
> (Byron, *Childe Harold's Pilgrimage*, Canto 4, Stanza 178)

This emphasis on solitude, sublimity and grandeur, William Cronon points out, can become a cult which 'tends to privilege some parts of nature at the expense of others'. Instead he invites us to celebrate 'the wildness in our own backyards ... the nature that is all around us if only we have eyes to see it.' He goes on: 'Indeed, my principal objection to wilderness is that it may teach us to be dismissive or even contemptuous of such humble places and experiences. Without our quite realizing it, wilderness tends to privilege some parts of nature at the expense of others' (Cronon, 1996: 22). Thus we develop notions of what amounts to first-class and second-class wilderness; and increasingly, though paradoxically, the more 'first class' and apparently pristine wilderness is, the more it is being managed and shaped behind the scenes to maintain its apparently wild qualities.

As Cronon again says:

> Wilderness is not quite what it seems. Far from being the one place on earth that stands apart from humanity, it is quite profoundly a human creation – indeed, the creation of very particular human cultures at very particular moments in human history. It is not a pristine sanctuary where the last remnant of an untouched, endangered, but still transcendent nature can for at least a little while longer be encountered without the contaminating taint of civilization. Instead, it is a product of that civilization, and could hardly be contaminated by the very stuff of which it is made. Wilderness hides its unnaturalness behind a mask that is all the more beguiling because it seems so natural.
>
> (Cronon, 1996: 7)

Other writers also speak up for *nature* as a more fundamental and universal category then *wilderness.* For example, the American ornithologist Robert Winkler writes that 'on walks in the unpeopled parts of the suburbs, I've witnessed the same wild creatures, struggles for survival, and natural beauty that we associate with true wilderness' (Winkler, 2003: ix).

Certainly by this point in history there *are* no places on the planet untouched by humanity; and in fact this has been true for a very long time, though some of the touching has been indirect through long-range pollution and atmospheric effects. 'Given the interpenetration of the human and non-human, to speak of "pristine wilderness" (land devoid of humans) is to speak of something which does not, did not, and cannot exist, at least not on this planet' (Whitt et al, 2001: 6). Accordingly a compromise definition of wilderness has developed, as a place which is not *dominated* or *controlled* by humans.

However there is a paradox in this description too: it is human control which prevents humans from controlling these areas. Many states have established National Parks, fenced-off areas of land which are not for humans to live in or build on; these generally become an important part of the economy through tourism of various kinds. But despite the ambiguity of these managed wildernesses, their existence still seems to rest on a view of wilderness as ideally a place without humans, positioning us outside nature and in opposition to it, as if humans are no longer part of nature. Wilderness becomes the place of the other-than-human and more-than-human; which, as we shall see, has a profound *political* effect on those human beings who live there.

There are (at least) three terms in play here: nature, wilderness, and wildness. Each of these is used in many different ways. I have explored in Chapter 1 the many complex senses of 'wild', but unless I indicate otherwise, I will use it in this book to point primarily to senses of 'spontaneous', 'local' and 'complex'. By 'wilderness' I initially denote a place where human use is not primary, and which strikes most city-dwellers, at least, as self-shaping rather than shaped by humans (Shultis, 1999); but I will also explore more radical concepts of untouched wilderness. And by 'nature', I refer to the ground of being, the unfolding of material and organic processes (including the expression of those processes in consciousness and thought). In this sense, everything that is, is natural – nuclear weapons as much as whales, housing estates as much as climax forests.

In the aura of the term 'nature', though, will always hover some of the other ways in which it has been used, and also some of the ways in which 'unnatural' has been used. But however destructive of other natural beings we may be, we can never be separated from nature, any more than can locusts or earthquakes. In a sense, our destructiveness is simply that of any species with no effective predators in its ecosystem, and hence able to multiply until it destroys its own environment. (Apart from microorganisms, humans are now virtually our own sole predators – but however murderous we are, so far we have had no lasting impact on human numbers.)

Yet the narrative of Western civilisation has lured many into the view that we must transcend the messy, dirty, dangerous and unpredictably wild aspects of earthly nature in order to reach the purer place of blue skywards spirituality – the order of heaven. This split, and these projections, have supported the illusion not only that humans are separate from and superior to the other-than-human world, but that we must erase our own human earthly nature, the animal within. The idealised, spiritualised human and the dangerous wilderness form a split complementarity – one which is unstable and easily reverses into dangerous 'unnatural' humans versus idealised spiritual wilderness.

As I have already suggested, positioning the wilderness as unused by humans doesn't in practice stop humans from going there and using it. One use is for tourism, including eco-tourism and spiritual tourism; but alongside and overlapping with this is the use of wilderness for psychological growth and healing. This use continues ancient themes: certain areas have been felt by indigenous peoples to be sacred and these places have been used for millennia for rite of passage rituals. The desert has been revered precisely for its emptiness, a place in which humans can experience symbolic death and rebirth as at certain stages of life. Like a shaman, Christ went into the desert for forty days and nights and was transformed. Spending time in places without the daily routines, distractions and comforts allows for the possibility of inner struggles to emerge and be resolved. In the language of psychotherapy we might say that spending time in outer wilderness enables an exploration of inner wilderness, the unconscious.

The primary Western understanding of wilderness at the moment, then, is as a *resource*: an economic resource, a psychological resource, a spiritual resource: something to be used. Without drawing a simplistic parallel between these different kinds of use, I do suggest that they can have something in common. Certainly each can be conducted in sustainable and in unsustainable ways. A cultural practice like the Vision Quest becomes something very different when carried out by wealthy Westerners who fly in with copious suitcases expecting a daily shower. I want to outline two alternative pictures of wilderness to this use-based one: the first of these is wilderness as *forbidden to humans,* the second is wilderness as *co-created by humans*.

WILDERNESS FORBIDDEN TO HUMANS

For most indigenous cultures there are some wild places which humans can enter, and others which humans must not use. Mount Everest, which as I said above is fast becoming a garbage dump, is known by Sherpa people of northern Nepal as Chomolungma, Tibetan for 'Goddess Mother of the World'; the peak was sacred and not a place for humans. (Luckily, a lower and less challenging peak – and one therefore less attractive to Westerners – called Kumbhila (or Kumbu Yul-lha) is apparently even more sacred to the Sherpas.) Perhaps this current of feeling flows into deep ecology visions of establishing vast areas barred to human civilisation. Evan Eisenberg (1998) proposes a transformation in our relationship with wilderness:

> Take any geographical unit – country, state, province, county, town, borough, precinct, block, backyard. Let each unit devote one-seventh of its land to wilderness, or something as close to wilderness as circumstances permit. If the wilderness is already there, let it be preserved; if not, let it be created.
>
> (Eisenberg, 1998: 408)

And the way to 'create' wilderness, of course, is to leave it alone to create itself. In a surprisingly short space of time, an area untouched by humans will become wild again, and, if above a critical size, and if the inorganic elements of the ecosystem (soil, climate etc) remain relatively intact, will establish a full ecosystem (Eisenberg, 1998: 535ff). The clear-cutting of lowland rainforest in the Gogol valley of Papua New Guinea was devastating; but six months after logging, 90% of the area was covered by vegetation, and after eighteen months Lawrence Hamilton 'could hardly force my way through the woody regrowth' (Hamilton, 1993: 118). After ten years, 70% of trees were primary species. This is exceptional even for the tropics, but regeneration happens even in temperate climates, if more gradually – Rothamsted experimental agricultural station in the UK has left two previously farmed areas, covering about four acres between them, untouched since the late nineteenth century; both have now reverted to wilderness (Weisman, 2007: 162–4; see also Janzen, 2009).

'Reversion' is the traditional term for this process, the implication being that the domesticated state is more progressive, the wild state more primitive. Increasingly, though, researchers are writing instead about 'regeneration', and thinking of domesticated land as damaged and deficient, in need of 'bed rest' so that it can recover.

> Yards and gardens are a very particular and notably impoverished ecosystem that favours weediness in both plants and animals. ... Cultivated land resembles what ecologists call a serial community: it results from a local wound and acts as a bandage to cover the soil until the forest or prairie grows back. Yards are in an early stage of bandaging, a stage in which life is low in number of species, high in number of individuals, and typifies by rampant reproduction.
>
> (Stein, 1993: 12)

I return to the regeneration of biodiversity later in this chapter.

There is a practical aspect to Eisenberg's proposal – uninterfered-with wilderness is crucial for the survival of other-than-human species, and also for the mitigation of climate change. But there is also a powerful psychological aspect to it. Large-scale wilderness needs simply to be left alone, entirely alone. This reality seems to be very hard for us to take in; but once we accept it, I suggest that there can be something deeply challenging yet also deeply comforting about it. Imagine how we would be affected by the knowledge that there were whole vast areas of the planet where human beings simply did not go. No exceptions. The knowledge that life in its richness and abundance was going on *without us.*

If we can grasp what this would mean, then we perhaps have a true sense of the wild, the untamed, the undomesticated. There is something wonderful but also something tragic about it – that in order for the wild to exist we have to be out of it, civilised humanity excluded from the natural order, shut out of Eden, our noses pressed up against the glass of a complex and whole ecology. Rilke wrote of this in the *First Duino Elegy*:

Even the knowing animals are aware
that we are not really at home in our interpreted world.

Hence the eerie grandeur of Alan Weisman's book which imagines a planet recovering from human beings, *The World Without Us* (Weisman, 2007). The picture of humans excluded from nature is also, of course, a picture of humans imprisoned in consciousness, cut off from the vastness of unconscious life. The realisation that life can go on without humans is parallel to Jung's assertion that individuation can go on without consciousness. 'Life going on without humans', however, is more usefully reconceptualised as 'life going on without capitalist-industrialist civilisation': this latter is not, despite its ambitions, synonymous with humanity.

WILDERNESS CO-CREATED BY HUMANS

We in the West are struggling, it seems, with several archetypes of wilderness, all overlapping yet all contradictory. There is wilderness as dangerous, worthless and marginal space; wilderness as resource, to be exploited; wilderness as teacher, to be approached respectfully; and wilderness as numinous, sacred, to be left alone. These images intertwine and interact in our relationship with the wild. But there is also at least one other sort of wilderness: although our view of it is, inevitably, shaped by our Western experience, it is an 'out there' actuality – a wilderness *in which real human societies turn out to always already be living*.

These are the First Nation societies of indigenous peoples, who have always lived in the wild, and have been pushed steadily back into land defined as 'wilderness' in the sense of 'not exploitable by Western civilisation'. Now, of course, pretty much everywhere is exploitable by capitalism and its technologies, and indigenous peoples are struggling to hold on even to what they have. But everywhere they have lived without being forcibly removed turns out to be a rich and fruitful environment for humans – when we relate to it as indigenous cultures do, as an integral, active and self-aware part of the ecosystem. In the Arctic tundra, the Kalahari or Central Australian desert, the Amazon jungle, indigenous cultures make a living without damaging their environment – in fact, make a living while at the same time *enriching* their environment. I will look in more detail at one example of this relationship between humans and ecosystem in Chapter 4, but it is now well documented as a common phenomenon (e.g. Plenderleith, 1999; Slikkerveer, 1999; and references therein).

This inhabited wilderness, then, is notable for its order and meaningfulness – every element of the environment is actively related with, understood and made sustainable use of. Hence some indigenous peoples *reverse* the current Western wilderness-worship, seeing the 'civilised' landscape as 'wild' in the sense of disordered, formless, meaningless. Jeanette Armstrong, a Native American, remembers:

> My grandmother said (translated from Okanagan), 'The people down there are dangerous, they are all insane.' My father agreed, commenting, 'It's because they are wild and scatter anywhere'.
> (Armstrong, 1995: 317)

Later she explains:

> Unless place can be relearned, it compels all other life forms to displacement and then ruin. This is what is referred to as 'wildness': a thing that cannot survive without special protective measures and that requires other life forms to change behavior in its vicinity.
> (Armstrong, 1995: 323)

The Okanagan are agriculturalists, but a hunter-gatherer culture on the other side of the earth takes the same view. Daly Pulkara, a senior custodian of Australian Aboriginal Ngarinman land, is asked what he calls the heavily cattle-eroded area:

> He looked at it for a while and said, 'It's the wild, just the wild' ... where life is absent, where all the care, intelligence and respect that generations of Aboriginal people have put into the country have been eradicated in a matter of a few short years.
> (Rose, 1988: 386)

This way of using the term 'wild' is powerfully corrective: it simplifies the ambiguity of positive and negative connotations in our usual Western usage, brought out in Tuan's gnomic observation: '"Wilderness" is now a symbol of the orderly processes of nature. As a state of the mind, true wilderness exists only in the great sprawling cities' (Tuan, 1974: 112). And it emphasises that wildness and wilderness in their earlier sense of chaotic and disordered places were largely the product of Westerners' *failure to see* the meaningful complexity under their noses: both a highly structured ecology and, as I will discuss in Chapter 4, a profoundly ordered, mutually beneficial and generous relationship between humans and other-than-humans.

This reversal in how 'wilderness' is applied has a powerful political meaning for indigenous peoples, who have suffered from the legalisation of the concept of wilderness as *terra nullius*, land which belongs to no one – no one worth considering! – and is therefore available to be appropriated (Lindqvist, 2008). For many indigenous cultures, the land *can* belong to no one, but belongs to itself; and humans, like other species, belong to the land.

WILDNESS AND WEEDINESS

> Generations have trod, have trod, have trod;
> And all is seared with trade; bleared, smeared with toil;
> And wears man's smudge and shares man's smell: the soil
> Is bare now, nor can foot feel, being shod.
>
> And for all this, nature is never spent;
> There lives the dearest freshness deep down things ...
> (Gerard Manley Hopkins, *God's Grandeur*)

So far I have been discussing different pictures of the wilderness 'out there', the opposite pole to Western urban environments. But in the same way that with the Chinese Yin-Yang concept taking either polarity to its extreme precipitates a phase-shift into the opposite polarity, Yin to Yang, Yang to Yin, so the extremes of urbanism constantly recreate micro-wildernesses within the cityscape, weeds springing up between the paving stones. Manuel De Landa (2000: 122) points out that cities never entirely succeed in 'socialising' the flows of energy and matter which pass through them: they are dynamic open systems, where multiple forms of matter-energy (including minerals, biomass and genes) enter into complex, non-linear and therefore unpredictable relationships (De Landa, 2000, Part II).

Through their complexity, cities develop wild aspects; in interstitial areas which fall between fields of human use, spontaneous ecologies develop and flourish:

> Although often heavily polluted and disturbed by human activity, interstitial wilderness sites can be important wild life habitats and may also be high in biodiversity, ... containing, *inter alia*, native plant species, naturalized non-native garden escapes ... and, remarkably, spontaneously occurring new hybrid plant species ...
> (Jorgensen & Tylecote, 2007: 453)

As I have said in Chapter 2, wildness and complexity go hand in hand: a patch of waste ground is often more complex, and in that sense more genuinely wild, than a carefully tended garden of rainforest plants.

A common pattern is for a successful, partially regenerated wild urban ecosystem – an abandoned railway line, for example – to be recognised, taken up as a community resource, a 'nature trail', and gardened back into something showier but actually much simpler, as happened recently to much public acclaim with the abandoned elevated railway in West Manhattan (Planning Pool, 2009). Jorgensen and Tylecote suggest that, instead, interstitial spaces might be approached by planners on their own terms:

> They are evolving landscapes which re-connect our natural-cultural selves in the context of our urban existence. Their ambivalence and ambiguity should not be seen as a failing but as a reservoir of meanings, which may be constantly elaborated and explored. They have an important role both in terms of their physical functions and as a means of unlocking imaginative truths and questions about the human condition. ... Their essential qualities ... include their ability to accommodate the spontaneous development of wild nature, the freedom and flexibility they offer to human thought and action; but above all the ways in which human and natural agency have become enmeshed over time.
> (Jorgensen & Tylecote, 2007: 458)

If a 'weed' is a plant growing where humans don't want it, then, since humans are indifferent to them, urban wildlife species are not weeds. But David Quammen (1998) offers a wider definition of weeds, one which includes animals as well as plants:

> What do Mediterranean fruit flies, boll weevils, and water hyacinths have in common with crab-eating macaques or Nile perch? Answer: they're *weedy* species, in the sense that animals as well as plants can be weeds. ... They reproduce quickly, disperse widely when given a chance, tolerate a fairly broad range of habitat conditions, take hold in strange places, succeed especially in disturbed ecosystems, and resist eradication once they're established. They are scrappers, generalists, opportunists. They tend to thrive in human-dominated terrain because in crucial ways they resemble *Homo sapiens*: aggressive, versatile, prolific, and ready to travel.
> (Quammen, 1998: 66–7)

Humans, in other words, are the ultimate 'weeds', clogging the growth of many other species. But on Quammen's definition, more and more species are becoming 'weedy', especially at what Mike Davis calls the 'increasingly fractal edge of development' of cities (Davis, 1998: 237): Davis suggests that in Southern California mountain lions are gradually joining coyotes, raccoons and other wild species as opportunist urban scavengers. 'What we are witnessing may be nothing less than a behavioral quantum jump: the emergence of nonlinear lions with a lusty appetite for soft, slow animals in spandex' (Davis, 1998: 249).

This process of adaptation to urban existence is termed 'synurbization' (Luniak, 2004). Among species which have become synurbic in various areas of the world are squirrels, rabbits, red foxes, striped field mice, badgers, stone martens, Mandarin ducks, Canada geese, parakeets, blackbirds, and magpies; in Tokyo, 71 species of birds have adapted to the city (all from Luniak, 2004: 51–2). New York State suburbs have seen a seven-fold multiplication in their deer population since 1970, with similar increases in woodpeckers, chickadees, grouse, hawks, squirrels, chipmunks, opossums, raccoons, and foxes (Dunn, 1999: 3). And synurbization involves changes in behaviour: among others Luniak lists increased population density, reduced migration, prolonged breeding season, greater longevity, and change in feeding habits. As we have just seen, this can involve feeding directly off humans as well as off human property or garbage. As David Baron says in his book on urban mountain lions, *The Beast in the Garden*, 'America [and the rest of the urban world] is engaged in a grand and largely unintentional experiment. As wildlife invades suburbs, and as suburbs invade wildlife habitat, we are changing animal behavior in unexpected and sometimes troubling ways' (Baron, 2004: 233).

The distinction of essence which often appears to exist between city and wilderness is in many ways more a difference of degree. The same natural processes that operate in the wilderness operate in the city – not only in official 'green areas', but also in every square inch of urban landscape (Spirn, 1984). A consequence of the cult of absolute wilderness, according to Michael Pollan, is that 'once a landscape is no longer "virgin" it is typically written off as fallen, lost to nature, irredeemable' (Pollan, 2003: 188). But the relationship between the wild and the urban is much more complicated than that. Peter del Tredici points out that carefully maintained native wilderness is effectively a form of garden, while conversely, a piece of urban waste ground is better understood as 'emergent forest' (Humphries, 2010: 1), an ecosystem self-creating without human intervention. Del Tredici and his co-workers explore the manifold ways in which urbanised plant life can contribute to environmental regeneration: controlling erosion, stabilising stream and river banks, building soil on degraded land, filtering water and air, absorbing heat, recycling minerals, and storing carbon (Del Tredici, 2006: 50; Del Tredici et al, 2010).

In a sense, then, there is a polarity between the fragile complexity of wilderness and the robust simplicity of 'weediness'. But as Del Tredici makes very clear, weediness is a necessary precursor stage of wilderness, re-establishing the conditions for wild growth in a devastated landscape: weediness is 'emergent forest'. Another poem by Gerard Manley Hopkins celebrates this relationship:

> What would the world be, once bereft
> Of wet and wildness? Let them be left,
> O let them be left, wildness and wet;
> Long live the weeds and the wilderness yet.
> (Gerard Manley Hopkins, *Inversnaid*)

Some view the celebration of urban wilderness as wishful thinking:

> In the context of claims that even the most remote tracts of 'wild' nature bear the imprint of the social, there is an understandable attraction to the idea that in the very heartland of the social – be it the sprawl of suburbia or the depths of the datasphere – there is a resurgence of 'nature', and efflorescence of 'life'.
> (Clark, 2000: 28)

There is undoubtedly some truth to this; and no urban resurgence can make up for the destruction of ecological complexity. In *The End of the Wild,* Stephen M. Meyer eloquently points out that 'the extinction crisis ... is over, and we have lost' (Meyer, 2006: 5). He divides the biosphere into 'relic species', whose habitat has been largely destroyed but who may survive indefinitely in artificial habitats managed by humans; 'ghost species', which may still be plentiful but which are certain to become extinct in the relatively near future; and 'weed species' which can thrive under human-dominated conditions (Meyer, 2006: 11–17).

> Over the next hundred years, perhaps half of the Earth's species are destined to become relics or ghosts in the wild, while weedy species will constitute an ever-growing proportion of the plants and animals around us. ... Ecosystems will experience a dumbing-down as built-in redundancies are eliminated. The web of life will become the strand of life.
> (Meyer, 2006: 16–17)

Perhaps it is a matter of personality how far one can enthuse about the continual rewilding of urban environments, and how far one mourns instead for the loss of fragile primal habitats. It is possible simultaneously to do both, which may be the most adequate response to the reality in which we live. In his book *The Wild Places,* Robert Macfarlane describes his travels around Britain searching for the truest wilderness. At the end, he returns to his own home in the suburbs of Oxford, and climbs a tree.

> I imagined the wind moving through ... places that were separated from each other by roads and housing, fences and shopping centres, street-lights and cities, but that were joined across space at that time by their wildness in the wind. We are fallen in mostly broken pieces, I thought, but the wild can still return us to ourselves.
>
> ...
>
> Wildness was here, too, a short mile south of the town in which I lived. It was set about by roads and buildings. Much of it was menaced, and some of it was dying. But at that moment the land seemed to ring by a wild light.
>
> (Macfarlane, 2007: 320–1)

INNER WILDERNESS

> 'Wilderness' cannot be defined objectively: it is as much a state of the mind as a description of nature.
>
> (Tuan, 1974: 112)

The different notions of wilderness I have been describing are important and interesting in their own right. A further notion of particular relevance to this book is of wilderness as a metaphor or symbol for certain qualities of the psyche. Even urban micro-wilderness is still 'out there' compared to the 'wilderness in here' which will be a major theme of this book.

This in some ways takes us back to the Romantics and their so-called 'pathetic fallacy' that our environment can reflect our feelings back to us. Shelley wrote in *Julian and Maddalo* (I, 14):

> ... I love all waste
> And solitary places; where we taste
> The pleasure of believing what we see
> Is boundless, as we wish our souls to be.

The Romantics condensed and focused this perception, but it seems to express a universal human impulse. In the *Gilgamesh* epic, inscribed on clay tablets in ancient Mesopotamia, we find this, or at any rate something which can be translated like this:

> As when one comes upon a path in woods
> Unvisited by men, one is drawn near
> The lost and undiscovered in himself
> (Mason, 1970: 35)

The correspondence that we can experience between the wilderness and the psyche is very much to do with what *Gilgamesh* calls 'the lost and undiscovered' in ourselves. The deepest inner wilderness is the unconscious. As Gary Snyder writes:

> The depths of mind, the unconscious, are our inner wilderness areas ... The conscious agenda-planning ego occupies a very tiny territory, a little cubicle somewhere near the gate, keeping track of some of what goes in and out (and sometimes making expansionist plots), and the rest takes care of itself.
> (Snyder, 1990: 17–18)

This is what, in the next chapter, I will describe as 'Wild Mind'. And just like physical wilderness, wild mind can never be eliminated so long as life survives, though it can be impoverished, marginalised, reduced to a patch of scrub on a corner of waste ground, to dreams, involuntary movements and slips of the tongue. Given the slightest opportunity, wilderness always renews itself: seeds sprout in the rubble, in a few years trees will grow up through abandoned stretches of tarmac. Wilderness is, in a sense, the *tendency to connect*, to become more complex; it is innate in all living systems, including ourselves.

WILDERNESS/WORDLESSNESS

> These words are written to those of us whose language is not heard, whose words have been stolen or erased, those robbed of language, who are called voiceless or mute, even the earthworms, even the shellfish and the sponges, for those of us who speak our own language.
> (Griffin, 1984, dedication)

We can also think of wilderness as the place untamed by language, the place without names. If wilderness lies, in Lord Dunsany's mantric phrase (e.g. 1924/1982), 'beyond the fields we know', then that includes the field of verbal representation. Lewis Carroll gives a very clear sense of this in *Through the Looking Glass, and What Alice Found There*, when Alice encounters 'the wood ... where things have no names', and thinks '"I wonder what'll become of my name when I go in? I shouldn't like to lose it at all – because they'd have to give me another, and it would be almost certain to be an ugly one."' She enters the wood, and loses not only her own name, but the names of the wood and of the trees.

> Just then a Fawn came wandering by: it looked at Alice with its large gentle eyes, but didn't seem at all frightened. ...
> 'What do you call yourself?' the Fawn said at last. Such a soft sweet voice it had!
> 'I wish I knew!' thought poor Alice. She answered, rather sadly, 'Nothing, just now.'
> 'Think again,' it said: 'that won't do.'
> Alice thought, but nothing came of it. 'Please, would you tell me what you call yourself?' she said timidly. 'I think that might help a little.'
> 'I'll tell you, if you'll move a little further on,' the Fawn said. 'I can't remember here.'
> So they walked on together though the wood, Alice with her arms clasped lovingly round the soft neck of the Fawn, till they came out into another open field, and here the Fawn gave a sudden bound into the air, and shook itself free from Alice's arms. 'I'm a Fawn!' it cried out in a voice of delight, 'and, dear me! you're a human child!' A sudden look of alarm came into its beautiful brown eyes, and in another moment it had darted away at full speed.
> (Carroll, 1871, Chapter 3)

Several feminists have seen connections between women, wilderness, and wordlessness. In her tremendous paper 'Feminist criticism in the wilderness' (1981), Elaine Showalter draws on the anthropologists Shirley and Edwin Ardener's theory (Ardener, 1977/1989) of the relationship between dominant male cultures and overlapping, 'muted' women's cultures, which represents the two by intersecting circles; much of the women's circle falls within the men's one, but there is also a 'wild' crescent not overlapping but falling outside it.

> We can think of the 'wild zone' of women's culture spatially, experientially, or metaphysically. Spatially it stands for an area which is literally no-man's-land, a place forbidden to men, which corresponds to the zone in X which is off limits to women. Experientially it stands for the aspects of the female life-style which are outside of and unlike those of men; again, there is a corresponding zone of male experience alien to women. But if we think of the wild zone metaphysically, or in terms of consciousness, it has no corresponding male space since all of male consciousness

> is within the circle of the dominant structure and thus accessible to or structured by language. In this sense, the 'wild' is always imaginary; from the male point of view, it may simply be the projection of the unconscious. In terms of cultural anthropology, women know what the male crescent is like, even if they have never seen it, because it becomes the subject of legend (like the wilderness). But men do not know what is in the wild.
> (Showalter, 1981: 200)

Ursula Le Guin comments on Showalter:

> Men live their whole lives within the Dominant area. When they go off hunting bears, they come back with bear stories, and these are listened to by all, they become the history or the mythology of that culture. So the men's 'wilderness' becomes 'Nature,' considered as the property of 'Man.'
>
> But the experience of women as women, their experience unshared with men, that experience is the wilderness or the wildness that is utterly other – that is, in fact, to Man, unnatural. That is what civilization has left out, what culture excludes, what the Dominants call animal, bestial, primitive, undeveloped, unauthentic ... what has not been spoken, and when spoken, has not been heard ... what we are just beginning to find words for, our words, not their words: the experience of women. For dominance-identified men and women both, that is true wildness. Their fear of it is ancient, profound, and violent. The misogyny that shapes every aspect of our civilization is the institutionalized form of male fear and hatred of what they have denied, and therefore cannot know, cannot share: that wild country, the being of women.
> (Le Guin, 1989: 163)

Both these writers are of course well aware that they are using (highly eloquent) language to describe this unlanguaged wilderness. But the connections they are making allow the concept to arise of a *remainder* that cannot be included within the mainstream – of language, of consciousness, of civilisation. This remainder is equally embodied in the primal forest – insofar as this still has physical existence – and in the weedy, litter-strewn edges of motorways. It is *the fact of being left out* which is more significant than anything else. In Terry Bisson's extraordinary story, *Bears Discover Fire* (Bisson, 1994), Americans realise that bears have discovered fire, come down from the mountains, and are living in the forest-like interstitial space of motorway medians (central reservations), eating the previously unknown 'newberries'.

The narrator's mother runs away from her old people's home and dies quietly sitting around the fire with the bears. Important things can happen in the gaps – including the gaps between words, and indeed the gaps between phonemes that allow language to exist as a meaningful system.

LOST IN THE WILDERNESS

> Remarkably, the growing distance between people and nature has gone hand in hand with more positive attitudes toward wilderness ... Even so, ancient fears of nature have not vanished, and they may reemerge when people are exposed to wilderness ... Modern individuals have thus come to feel deeply ambivalent toward wilderness, finding it both beautiful and terrifying, both awesome and awful.
>
> (Koole & Van den Berg, 2005: 1014)

Only domesticated people can become lost in the wilderness; not because wild humans always know their way around, but because for them there is no wilderness in which to become lost – or only what Tuan calls the 'true wilderness' of 'the great sprawling cities' (Tuan, 1974: 112). It was in the earlier days of domestication that the other-than-human wilderness was truly terrifying, because it was no longer our home but not yet something we could completely keep out or protect against. Our relationship with it now is, as Koole and Van den Berg say, ambivalent. It only takes complete darkness to fall for a beautiful rural landscape to become something much more alarming and confusing.

Jorgensen and Tylecote point out that urban interstitial land, too, has its frightening aspect:

> It may be regarded as a dangerous place, particularly by women, elderly people and members of ethnic groups, who may feel themselves to be vulnerable and liable to be victims of physical or sexual assault, or robbery or mischief from gangs of young people ... In general, these woodland landscapes are often perceived as lawless, disordered places disfigured by the traces these crimes and incivilities leave behind in the form of dens, camps, fires, burnt out cars, fly tipping, collections of cans and bottles and evidence of drug abuse. ... There is evidence that some people invest these environments with good and bad meanings simultaneously. [In one local survey] a quarter of those who identified local green and woodland spaces as their favourite places in the locality also said that they would feel unsafe if they were

> alone in them ... It seems likely that this ambivalence is widespread, probably applying to a wide range of urban landscapes.
>
> (Jorgensen & Tylecote, 2007: 444)

In the UK, the predator we fear is human (perhaps also supernatural); in other parts of the world, wilderness still holds real physical threat from other-than-human predators.

Now that we feel ourselves masters of the wilderness – at least provisionally, accompanied and in daylight – now that it is nearly extinguished, we can afford to feel protective of it. That at least is the cynical take on our current relationship with wilderness; but there is also a genuine deep love of its otherness, and a desperate sense of its fragility. Perhaps the urbanite who claims to believe in the importance of wilderness, but has no desire to go near it, is not such a figure of fun. We need more human beings prepared to stay away. Robert Greenway is a pioneer of ecopsychology, one of the early people to take therapeutic groups into the wilderness. Recently he wrote:

> Perhaps ... we can come to see 'the wilderness experience' as a vision or a model of modes of healing that don't require wilderness. Perhaps the clearest evidence of our recovery will be that we do not demand that wilderness heals us. We will have learned to let it be.
>
> (Greenway, 1995: 134)

4

Wild Mind

> Knowing is a matter of part of the world making itself intelligible to another part. ... We do not obtain knowledge by standing outside of the world; we know because 'we' are *of* the world. We are part of the world in its differential becoming.
>
> (Karen Barad, 2003: 829)

> The foraging way of life is as much a mode of spirituality as a mode of subsistence.
>
> (Barker, 2006: 409)

LOCAL KNOWLEDGE

The French anthropologist Claude Levi-Strauss wrote an influential book which appeared in English as *The Savage Mind* (1966). This drastically contradicts the sense of the original title, *La Pensée Sauvage*, or 'Wild Thought'. To underline the point, the French edition had a cover illustration of the wild pansy, *pansée sauvage*, which is pronounced identically. While earlier Western anthropologists thought of tribal cultures as 'savages' – a word which originally simply meant 'living in the woods' – Levi-Strauss helps us recognise them as what I am calling 'wild' or 'undomesticated' cultures – participating human members of wild ecosystems.

These wild cultures will generally be hunter-gatherers, or what many anthropologists now refer to as foragers, perhaps most exactly defined as societies which 'exercise no deliberate control over the *gene pool* of exploited resources' (Panter-Brick et al, 2001: 2, original italics): in other words, they do not breed either crops or animals for increased human benefit, although spontaneous co-evolution may well take place. (As we will see below, jungle gardening, for example, is in many ways much more closely aligned with foraging than with agriculture.) It is not difficult to envisage the difference that this fact alone makes to a society's relationship with the other-than-human. A relationship where one participant deliberately physically alters the other for their own benefit is one of ownership.

There are huge controversies among anthropologists and archaeologists about the nature of forager societies, their relationship with agricultural and urban societies, whether 'pure' foragers still exist, and whether how contemporary foragers live can tell us anything about prehistoric foragers (as well as the works referred to above and below, for perspectives which challenge the approach taken here see e.g. Sassaman, 2004; Schweitzer et al, 2000). We do not need to go too far into these issues, but will focus instead on exploring elements of the forager world-view like those touched on by Graeme Barker:

> Commonly the environment is regarded as a benign spiritual home ... relations with it are modelled on the same principle of sharing that applies within the human community: it is the source of all good things, 'a giving environment' ... Foragers ... commonly do not have words for distinguishing between people, animals and plants as separate categories ....
>
> (Barker, 2006: 58–9)

Barker is describing a culture that *includes rather than excludes.* It includes the other-than-human within the same systems of knowledge and relationship as the human; and it models both these communities as essentially generous, essentially sharing. It is able to do this because it doesn't seek to *own* the world, but only to live within it, to pass through it: humans belong to the land, not the land to humans. 'Land needed for living is appropriated not by fences and boundaries, in the way of farmers, but by moving through it along paths. Thus a forager's territory is something to be *related to* and *associated with*, not *owned*, and tracks and paths are symbolic of the process of life itself' (Barker, 2006: 58, original italics). And this relationship with the world both allows and requires humans to understand what happens where they live, and to persuade and encourage, rather than force, the world to satisfy their needs.

Some people would consider that this way of being-in-the-world is inherent to an existence unmediated by technology, including the technologies of agriculture. However, Bird-David (1990), from whom Barker takes the concept of the 'giving environment', argues that even when two societies exist side by side with quite similar mixes of hunter-gathering and agriculture, foragers can be distinguished by their fundamental world-view, which experiences the world around them as a generous parent. 'They view their environment as giving, and their economic system is characterized by modes of distribution and property relations that are constructed in terms of giving, as within a family, rather than in terms of reciprocity, as within kin' (Bird-David, 1990: 189; see also Turnbull, 1976). Interestingly, in the specific neighbouring societies Bird-David describes, both recognise a deity under the same name; but the foragers describe him as a 'parent', and the farmers as an 'ancestor'. It is as if the shift to an agriculturalist mode has pushed the relationship with the world, as mediated through the deity, one remove further away.

Certainly there are at least two features of forager life which strongly support the 'giving' way of being. One emerges from Lee and Devore's neat summary: 'We make two basic assumptions about hunter-gatherers: (1) they live in small groups, and (2) they move around a lot' (Lee & Devore, 1968: 11). These characteristics are more than accidental: they have important effects on the social and psychological structures of forager cultures. It is necessary to their survival that they cooperate and share, which is much easier in a small group with face-to-face relationships; and necessary also that they do not attach closely to any single spot, since no one spot will be able to meet their needs for sustenance.

The other feature is that for children to survive and reach adulthood, they must be constantly supported by grown-ups. Infants in forager cultures are held and carried at all times – not only by mothers, but by relatives and allies of all kinds (Hrdy, 2009: 73–82; Sorenson, 1998: 83–4). To grow up in this way – cherished and nurtured by all around you – is to directly experience the world as 'a giving environment'; and this upbringing facilitates the development of an ecological self, a Wild Mind.

When we write that foragers 'cooperate and share', it communicates very little of the real texture of connectedness between individuals in forager culture. Richard Sorenson offers a vignette of adolescent boys hunting:

> One day, deep within the forest, Agaso, then about 13 years of age, found himself with a rare good shot at a cuscus in a nearby tree. But he only had inferior arrows. Without the slightest comment or solicitation, the straightest, sharpest arrow of the group moved so swiftly and so stealthily straight into his hand, I could not see from whence it came.
>
> At that same moment, Karako, seeing that the shot would be improved by pulling on a twig to gently move an obstructing branch, was without a word already doing so, in perfect synchrony with Agaso's drawing of the bow, i.e., just fast enough to fully clear Agaso's aim by millimeters at the moment his bow was fully drawn, just slow enough not to spook the cuscus. Agaso, knowing this would be the case made no effort to lean to side for an unobstructed shot, or to even slightly shift his stance. Usumu, similarly synchronized into the action stream, without even

> watching Agaso draw his bow, began moving up the tree a fraction of a second before the bowstring twanged.
>
> (Sorenson, 1998: 90)

As Sorenson remarks, this sort of synchrony is:

> alien to my Western consciousness ... when trying to describe that kind of unity in English, the words bump up against each other as if contradictions – as in *individualistic unified at-oneness,* a phrase self-contradictory in English, and yet another indication of the magnitude of the gap separating these two types of consciousness.
>
> (Sorenson, 1998: 90)

As we have seen in Chapter 2, this 'individualistic unified at-oneness' is exactly the way in which an ecosystem functions: each being pursuing its own needs, in perfect synchrony with other beings. To live as part of an ecosystem, one has to *be* part of an ecosystem.

THE KAYAPÓ

> The science of the concrete was necessarily restricted by its essence to results other than those destined to be achieved by the exact natural sciences but it was no less scientific and its results no less genuine. They were secured ten thousand years earlier and still remain at the basis of our own civilization.
>
> (Levi-Strauss, 1966: 16)

We in the mainstream culture can now have some grasp of the deep and rich understanding with which wild cultures approach and participate in their host ecosystems, and it becomes clear how profoundly the mainstream has misperceived such societies as ignorant and incompetent. For example, 'slash-and-burn' has been the Western name given to shifting cultivation, or 'swidden', the most common form of agriculture in the world's rain forests. As carried out by Western or Westernised farmers, it destroys the soil and permanently eliminates rain forest from the areas where it is used. However as practised by indigenous peoples swidden can be deft, subtle and sustainable.

The semi-nomadic Kayapó of the Amazon basin clear a forest plot by felling the largest central trees outwards, bringing smaller trees and brush down with them. While all this is baking in the sun they plant some of their root crops within this wheel of fallen trees and brush, and then slow-burn it so that the crops draw up the nutrients released as ash. Once the ashes have cooled, the rest of the root crops are planted; a week or so later, remaining twigs and branches are burnt in piles, and heavy-feeding crops like beans and squashes are planted in these ashes (Hecht & Posey, 1989: 182–6).

After a few seasons, the garden is left to revert to forest. It will be used for years as a permaculture plot, with some crops bearing for thirty or forty years, together with self-seeding successional plants like fruit trees, palms and medicinal herbs, and berries that attract birds and wildlife for hunting. These gardens need no attention for months or years at a time. They give high yields for very little work – far more so than most Western agriculture – and through the use of biochar (Petersen et al, 2001; Bruges, 2009) they actually *improve* the rainforest soil, in stark contrast to agribusiness.

The anthropologist Darrell Posey wrote extensively about the Kayapó; he emphasises that the community he contacted and lived among was a small and deeply wounded remnant of a much larger culture, struggling to preserve and recover its way of life after the shocking impact of contact with Western civilisation (Posey, 2002: 30), an impact both cultural and physical. 'European diseases swept with unimaginable speed through indigenous populations with devastating effects' (Posey, 2002: 59), creating what Hemming (2006: 13) describes as 'the world's worst demographic catastrophe': it is estimated that initial contact with Europeans reduced Amazonian populations to a twentieth of their previous size, with death rates as high as 70–80% from a single epidemic (death rates can still can be 30–40% even in inoculated indigenous groups). 'First contact' was generally post-disease rather than pre-disease, since infections such as smallpox, measles, cholera and TB swept ahead of Europeans, giving them a highly distorted picture of Amazonian culture which they encountered only in a recently fragmented and traumatised form (Posey, 2002: 59–60).

Having previously lived in one large town of perhaps 5,000 people, fatal diseases splintered the Kayapó subtribe which Posey knew into small villages of 200 or 300. Women chiefs disappeared because whites preferred to deal with males (Posey, 2002: 27). Most shamans died or were killed, replaced by apprentices or 'weak shamans'. 'Plant knowers', who carried an understanding of how to relate to the plant communities without the spiritual context within which this information was previously framed, filled the gap as best they could (Posey, 2002: 26).

Despite this physical and psychological trauma, the Kayapó still practice an environmentally sensitive agriculture beyond anything which Western expertise can match. On the savannah and grasslands where the Kayapó villages are situated are islands of forest known as *apete* (the following account is from Posey, 2002: Ch 18). Anthropologists have long assumed them to be natural, and only recently realised that most are deliberately created by 'infecting' new areas with a mulch created out of compost heaps from existing *apete,* filling a natural depression with the mulch and then mixing this with soil from termite nests and smashed up bits of a particular ants' nest (including living ants and termites in the mixture). The resulting mounds are nurtured by the Kayapó as they pass along savannah trails, adding especially useful trees and plants; over the years, they grow into full-scale *apete.*

The *apete* are crammed with useful trees and plants, providing food, medicines (for fevers, bleeding, diarrhoea, body aches, dizziness, headaches, toothaches, abortion, and contraception), materials for baskets, cords, needles, bows and arrows and ceremonial items, firewood, body paint, poisons, and containers and wrappings. Some trees are planted specifically to attract game and birds; vines that produce drinkable water are transplanted to the *apete*. *Apete* are used as places of rest, to pass the hottest time of the day under shade, to paint bodies of relatives, or for supervised play for children. They are also a favoured spot for lovers. In times of war or epidemic they are used as self-sufficient refuges, and also as ambush spots for warriors.

But these complex, incredibly rich, humanly co-created resources appear to the non-local eye as 'natural' occurrences – which in a deeper sense is of course exactly what they are! Darrell Posey reached some understanding of Kayapó techniques by living with them, talking with them. Far from using fire to clear the *campos,* as anthropologists assumed, the Kayapó use it to protect and encourage the *apete*. Kayapó 'do not make a clear distinction between field and forest nor between wild and domesticated species' (Posey, 2002: 10) – not because their categories are inadequate, but because there *is* no clear distinction.

'Gathered plants are transplanted, concentrated in spots near trails and campsites, to produce "forest fields". The sides of trails themselves are planting zones' (Posey, ibid; see also Panter-Brick et al, 2001: 2). 'Old fields' of semi-domesticated species can easily be confused by non-natives with wild forest (Posey, 2002: 29).

> One must also think of how artificial are our own categories and how they have limited our own investigation of human manipulation of nature. For example, while we distinguish between 'campo' and 'forest', the Indians recognize the many different proportions, types and configurations of campo-cerrado-forest. And while our categories include such opposing entities as 'domesticated' and 'wild', to the Indians manmade *apete* are mirrors of forest openings. For example, whilst gallery forests and swampy forests close to Gorotire were cleared to decrease mosquitoes and lower the risk of malaria, nearby, but in another direction, forest islands were being formed in campo for protection

> and the production of useful materials. Thus at the same time clearings were being formed in forests and forests were being created in campos.
>
> (Posey, 2002: 204)

Does it make sense to say that plants so useful to the Kayapó, so carefully selected, transplanted and nurtured for countless centuries, are 'wild'? Only because the Kayapó themselves are wild. In *campo* and *cerrado* environments, much of the 'natural' flora has in fact been planted or encouraged. Like several other modern writers, Clement (2006: 34; see also Neves et al, 2001: 14) believes that 'pristine environments were probably rare in Amazonia at contact' with Westerners. Like other investigators in various parts of the world, Posey (2002: 204) suggests that 'our ideas must be re-evaluated to admit the possibility that aboriginal management and manipulation of these ecosystems have been widespread' – co-creating their own ecological niche much like the earthworms I described in Chapter 2.

> It is impossible to ascertain the true extent of Indian influence in either forest or campo. Today's relatively small Kayapó villages are only remnants of ancient villages that were once linked by sizeable and extensive trails ... It is probable, moreover, that many tribes throughout Brazil once practised *campo* and *cerrado* management. Even in areas where Indians have disappeared, botanical evidence of human manipulation and management is still discernible, and we hope that further research will uncover information on the extent of management practices.
>
> (Posey, 2002: 204)

In support of this interpretation, throughout the Amazon basin (and in other places including Ecuador, Peru, West Africa and South Africa), patches of extremely fertile soil have been discovered in the midst of the usual jungle poor-fertility soil. Known as *terra preta* ('dark earth'), this soil is now understood to have been created by indigenous people at least a thousand years ago, using a mixture of charcoal, bone and manure – probably by methods similar to those of the Kayapó. Full of nutrients and microorganisms essential to plant growth, *terra preta* can be up to two metres deep; its nutrients are 'locked' against being leached away by tropical conditions, and it is reported to actually *grow* at the rate of up to a centimetre a year (for all the above see Petersen et al, 2001; Lehman et al, 2003; Mann, 2002; Glaser, 2007; Bruges, 2009).

All of this may have some bearing on recent reports (Heckenberger et al, 2003, 2008) backing up Posey's account of Kayapó cultural memory: satellite mapping and on-the-ground archaeological investigation of the part of the Upper Xingu region occupied by the Kuikuro tribe show a network of ancient, densely packed towns, villages, and hamlets arranged in an organised pattern of 'garden cities'. Such intensive settlement would not have been possible on the unimproved shallow soils of the Amazon rainforest: as Petersen et al write, *terra preta* is 'often the most monumental and enduring material testimony to the indigenous polities that once thrived in the Amazon' (Petersen et al, 2001: 103). Several people now believe that *terra preta* offers us a potentially crucial way to limit global warming, by locking up carbon permanently in a way that at the same time improves soil yields (Bruges, 2009).

Like the Kayapó, this Upper Xingu society, of which we know nothing, was apparently destroyed by catastrophic disease when Europeans arrived in South America. As Neves et al write:

> Amazonian indigenous groups can no longer be stereotyped as small, isolated communities living in the depths of the forest or dispersed along rivers. The perception of simple social structures and a low level of cultural achievement is largely the consequence of catastrophic population collapse, displacement and cultural loss.
> (Neves et al, 2001: 15)

This is a huge, and very recent, realisation – the discovery of an unknown civilisation or network of civilisations (in a sense confirming the many stories and fantasies of El Dorado, a lost golden city in the Amazon). But what is even more extraordinary about it is that this seems to have been *an urbanised forager culture* – not in the literal sense that they subsisted entirely by hunting and gathering, but in the more important sense that they experienced themselves as part of a 'giving' local ecosystem.

The Kayapó clearly don't *plan* how to farm in harmony with the local ecosystem – or not in the same sense that we plan, drawing on explicit theory backed by systematic research. On the other hand this is emphatically not instinctive behaviour – human beings don't *have* instinctive behaviour to any significant extent, intelligence being an alternative to instinct; the racist tendency to think of indigenous peoples as acting instinctively follows from the equation of primitive, natural, animal and inferior which we have already discussed. The point is that it would never occur to the Kayapó, or to many other indigenous peoples, to farm or live *out of* harmony; because they experience themselves as *part* of the ecosystem, a self-aware part of it. From this wild mind or ecological self flows a detailed and precise understanding of how things work in that place – which they describe in terms of 'plant energies' needing precise mixing and balancing through complex patterns of cultivation.

PRECONQUEST CONSCIOUSNESS

The Kayapó are only one example, recorded by an exceptional sensitive observer, of a human culture which is itself part of a wild ecosystem. Such local, indigenous knowledge is completely specific to the ecosystem in which it arises. It is creative and experimental, steadily incorporating outside influences and inside innovations to meet new conditions (Whitt, 1999: 71–2). The times when it goes wrong – when tribal peoples live in ways that mirror, on a far smaller scale, the destructiveness of mainstream culture – seem to occur when their environment has changed faster than they can adapt, but they go on trying to apply traditional strategies to their new situation – much as other-than-human species do in times of glut or famine (Johnson, 1992; Turnbull, 1980). This speed of change is, of course, the constant condition of modernity: Western culture is constantly failing to catch up with the environmental changes it itself creates.

The anthropologist Richard Sorenson has written extensively on what he calls 'preconquest consciousness', which he identifies as the primary mode of existence in many barely contacted non-Western cultures (for example in New Guinea, Micronesia and the Andaman Islands), with larger or smaller traces surviving in some other cultures (Sorenson, 2006: 11–20; see the list of societies showing various degrees of preconquest consciousness in Sorenson, 1997: 2). Sorenson offers a recipe for preconquest consciousness (all the following quotations are from Sorenson, 1998: 80):

- 'The outstanding demographic condition ... is small populations surrounded by tracts of open territory into which anyone can diffuse virtually at will.'
- 'The outstanding social condition is a sociosensual type of infant and child nurture [see below] that spawns an intuitive group rapport.'
- 'The outstanding psychological condition is heart-felt rapprochement based on integrated trust.'
- 'The outstanding economic condition is absence of private property, which allows constant cooperative usage of the implements and materials of life for collective benefit.'

He adds: 'The human ecology engendered by the interaction of these outstanding conditions makes the forcing of others (including children) to one's will a disruptive and unwholesome practice. It was not seen.'

Notice how Sorenson reiterates and gives life to Lee and Devore's observation about hunter-gatherer cultures: '(1) they live in small groups, and (2) they move around a lot' (Lee & Devore, 1968: 11). A crucial aspect of preconquest culture is its style of child rearing, in which:

> Infants were kept in continuous bodily contact with mothers or the mothers' friends – on laps when they were seated, on hips, under arms, against backs, or on shoulders when they were standing. ... [B]abies were simply not put down, not deprived of constant, ever-ready, interactive body contact – even when the group was on the move under difficult conditions. ... Eliciting delight from babies was a desired social norm, and attentive tactile stimulation was the daily lot of infants. It included protracted body-to-body caressing, snuggling, oral sensuality, hugging, fondling, and kissing.
>
> (Sorenson, 1998: 83–4)

The state of mind which follows from the ensemble of conditions listed above, Sorenson calls 'liminal awareness'.

> Liminal awareness, by definition, occurs on the threshold of consciousness. .... In the real life of these preconquest people, feeling and awareness are focused on at-the-moment, point-blank sensory experience – as if the nub of life lay within that complex flux of collective sentient immediacy. Into that flux individuals thrust their inner thoughts and aspirations for all to see, appreciate, and relate to. This unabashed open honesty is the foundation on which their highly honed integrative empathy and rapport become possible.
>
> (Sorenson, 1998: 82–3; see also Sorenson, 2006)

Although Sorenson does not directly discuss preconquest cultures' relationship to their environment, it is clear that this immediate, intuitive, heart-centred response is at the core of the way in which peoples like the Kayapó operate as an active and involved part of the wild ecosystem. Their rapport with each other is inseparable from rapport with their environment. Sorenson's description of preconquest 'sociosensual' childrearing is a recipe for the development of the ecological self. Sorenson in fact argues that all babies are 'liminally aware', but that outside preconquest culture they seldom get the support through 'constant empathetic tactile contact' to develop an adult form of this awareness (Sorenson, 1998: 84). This child-rearing style depends on a *collective* responsibility being taken for children; it cannot, of course, be abstracted from its social setting – if simply transplanted into Western culture, it will not create the same effects, and many parents who try to give their children this sort of start in life experience great difficulty and stress at they attempt to substitute, *on their own*, for an entire sociosensual society.

Alongside this, however, it is also clear that sociosensual 'wild mind' culture is not entirely an all-or-nothing phenomenon: there are degrees or shades of sociosensuality, of tenderness or cruelty to and among children and adults. In a classic study, the neuropsychologist James Prescott collated ethnographic data on 400 tribal societies, and found that:

> Those societies which give their infants the greatest amount of physical affection were characterised by low theft, low infant physical pain, low religious activity [that is, formal, institutional religion], and negligible or absent killing, mutilating or torturing of the enemy.
>
> (Prescott, 1975: 12)

Conversely, 'deprivation of bodily pleasure' throughout life, but especially in the younger years, correlated with high levels of war and violence (Prescott, 1975: 14): the more people are themselves positively embodied, the less they want or are able to impose pain on other bodies.

Societies can be closer to or further away from the sociosensual paradise which Sorenson describes, to any degree; and even within cruel and dissociated societies – like our own – many subgroups, families and individuals can preserve some of these qualities. Following Tibetan Buddhist traditions, Joanna Macy (1991: 179–80; Macy & Brown, 1998: 60–1) speaks of 'Shambhala warriors' in the modern world, those who struggle with great courage, publicly or privately, to oppose the direction of the mainstream. Yet of course these unavoidably necessary qualities of struggle and warriorship are ultimately opposed to the values of liminal culture. I discuss Sorenson's work further in Chapter 5.

THE ECOLOGICAL SELF IN THE MODERN WORLD

The Jungian analyst Jerome Bernstein (2005) also talks about 'liminal space' in his work on what he calls 'Borderland consciousness'. Bernstein developed the Borderland concept to describe some individuals he encountered in psychotherapy. He concludes:

> There are thousands of people in our culture – people I refer to as 'Borderland personalities' – whose transrational experience is nothing short of sacred. There are many who would not be able to function in our culture without their deep personal connection to that domain. And most of them feel forced to conceal that dimension of their experience, even from their loved ones, out of fear of being ostracized and branded as abnormal.
> (Bernstein, 2005: xvi)

Bernstein describes the 'Borderland personality' as experiencing reality primarily through feeling rather than thinking. Such individuals are highly intuitive, often to the degree which we call 'psychic', and directly and rawly exposed to the suffering inflicted on human and, especially, other-than-human beings through domesticated culture and environmental damage. Often they experience environmental illnesses. Borderlanders' open hearts have to try to process our ecological crisis not intellectually but directly.

Bernstein is speaking of the survival within our society of Sorenson's preconquest consciousness. Inevitably, it survives in a wounded and damaged form. 'Borderland people *personally* experience, and must live out, the split from nature on which the western ego, as we know it, has been built' (Bernstein, 2005: 9, original italics). He perhaps underestimates the importance of the split from our own embodied nature – the destruction of 'sociosensual awareness' – which accompanies the 'split from nature' he describes, and in some ways makes it possible: as we have indicated, diminished contact with our own embodiment leads to diminished empathy with the suffering of other beings.

Bernstein suggests (2005: 81–101) that there are three 'portals' to Borderland consciousness – three ways in which a person may be opened up to liminal awareness: evolution, personality structure, and trauma. In his view, Western culture as it faces environmental crisis is collectively evolving towards Borderland consciousness: 'the western ego is being pushed into that reconnection with nature ... in the name of species preservation – if not the preservation of all life as we know it' (ibid: 81). But this awareness also comes naturally to certain individual personalities which 'have not fully adapted to the apparent split from nature that is apparent in the mainstream' (ibid: 83).

To be in this position is itself inherently traumatising to anyone growing up in our culture; and Bernstein suggests that children up to the age of six or seven are natural Borderlanders, but then mostly block off this side of themselves in order to survive. Conversely, severe trauma in childhood, or even in adulthood, can itself 'open a portal to the Borderland world' (ibid: 91). The psychoanalyst Sandor Ferenczi wrote similarly long ago of 'the sudden, surprising rise of new facilities after a trauma, like a miracle that occurs upon the wave of a magic wand, or like that of the fakirs who are said to raise from a tiny seed, before our very eyes, a plant, leaves and flowers' (Ferenczi, 1933/1999b: 301). Bernstein might also have spoken of the role of relatively undamaged individual families in nurturing Borderland consciousness in their children.

There is something magical, in fact a definite ring of Fairyland, about Bernstein's Borderland – and I suggest that this reflects a real and common experience, the experience which attracts so many children to fantasy and fairytale. The great fantasy writer Lord Dunsany crystallised this in his repeated phrase 'beyond the fields we know': the sense that magic is a hairsbreadth away from ordinary awareness, requiring only a *shift of attention,* only looking up from the routines of everyday life (see also Abram, 1997). In many of Dunsany's writings, for example *The King of Elfland's Daughter* (Dunsany, 1924/1982), humans can enter Elfland simply by becoming aware of its presence, as the human Prince Alveric does:

> To those who may have wisely kept their fancies within the boundaries of the fields we know it is difficult for me to tell of the land to which Alveric had come ... [S]o strong lay the enchantment deep over all that land, that not only did the beasts and men guess each other's meanings well, but there seemed to be an understanding even, that reached from men to trees, and from trees to men.
>
> (Dunsany, 1924/1982: 11–12)

DIRECT ECOLOGICAL KNOWLEDGE

The question has often been raised of how indigenous cultures know what they know about their ecosystem – how they identify which plants are medicinal, or how in both Africa and South America they know that cassava, a staple crop in the tropics, needs to go through a complex procedure of grating, sun drying, and fermenting to reduce the cyanide content before it can be eaten (Vasconcelos et al, 1990); or how Australian aborigines know the equally elaborate procedures involved in removing the toxicity from zamia palm nuts and from round yams (Worsley, 1997: 23); or how the Kayapó know to plant their crops in the way they do. Western anthropologists suggest that, over sufficiently long periods of time, trial and error can account for even very complex processes like these. Indigenous peoples themselves will generally say that they were *told*, by gods, by animals – especially bears: one researcher offered a plant called bear root, used medicinally by the Navaho, to bears in a zoo, who immediately started chewing it and rubbing it on their bodies just as the Navaho say bears showed them to do (Andrews, 1992) – or by the plant itself.

The 'understanding' which Dunsany describes between humans and animals, humans and trees, suggests the possibility of direct perception, direct communication, an idea which has been taken up by Stephen Harrod Buhner in his book *The Secret Teaching of Plants* (Buhner, 2004). In the first half of the book, Buhner assembles research evidence to support the general indigenous view that humans can acquire knowledge and wisdom *through the heart* – not the heart as a metaphor, but the heart as a physical organ. He points out that 'between 60 and 65 per cent of the cells in the heart are neural cells' (Buhner, 2004: 82), and that the heart is 'directly wired into the central nervous system and brain', and is a repository of memory, in particular emotional memory (ibid: 82–3). He shows that the heart is a powerful electromagnetic source, which 'continually senses electromagnetic patterns from its environment and works to decode the information contained within them' (ibid: 111).

Buhner quotes considerable research on the heart as an organ of communication between humans, especially those in intimate relationship. But he also argues that anthropomorphism has prevented researchers from giving equal attention to the heart as an organ of communication with the other-than-human, and specifically with plants.

> In many respects, plant nervous systems are nearly as sophisticated as our own ... Plant nervous systems ... help process, decipher, and coordinate external and internal impulses to maintain the functioning of the organism. ... Plant nervous systems are as highly sensitive to electromagnetic fields as ours. ... And we, like plants, are evolutionarily designed to encounter such fields, just as the generators of such fields are designed to encounter us. The meanings embedded within these fields, experienced by us as emotions, affect the heart's rate, hormonal cascade, pressure waves, and neurochemical activity. ... Through such directed communication and perception, a living dialogue occurs between us and the world.
>
> (Buhner, 2004: 113–15)

In the second half of the book, Buhner focuses on practical, experiential approaches to learning directly from plants, warning:

> You must ask yourself, in the beginning, if you truly want to communicate with plants, just what is the status of the plant? Just how do you really feel about it? Is that plant there, the one

> near to your hand, your equal? If you do not feel that it is at least the same to you as a human being ... then I am not sure it will talk to you. ... The first step in learning to talk to plants is cultivating politeness.
>
> (Buhner, 2004: 133)

WILD MIND

At this point I am ready to attempt a synthesis of these various viewpoints into an account of a particular style of awareness which I suggest therapy can nurture and support, and which I also believe is a prerequisite for the Great Turning (Korten, 2007; Macy & Brown, 1998), a cultural change of direction which may allow the world's ecosystems, and humanity as a part of those ecosystems, to survive. As I hope I have already made clear, I am not proposing a dualistic opposition between 'wild' and 'domesticated', where 'wildness' is idealised; nor am I beating the drum for a return to forager-gardener culture (incidentally wiping out 99% of the human race). We cannot go back. Instead I want to indicate a possible way *forward*, by identifying an aspect of human psychology which operates to a greater or lesser extent in all cultures and societies, and which we can call 'wild mind', as ecologists speak of 'wild ecosystems': undamaged, complex systems of interaction where each part supports and is supported by the whole.

Wild mind is privileged in most or all indigenous cultures, and runs as an often invisible thread through other human societies, often carried in individual families, or in subcultures – recently in the West, bohemians, beatniks and hippies. It is also expressed in wisdom traditions like Buddhism and Taoism, and increasingly in modern psychology, ecopsychology and psychotherapy. Here are six properties of wild mind, each of which has powerful implications for therapy and counselling, and indeed for human life as a whole.

- Wild mind is embodied
- Wild mind is animal
- Wild mind is spontaneous
- Wild mind is co-creative
- Wild mind is self-balancing
- Wild mind is inherent wisdom

Wild mind is embodied

In some ways the foundational quality of wild mind is that it is not just a *mind*, residing in a body: it is itself directly *embodied*, drawing from that fact its being and its nature. Embodiment is not a fixed state, but a process, something that we are both doing and having done to us; terms like 'corporeality' are much weaker than 'embodiment', because they do refer to a fixed state, something apparently completed and passively experienced (Totton, 2010: 23). Embodiment, however, is *an ongoing process of embodying*, an always provisional experience of coming to be, in which the witnessing aspect of mind rhythmically leaps dolphin-like above the surface of the body's sea then dives down into it again, stitching together air and water, self-awareness and embodied immediacy.

And being a body, we are part of the material universe. Wild mind calls on us to make a shift from the ego 'I', marooned in our heads, to a sense of a permeable self within an embodied larger whole. This is what some writers call an experience of the Ecological Self, defined by Arne Naess (1995: 13) as a 'widened and deepened self' which identifies with all life – directly knowing and feeling that we are a cell within a living body of the earth, which is in turn a cell within a larger universe. Native American Jeannette Armstrong of the Okanagan tribe describes this:

> We survive within our skin inside the rest of our vast selves. ... Okanagans teach that our flesh, blood and bones, are Earth-body; in all cycles in which the earth moves, so does our body ... Our word for body literally means 'the land-dreaming capacity'.
> (Armstrong, 1995: 320–1)

In his book *Mind and Nature: A Necessary Unity*, Gregory Bateson (1980) argues cogently that mind is never a thing in itself, but always an emergent property of the relationship between things: most particularly, in our human case, between brain, body and environment. The brain does not 'control' the body, it responds with feedback to events in the body, just as the organism responds with feedback to events in the outside world, and vice versa: body, brain and world are each in a sense part of the environment for the other two. And this complex systemic relationship of mutual feedback is what we call 'mind'.

This position has been developed more recently, with the support of much new research, by the distinguished neuroscientist Antonio Damasio in books like *Descartes' Error* (1994) and *The Feeling of What Happens* (2000). Damasio emphasises that 'the representations your brain constructs to describe a situation, and the movements formulated as response to a situation, depend on *mutual* brain-body interactions' (Damasio, 1994: 228; italics added). As Thomas Fuchs writes, 'there is no such thing as a brain' (Fuchs, 2002: 264) – *on its own*: brain and body dependently co-arise, and together with each other and with the environment they give rise to an embodied mind. (For an extended discussion, see Totton, 2003a: 29ff.) Wild Mind, then, is actually a relationship between Wild Body, Wild Brain, and Wild World!

Wild mind is animal

Our lived embodiment holds us to the reality that we are physical organisms, animals, with some unusual talents and some unusual failings but with no inherent privilege over other animals. The poet Gary Snyder describes this as:

> A wonderful piece of information: I have been enjoying it all my life. ... But many people ... have not absorbed the implications of it, perhaps feel remote from the nonhuman world, are not sure they are animals. They would like to be something better than animals. ... [W]e must contemplate the shared ground of our biological being before emphasizing the differences.
>
> (Snyder, 1990: 17)

There is a huge freedom in this 'wonderful information', as if we no longer have to do all the painful, impossible work of raising ourselves up above our bodies and above other beings. We can relax into the understanding that we are really just the same, and that much of life will happen of its own accord. As Mary Oliver puts it in her poem *Wild Geese*:

> You do not have to be good.
> You do not have to walk on your knees
> for a hundred miles through the desert, repenting.
> You only have to let the soft animal of your body love what it loves.
>
> (Oliver, 1992: 110)

Most indigenous cultures work within this basic understanding that human beings are animals, on an equal footing with other species.

> Foragers with animistic belief systems commonly do not have words for distinguishing between people, animals and plants as separate categories, using instead classification systems based on terms of equality rather than the hierarchies of our own Linnaean taxonomies.
>
> (Barker, 2006: 58–9)

This has conventionally been understood as a lack of discrimination on their part; now we are beginning to see that the distinction they omit to make is actually in many ways unreal (see Chapter 7). Apffel-Marglin and Rivera show how Andean Native Americans take this world-view to its full extent, paralleling mystical writers of the West – not as a rarefied mystical apprehension, but as the practical basis on which their culture is founded: 'the stars, the sun, the moon, the hills, lakes ... the plants and animals ... along with the rocks and the human beings ... they are all relatives and are at once children, parents and siblings' (Apffel-Marglin & Rivera, 1995: 25).

To know that we are animal bodies, living amidst other bodies that are 'all relatives' (and all relative), gives Wild Mind a foundation of sober yet ecstatic humility. Humans specialise in thinking. Rocks specialise in being. As Alice Walker says, 'everything has equal rights because existence itself is equal' (Walker, 1983/2005: 148). She goes on to quote from a nineteenth-century book (Mooney, 1900/1996) describing how a white trader visiting the Ojibway in 1764 came upon a poisonous snake:

> I no sooner saw the snake than I hastened to the canoe, in order to procure my gun; but, the Indians observing what I was doing, inquired the occasion, and being informed, begged me to desist. ... On returning, I found the snake still coiled. The Indians, on their part, surrounding it, all addressing it by turns, and calling it their *grandfather* ... They filled their pipes; and now each blew the smoke toward the snake, who, as it appeared to me, really received it with pleasure. ... It stretched itself along the ground, in visible good humour [and] at last it moved slowly away, the Indians following it, still addressing it by the title of grandfather ... One of the chiefs added a petition, that the snake would take no notice of the insult which had been offered by the Englishman ....
>
> (Mooney, 1900/1996: 457)

The trader is patronising; the Indians know better.

Wild mind is spontaneous

Gary Snyder describes the spontaneity that is intrinsic to embodiment:

> Our bodies are wild. The quick involuntary turn of the head at a shout, the vertigo at looking off a precipice, the heart-in-the-throat in a moment of danger, the catch of the breath, the quiet moments relaxing, staring, reflecting – all universal responses of this mammal body.
>
> (Snyder, 1990: 17)

Wild mind's quality of spontaneity follows from not resisting identification with the animal body, and through this with the body as an aspect or part of the whole system. Wild mind is the whole of our bodymind self, not just the fraction isolated by consciousness (Metzinger, 2003, and the more accessible account in Metzinger, 2009; also Nørretranders, 1999).

Like an ecosystem, like our physiological functions, wild mind *happens of its own accord*, as the sum product of local reality: we do not have to bring purpose or intention to bear on the situation, as if from the outside – they arise as spontaneous expressions of the situational gestalt. Like the body, wild mind opens up no gap between impulse and execution: as Gary Snyder says, 'the body does not require the intercession of some conscious intellect to make it breathe, to keep the heart beating' (Snyder, 1990: 17). In fact, such conscious intervention would complicate and confuse autonomic processes, cause them to stutter, as when we try to think about riding a bicycle. A great deal of crucial internal processing happens outside awareness – often referred to as '*below the level of* awareness', with the usual automatic 'lowering' of the bodily and the spontaneous (Dixon, 1981).

Equally the *mind* does not require conscious intervention to function! When I experience myself making decisions, neural imaging shows that I have already 'made' that decision fractions of a second earlier – or rather, the decision has already made itself, since 'I' was not involved (Libet, 1985; see also Wegner, 2002). This feels intuitively impossible to the Western-conditioned mind; we cannot easily get hold of the concept (Libet himself seems to have problems interpreting his own results intelligibly: Libet, 2003). But think about catching a ball that someone has thrown to us: we make complex subliminal calculations of direction and velocity, and our hand reaches for the ball 'of its own accord', catching it sometimes before we are consciously aware that it has been thrown. What would it be like to do that 'on purpose'? Surely this would be truly impossible. Similarly, our emotional response to events and situations, especially interpersonal ones, is an instant, preconscious summation of all available information, far superior to anything our conscious mind could come up with (Totton, 2003a: 33–6). 'The depths of mind, the unconscious, are our inner wilderness areas ... The conscious, agenda-planning ego occupies a very tiny territory, a little cubicle somewhere near the gate' (Snyder, 1990: 17).

In the nineteenth century T.H. Huxley similarly concluded that 'the feeling we call volition is not the cause of the voluntary act, but simply the symbol in consciousness of that state of the brain which is the immediate cause of the act' (Huxley, 1874/1893: 245). He did this as part of a rather neat reversal: in a paper called 'On the hypothesis that animals are automata, and its history', Huxley argues that to diminish animals by claiming that they are not conscious is like people in glass houses throwing stones.

> The argumentation which applies to brutes holds equally good of men [*sic*]; ... all states of consciousness in us, as in them, are immediately caused by molecular changes of the brain-substance. It seems to me that in men, as in brutes, there is no proof that any state of consciousness is the cause of change in the motion of the matter of the organism. ... We are ... parts of the great series of causes and effects which, in unbroken continuity, composes that which is, and has been, and shall be – the sum of existence.
>
> (Huxley, 1874/1893: 244–5)

William James reached similar conclusions a generation later in his much-disputed paper 'Does "Consciousness" Exist?' (James, 1904/2003). This view of consciousness as in a sense imaginary is often experienced as disturbing and alienating: the idea of 'being no one', as Metzinger (2003) entitles his book, is not generally very welcome, despite its ubiquity in wisdom traditions like Buddhism and Taoism. I am suggesting, though, that it is more a matter of 'being everyone': rather than identifying as a beleaguered and isolated individual consciousness, we can identify as a collective co-creation, a selfhood which is simply a point of view, gradually attenuating as our awareness moves further out from the embodied organism.

I think this is what the Hindu teacher Sri Nisargadatta Maharaj was referring to when he said: 'When I look inside and see that I'm nothing, that's wisdom. When I look outside and see that I'm everything, that's love. And between these two, my life turns' (quoted in Pfister, 2009: 293). It is our degree of embodiment, our willingness to let our body take the lead, which makes the difference between an alienated, schizoid experience of non-self – 'I am just a biological robot, a meat machine' – and a rich, multidimensional experience of non-self or 'emptiness' as the summed mammalian wisdom of many million years, everything 'just happening' of its own accord, so that our infinitely weary consciousness can rest and relax from continual responsibility for its own existence.

Where consciousness does relax its control, we often have experiences of wholly or partially leaving what Metzinger (2009) calls 'the Ego Tunnel', the blinkered and filtered experience of the world which is all that normally seems safe for us to allow. As Aldous Huxley (1954: epigraph) famously quotes Blake (*The Marriage of Heaven and Hell*, Pl. 14), 'If the doors of perception were cleansed every thing would appear to man as it is: infinite.' I have already quoted the connection Perls et al make between spontaneity and perception:

> The relaxation of deliberateness and the vanishing of boundaries is the reason for the extra brightness and vigour – e.g. the 'flash of insight' or the 'shock of recognition' – for the energy that went into withholding oneself or aggressively putting connections into the environment is now suddenly added to the final spontaneous experience.
>
> (Perls et al, 1951/1973: 474)

Wild mind is co-creative

Wild mind is an expression of the situational gestalt: an expression of how the entire universe operates as it comes to bear on this local moment (see the discussion of 'dependent co-arising' in Chapter 2). Co-creation is intimately bound up with self-balancing: just as, in a therapy session or a therapy group, each participant expresses one aspect of a whole relational pattern of transference, countertransference and projection within the dyad or group, so wild mind is balanced in and with its whole environment, including the environment provided by other humans. Gregory Bateson shows that mind, like all complex systems (including mycorrhiza), operates through homeostatic loops, mechanisms for rebalancing the system whenever it goes out of equilibrium. For him, the processes which produce healing in organs, growth in organisms, development in societies, or balance in large ecosystems are *all minds* – aspects of 'that wider knowing which is the glue holding together the starfishes and sea anemones and redwood forests and human committees' (Bateson, 1980: 3).

James Gibson developed the concept of 'ecological perception', countering mainstream dualistic theories of perception as a transaction between two separate entities, perceiver and perceived. He suggested that we and our bodies 'exist along with the environment, they are co-perceived' (Gibson, 1982: 418): the perceiving 'subject' at any particular moment is also the perceived 'object', defining and defined by the whole network within which each perception is held (see also Sewall, 1999). These ideas are difficult at first encounter, but ultimately illuminating; as is Gregory Bateson's insight that mind is not bounded by our skin but necessarily an interrelationship of brain, body and environment. And part of mind's environment consists of other minds, all mutually co-arising with and co-influencing each other.

In his wonderful book *The Lost Language of Plants* (2002), Stephen Buhner describes how plant communities exist within and communicate through huge networks of coevolved, symbiotic fungi around their roots, mycorrhizal systems extending sometimes for hundreds of acres below ground, forming sophisticated biofeedback loops which exchange information with and between plants – so much so that, in a sense, the plants are no more separate individuals than are mushrooms sprouting from the same mycelium. Very recently, a previously unknown elaborate system of 'tunnelling nanotubes', ultrafine microscopic pipes, has been discovered linking the cells within humans' and other animals' bodies, and facilitating a similar exchange of information and materials – which on this scale amount to much the same thing – between cells (Gerdes & Negrão Carvalho, 2008; Hurtig et al, 2010).

Mycorrhiza and tunnelling nanotubes are vivid examples of how ecosystems work – how the *universe*, including the human universe, works: a universe mirrored in the unconscious and emerging in our frequent dreams of networks of secret tunnels and passages. This joined-up universe is 'Indra's Net', which I described in Chapter 2: an infinite network with a jewel at each node, reflecting every other jewel within itself. All beings, all minds, mutually condition and create each other, forming larger wholes through these interconnections. Wild mind is one.

Wild mind is self-balancing

The conscious mind's impression that it is in control of the bodymind is simply an illusion, and maintaining that illusion creates tremendous stress and anxiety. Actually, *nothing* controls (though many things affect) the bodymind: everything just happens. Wild mind seeks constantly to communicate this reality to consciousness, as a rebalancing – through dreams, visions, slips, symptoms, psychoses and sudden enlightenment. It also expresses itself through 'ideomotor movement', the spontaneous and unconscious body actions which accompany us through life (Dorko, nd; see also Spitz, 1997), and which I will discuss in relation to children in Chapter 5.

This rebalancing function of wild mind is a constant theme of Jung's work, and one of his deepest insights: 'As I have repeatedly indicated, I regard the attitude of the unconscious as compensatory to consciousness' (Jung, 1921/1971: para 568). At the extreme, in Jung's view, it will impose a neurotic symptom on us if this is the only way available to force us to rebalance:

> The reader will doubtless ask: What in the world is the value and meaning of a neurosis, this most useless and pestilent curse of humanity? To be neurotic – what good can that do? ... I myself have known more than one person who owed his whole usefulness and reason for existence to a neurosis, which prevented all the worst follies in his life and *forced* him to a mode of living that developed his valuable potentialities. These might have been stifled

> had not the neurosis, with iron grip, held him to the place where he belonged.
>
> (Jung, 1917/1928/1966: para 68)

From this perspective, the environmental crisis looks very much like a drastic collective symptom, trying to 'hold us to the place where we belong', force us to become aware of the need for rebalancing.

Wild mind is inherent wisdom

The inherent wisdom of wild mind follows from and sums up all of these qualities. In her novel *The Telling*, Ursula Le Guin describes a human 'wild culture' on another planet, where a teacher says:

> Animals have no language. They have their nature. You see? They know the way, they know where to go and how to go, following their nature. But we're animals with no nature. Eh? Animals with no nature! That's strange! We're so strange! We have to talk about how to go and what to do, think about it, study it, learn it. Eh? We're born to be reasonable, so we're born ignorant.
>
> (Le Guin, 2000: 143)

Wild mind, however, is not ignorant – although it doesn't 'know' anything (we project knowledge onto its unknowing wisdom). Rather, it is the summation of all our experience, of the entire local situation (including our physiological and genetic resources); through our co-creation with the rest of the universe, it mirrors and expresses everything the universe is – just as a cork floating on the ocean *expresses*, without *knowing*, every detail and shift of the tides, winds and currents. Summing up his perception of indigenous wisdom, the process psychotherapist Arnold Mindell writes:

> When the world speaks to you, it is impossible to tell whether the world is doing things to you or you are doing things to it. You may perceive yourself as causing some events and being the recipient of others, but you never know for sure whether you send messages and get responses or whether the world sends you messages to which you respond. ... You are an aspect of the world.
>
> (Mindell, 1993: 46)

Again, wild mind's response to events is a *rebalancing* one: it seeks to restore peace, to re-establish harmony. Often this can only happen through intensified conflict and disharmony! It of course doesn't come about through eliminating our conscious, domesticated, 'no nature' mind, but through reuniting it with its source in wild mind – re-minding us that we are in fact animals who control nothing. 'To neither come nor go, but to remain as you innately are, without allowing the mind to become obscured – this is what's meant by Buddha', said the Zen master Bankei (Besserman & Steger, 1991: 107).

SHAMANISM AS WILD MIND

> The traditional magician cultivates an ability to shift out of his her common state of consciousness *precisely in order to make contact with other species on their own terms*. ... It is this, we might say, that defines a shaman: the ability to readily slip out of the boundaries that define his or her culture ... in order to make contact with and learn from, the other powers in the land. Shamanic magic is precisely this heightened receptivity to the meaningful solicitations – songs, cries and gestures – of the larger, more-than-human field.
>
> (Abram, 1997: 307)

Reading this paragraph, Andrew Tovey, a student on the Ecopsychology module offered by the Centre for Human Ecology in Edinburgh, found that it:

> stopped me in amazement ... I exclaimed out loud. When I go out to Blackford woods seeking guidance, I enter what I refer to as Wild Mind, an ASC (Altered State of Consciousness) I've come to recognise and bring about purposefully in order to be open and receptive to 'tugs' and meaningful patterns surrounding me.
>
> (Tovey, 2009a)

(All quotations are from Tovey's unpaginated course journal, 2009a; see also his dissertation, 2009b.)

Tovey goes on to describe 'the process by which Wild Mind is entered':

> Firstly it is important to build intent beforehand. ... The next stage entails presencing. All thoughts of past and future are cleared, and in this respect it is very similar to meditative preparation. However the body remains active and the senses alert. In fact I find that my senses all sharpen when I enter this state. ... The mind must be totally clear but actively receptive to the slightest influence. It is no good actively looking for signs, objects, trees or meanings ... this necessarily blocks out the subtle

> 'tugs' from outside ... strange little compulsions to 'veer off to the right here' or to 'climb over that wall there'. Sometimes, amongst these, I will get inauthentic tugs, which is my ego struggling to find voice again, but these are always visible for what they are and with practice can be ignored. The path taken, in response to these 'tugs' from outwith my own ego, involves me remaining totally in the present. ... As a result, time takes on a different quality. When I 'arrive' at a given location, a scene is presented to me, and that scene *always* contains meaningful coincidence that can be read.

Here is a small example of the process at work:

> I had been busily working on an essay for days and felt thoroughly frazzled and ungrounded. I decided to go out to Blackford woods for grounding and guidance before the interview and to hell with the essay! Having arrived I slipped into Wild Mind and entered the woods. I was having difficulty with it as there was so much noise in me and, as I say, I hadn't grounded myself for some time. I was also looking for an acorn seedling to take to the interview. I wasn't finding any acorns at all to start with, but as I eased closer to Wild Mind I found myself crouched by a hollow at the base of a tree. It was full of acorn husks. It was almost like I was being told 'you're coming here with the wrong attitude and the wrong questions, and that's because you're out of touch with the land of late. All the acorns have been eaten. You'd be wise to pay more attention.' From there I was able to release more fully and found myself next stood on the very edge of a 30m high cliff overlooking a deep wooded gorge. It was there that I had a profound feeling of joyous and unrestrained death ... not what I was expecting at all. It was so powerful that I literally had to fight to stop myself from stepping forward over the edge.

Tovey seems to be channelling the Fool from the Tarot, who is portrayed teetering on the edge of an abyss. He concludes:

> So to return to Abram ... it seems that what I have been doing, by his definition, is Shamanic magic. That sounds strangely grandiose to me, but perhaps that is indeed what is.

We need to be very careful in talking about shamanism, a term which has been promiscuously applied to all sorts of New Age practices, many of them a good deal blander and less demanding than authentic indigenous practices, which are not simply individual activities but defined and supported by an entire cultural context. Shamanism is both more specific and much harder to pin down than it may appear. But if we think of shamanism as the spiritual practice that accompanies and flows from contact with Wild Mind, then Tovey's description does indeed correspond to this; and many individuals, including therapists, are consciously or unconsciously including shamanic elements in their life and work.

> Indigenous healers have taught me that the quality of life depends upon body sensations that are linked to dreams and the environment, to what I call the shaman's body. According to medicine people living in native settings around the world, and to mystical traditions, the shaman's dreamingbody, when accessed, is a source of health, personal growth, good relationships, and a sense of community.
>
> (Mindell, 1993: 3)

In his book *The Spell of the Sensuous*, David Abram describes the shaman's role:

> By his [*sic*] constant rituals, trances, ecstasies, and 'journeys,' [the shaman] ensures that the relation between human society and the larger society of beings is balanced and reciprocal, and that the village never takes more from the living land than it returns to it – not just materially but with prayers, propitiations, and praise. ... *The medicine person's primary allegiance, then, is not to the human community, but to the earthly web of relations in which that community is embedded.*
>
> (Abram, 1997: 7, italics added)

This already implies a split, a wedge driven into preconquest consciousness which causes the appearance of an 'us' and 'them', and necessitates the shaman siding with the other-than-human and more-than-human so as to help rebalance the human community's relationship with the larger community of beings.

WILD ETHICS

The primary ethical approach of Western society has been to establish a set of *principles* which we can then attempt to apply to (or impose on) situations. Usually, these principles are seen as transcending or even opposing what is natural – 'human nature', 'fallen nature' as Christianity called it. This basic mindset has been transferred from Christianity to more modern theories, down to the famously atheist

Richard Dawkins, who ends *The Selfish Gene* by saying that 'We, alone on earth, can rebel against the tyranny of the selfish replicators' (Dawkins, 1989: 201) – we alone, that is, are capable of altruism. As John Gray (2007: 26) points out, this 'assumes a discontinuity between the biology of humans and other animals' which is completely non-Darwinian (and which Dawkins himself rejects elsewhere in his writings, e.g. Dawkins, 1993). As we have already seen, the supposed break in continuity between us and other creatures is one of the fundamental issues here.

There is an alternative view that ethical behaviour is the *expression* rather than the contradiction of our naturalness: that humans will spontaneously act in an ethical way unless interfered with. Not only humans, but also other animals – there are many examples of empathic behaviour, for instance, in other-than-human species, even between different species:

> A female bonobo ... had captured a starling and been urged by her keeper to let it go; she climbed to the highest point of the highest tree in her enclosure, carefully unfolded the bird's wings, and spread them wide open before trying to throw it out of the enclosure. When the bird fell short, the bonobo guarded it for a long period.
>
> (Gray, 2007: 28; see also Bekoff & Pearce, 2010)

I discuss other-than-human empathy further in Chapter 7. The belief in our spontaneously ethical nature was also held by Wilhelm Reich, the founder of body psychotherapy, who wrote that, beneath the layers of repression, humanity 'is an essentially honest, industrious, cooperative, loving, and, if motivated, rationally hating animal' (Reich, 1946/1975: 13). Reich believed in self-regulation on all levels, from the individual to the social and political: 'love, work and knowledge,' he wrote as his personal motto, 'are the wellsprings of life; they should also govern it.'

The most developed statement of such ideas that I know of is in Taoism, the 'Watercourse Way' (Watts, 1979), which identifies as the highest human achievement the capacity to be spontaneous in the sense that animals or clouds are spontaneous; to follow the path of least resistance like water. Hence Taoism praises the quality of *wu-wei*, non-action – not that one does not do anything, but that one does not *interfere* with things, including with oneself – does not force one's actions, rehearse them and measure them against an ideal standard (Wong, 1997: 24–5).

> The world is ruled by letting things take their course.
> It cannot be ruled by interfering.
> (*Tao Te Ching*, Feng & English, 1972: Section 48)

This has implications not only for the individual, but for social action. If the universe cannot be improved by conscious effort, then our best path is humility and ordinariness:

> Give up sainthood, renounce wisdom
> And it will be a hundred times better for everyone.
> (Feng & English, 1972: Section 19)

Wild ethics, then, derive not from a set of abstract or revealed standards, but from an understanding of what human beings *are*: embodied creatures, domesticated wild animals with self-aware, symbolising brains, an unusual aspect of the natural order uniquely capable of experiencing the natural as *other*. All of these things are surely enormously important for thinking about a sustainable human ethics; many of them have been left out, it seems to me, from most previous attempts.

WILD MIND AND THERAPY

> Something inside me has reached to the place
> Where the world is breathing.
> The flags we cannot see are flying there.
> (Kabir, in Bly, 1977: 52)

All this has implications for the practice of therapy. From the point of view of the ecology of mind, our work as therapists is to interrupt purpose-obsessed consciousness and relax into wild mind, so as to facilitate the same process in our clients. Insofar as therapy has a 'goal', it is to let go of goals and settle down to what *is*. Freud called this 'free association', roaming the networks of wild mind. If consciousness can abandon its mad, quixotic quest to control reality, a radical lessening of anxiety follows, through a reappraisal of our situation as human beings: we become aware that we experience ourselves as subject to impossible demands, and that these demands are, indeed, *impossible* – in other words, they do not really exist. Something which previously seemed hugely important and hugely difficult is now quite unimportant. Our domestication becomes rebalanced with our wildness. This is an enormous and life-changing relief.

Wild mind relates directly to clear perception of the world, what Zen Buddhists call the polished mirror. The founder of ecological psychology, James J. Gibson writes: 'Ask yourself what it is you see hiding the surroundings as you look out upon the world – not darkness, surely, not air, nothing but the ego' (Gibson, 1979: 112). This links with a profound remark by W.H. Bates, the inventor of the Bates Method: 'When the eyesight is normal, the mind is always perfectly at rest' (Bates, 1920/2008: 218). Relaxation and spontaneity are the foundations of wisdom. But sight should not be privileged over the other channels of experience: we make contact with our environment through all the senses, especially the intimate senses of touch, smell, taste, kinesthesia and proprioception.

In Chapter 3 I quoted Rilke's lines about humans not being 'at home in the interpreted world' – the world after it has been passed through the filter of consciousness. Consciousness doesn't intrinsically mean alienation, but it does open the way to it: an 'interpreted world' is a world with two positions, myself and my environment. To avoiding splitting this world in two, our awareness, our story of reality, needs to *include* our continuous act of interpretation. And this is after all what we do in sophisticated forms of relational therapy: we're not seeking 'reality' at all, let alone seeking it across the abyss of interpretation, instead we're taking the *whole* of what is going on, interpretation and all, projections, transferences and counter-transferences, as 'reality'.

What I have described in this chapter is, naturally, nothing new: many people, including therapists, have talked about a similar process. We need to access wild mind, both for our own sakes and for the sake of the whole: any radical change in our behaviour towards the rest of the wild world depends upon making friends with our own wilderness inside. Until then we are Toad of Toad Hall, egos posturing in the mirror and trying to ignore the Wild Wood.

I am arguing, then, that psychotherapy, and body psychotherapy in particular, can hold the role of guardian and cultivator of wild mind, human ecological consciousness. If this is to happen, it must be in the context of the millennia-long persecution and attempted suppression of wild mind: a process which has not wholly succeeded, perhaps *cannot* wholly succeed, but which has already inflicted enormous damage on human beings and on the other-than-human and more-than-human world. It is to this process of malignant domestication that I will now turn.

5

Domesticating Wild Mind

> The domestication of nature appears to be a universal process of humankind, the unfolding of laws of evolution which made humans lords of creation and animals our organic hosts.
>
> (Anderson, 1997: 464)

> The unconscious domestication of humans by agriculture that began over 10,000 years ago is still underway.
>
> (Diamond, 2002: 706)

This chapter and Chapter 6 may feel like difficult reading, because they are in a sense negative: they focus on what seems to me problematic and in many ways destructive about human culture. To discuss this is also difficult in another way. In the process of human development certain things seem to have happened, certain thresholds seem to have been crossed; but from a position in time after such events, we can approach them only mythically, and we need to remember that our accounts are only mythical – as Derrida famously says (e.g. Derrida, 1998), these things have 'always already' happened, and because their mark on our perception is indelible we cannot really grasp how things were 'before'.

The myths, however, are important and illuminating in themselves; and one key mythic threshold for humanity which we need to explore here is domestication. 'Domestication' literally means coming to live in the 'domus', the home; and this is the movement hunter-gatherer humans have carried out, not once, but repeatedly, at different moments in time and in different parts of the world. As soon as there is a home, a place where we live permanently, rather than moving around from place to place, then there is also a *non*-home, a wildness that surrounds and counterpoints the safe and familiar. In German, *unheimlich* literally means 'not part of the home', but it is actually used to mean 'uncanny, sinister'. The project then arises of domesticating the wild, turning it into a secure place for domesticated humans: a garden, a farm, a park, a zoo.

As Kay Anderson says, through domestication – understood both as fixed settlement and as the taming and selective breeding of animals and plants – 'that which is culturally defined as nature's "wildness" is brought in and nurtured in some guises, exploited in other guises, mythologized and aestheticized in still other forms of this complex cultural practice' (Anderson, 1997: 464). Plants and animals come to be treated as objects of human will, 'incorporated into the social structure of human communities where they became objects of ownership, purchase and exchange ... progressively "improved" in human terms, and stripped of what came to be called their "wildness"' (ibid: 465–6).

Anderson also argues that:

> domestication frames relations that extend beyond animals to include other human groups encountered as people inhabit and move about the world ... Domestication practices have had a political content ... that not only defined the relationship of humans with certain animals but also intrahuman relationships between groups defined on the basis of race and gender.
> (Anderson, 1997: 464–5)

Just as other-than-human species become objects of human will, so other human cultures encountered by domesticated and urbanised peoples are treated as wild, 'savage' semi-humans who must be brought within the pale of civilisation, by persuasion or by force.

Anderson sees domestication as the original template for the human|animal divide, and beyond that for the mind|body, male|female, white|black and many subsequent polarities: the mythic origin, in fact, of the whole List which I discussed in Chapter 1. It is also the template for the Myth of Progress discussed in Chapter 2, the notion that we as a species are heading somewhere, and that there is in fact somewhere to head (Anderson, 1997: 472). She unequivocally identifies the cognitive/emotional split between humans and other animals – required for domestication to be carried out, since this involves treating animals in a way that most of us would not treat humans – as a crucial point in the development of alienated civilisation, the foundation for all the other splits between man and woman, white and black, adult and child, where in each case the first of the pair is identified with civilisation and humanity, the second, to varied extents, with the wild and animal.

> Man, in harnessing life-forms to his service, was said to be overcoming the force of instinct within himself. In so doing, he too did himself become 'civilized'. He became free, released from what the ancients pejoratively called his 'animal nature'. ... In short, a language of difference became expressed by the ancients in terms of a temporal metaphor of civilized and wild, human and

> animal, culture and nature. ... [I]nstead of acknowledging species-specific diversity, humans came to draw a sharp dividing line between human and nonhuman such that we have perceived ourselves as belonging to a totally different order (called culture), while all other beings and inanimate things are only nature.
>
> (Anderson, 1997: 472)

This is interestingly parallel to Jung's account of the primal split around domestication:

> Man became split into a conscious and an unconscious personality. The conscious personality could be domesticated, because it was separated from the natural and primitive man. ... This ... explains the really terrible fact that, the higher we climb the mountain of scientific and technical achievement, the more dangerous and diabolical becomes the misuse of our inventions.
>
> (Jung, 1933–1934/1970e: paras 1008–1009)

We need to be cautious with these models and metaphors, because they incorporate and reproduce the notion of the Fall, of some original sin which alienates us and splits us away from a primal state of grace. As I said at the beginning of this book, I am endeavouring to avoid the dualistic polarities that so easily insert themselves into our thinking. But why is it that such polarities are so hard to avoid and so easy to re-create? I will discuss these issues later in this chapter.

THE TRAUMA OF DE-WILDING

We can have no idea what the process of domestication was like when it 'first' happened. But we can get some sense of what it is like for a culture to be shocked out of its living relationship with the wild through a traumatic encounter with domesticated civilisation, thanks to Richard Sorenson, who experienced it at first hand in New Guinea and the Andaman islands. Sorenson had previously observed the striking fragility of what he calls 'preconquest' individuals in the face of strong negative emotions:

> Individuals from the most isolated regions became highly agitated when shown photographs of anger. Some went dumb, others became tongue-tied, many trembled, some perspired profusely or looked wildly about. Those from remotest hamlets reacted most dramatically. Not just confounded, they were fearful too. It was an astonishing and gripping spectacle.
>
> (Sorenson, 1998: 97)

In New Guinea, Sorenson was present in a 'preconquest' society – what I am calling a wild society – before overwhelming contact with Western culture, and then again a few years after such contact.

> In all cases the subtlest affect exchanges faded first with intuitive rapport going into irreversible collapse much later ... In large regions a grand cultural amnesia sometimes accompanied this collapse. Whole populations would forget even recent past events and make gross factual errors in reporting them. In some cases they even forgot what type and style of garments they had worn a few years earlier or ... that they had been using stone axes and eating their dead close relatives a few years back. ...
>
> The periods of anomie sometimes alternated with spates of wild excitement leading to a strange mixture of excess and restraint. It was during such disorders that abstract concepts of rights, property, and possession began emerging. So did formal names for people, groups, and places. These were then used argumentatively in defense of rights, property, and possessions. Negative emotions were applied to strengthen argument. Eventually they became structural aspects of society. As the art of political manipulation emerged, the selfless unity that seemed so firm and self-repairing in their isolated enclaves vanished like a summer breeze as a truth-based type of consciousness gave way to one that lied to live.
>
> (Sorenson, 1998: 98)

This is stirring and distressing enough; but far more so when Sorenson describes his experience of actually being on the spot, in the Andaman Islands, when a wild culture collapsed under the impact of 'an explosively abrupt tourism trade' (Sorenson, 1998: 99).

> To speak abstractly of the death of a way-of-life is a simple thing to do. To experience it is quite another thing. I've seen nothing in the lore of anthropology that might prepare one for the speed by which it can occur, or for the overwhelming psychic onslaughts it throws out. Nor does my profession forewarn of those communicable paroxysms that hover in the air which, without warning, strike down with overwhelming force, when a culture's mind gives way.
>
> Yet this is just what happened when the traditional rapport of those islands was undone, when the subtle sensibility of each to one another was abruptly seared away in a sudden unpredicted, unprecedented, uncognated whirlwind. In a single crucial week a spirit that all the world would want, not just for themselves but

> for all others, was lost, one that had taken millennia to create. It was suddenly just gone.
>
> Epidemic sleeplessness, frenzied dance throughout the night, reddening burned-out eyes getting narrower and more vacant as the days and nights wore on, dysphasias of various sorts, sudden mini-epidemics of spontaneous estrangement, lacunae in perception, hyperkinesis, loss of sensuality, collapse of love, impotence, bewildered frantic looks like those on buffalo in India just as they're clubbed to death ... Such was the general scene that week, a week that no imagination could have forewarned, the week in which the subtle sociosensual glue of the island's traditional way-of-life became unstuck.
>
> (Sorenson, 1998: 99–100)

There is a striking resemblance between this description and Doris Lessing's imaginative vision in her novel *Shikasta* of a harmonious society's disintegration when its city's relationship with earth energies is disrupted:

> Everywhere ... the Natives were hustling and jostling around in groups which continually formed and re-formed. They were always in movement, looking for something, someone ... they looked around wildly, uneasily, and their eyes, which now all had the lost, restless look that seemed the strongest thing in them, were never still, always searching, always dissatisfied. These groups took little notice of each other, but pushed and elbowed as if they had all become strangers, even enemies. ...
>
> These poor creatures already did not know what had been lost.
>
> (Lessing, 1981: 70–1)

Ursula Le Guin has parallel descriptions in her utopian novel *Always Coming Home* (Le Guin, 1988), in which a society of the sort I am describing as 'wild' comes into contact with a violent, dualistic culture, and barely manages to avoid irretrievable damage as it takes on some of the other culture's aggressive character in the act of defending against it. Note that Sorenson compares the Andaman islanders to buffalo suffering the ultimate fate of most domesticated species.

Why is it that wild cultures are so fragile in the face of aggressive domesticated cultures – not only physically, which is easily understandable, but with a crucial psychological vulnerability? Doris Lessing's parable is helpful here: a disruption of their relationship with earth energies is very much how wild people seem to experience confrontation between 'integrative human mental evolutionary development' and 'an adversarial one' (Sorenson, 1998: 101). Their way of being is founded in a sense of connectedness with each other, with the physical world, with the whole ecological web of which they are part; and this allows them to live in undefended psychic openness.

> With body language based on full-time accurate truth, infants became candid and open, and remained so as they grew. ... They didn't expect prevarication, deception, grandstanding, or evasion. And I could find no cases where they understood these concepts. Even teenagers remained transparently forthright, their hearts opened wide for all to gaze inside.
>
> (Sorenson, 1998: 97)

Exposure to a culture of aggression, manipulation and defensiveness demands a total change of posture towards other people and hence towards the world – including one's own embodiment: Sorenson argues that the necessary readjustment requires 'new relationships between the awareness and manipulation centers in the cerebral cortex and the centers of emotion in the mid and lower brains, ... physiological as well as psychological change' (Sorenson, 1998: 101). The dreadful scenes which Sorenson describes indicate that a psycho-physiological tsunami is taking place.

The most recent evidence suggests that something similar happened to forager societies in Europe. There are strong genetic indications of a population movement from the Middle East into Europe, corresponding closely to the spread of agriculture in the same direction at the same time and speed (Cavalli-Sforza, 2000: 96–113). While it used to be believed that agriculture diffused as an *idea*, because it was so manifestly superior to foraging, this is no longer plausible:

> The old way of obtaining food was as efficient as the new one, so agriculture could not have won over the European population because of its intrinsic superiority; instead, invasion and replacement of some local populations played a key role in spreading the new population across Europe.
>
> (De Landa, 2000: 114–15)

The trauma of de-wilding, then, reverberates down through the generations of our own culture too. And to imagine the dreadful shock that undomesticated people experience when confronted by Western culture is to see ourselves in a pitiless mirror: the 'prevarication, deception, grandstanding, [and] evasion,' the use of 'negative emotions ... to strengthen argument,' the 'strange mixture of excess and restraint' – these are all part of the cultural air we breathe, mingled of course with the direct symptoms of trauma: 'epidemic sleeplessness, frenzied dance throughout the night, reddening burned-out eyes getting narrower and more vacant as the days and nights wore on, dysphasias of various sorts, sudden mini-epidemics of spontaneous estrangement, lacunae in perception, hyperkinesis, loss of sensuality, collapse of love, impotence, bewildered frantic looks' – all these are familiar, especially among young people, and getting more so all the time.

THE NEOLITHIC BARGAIN

I should acknowledge that the picture of a contrast between peaceful, embodied liminal culture and aggressive, disembodied domesticated culture is strongly contested by certain writers. Authors like Keeley (1996) and Le Blanc (2003) insist that violence and aggression have been endemic throughout history and throughout the world; they accuse those like Fry (2007) who suggest that 'warfare is not inevitable and ... humans have a substantial capacity for dealing with conflicts nonviolently' (Fry, 2007: 1–2) of wantonly ignoring the evidence of continuous bloodshed and domination – while the other side make precisely equivalent criticisms against them. Even on-the-spot observers of the same culture can interpret it in opposite ways!

It is in a sense extraordinary that such apparently objective issues can be so plastic to individual interpretation; and certainly the two overall positions – that humans are by default cooperative and peaceable, and that humans are by default competitive and warlike – cannot be reconciled. But what does seem to emerge from the din of argument is a pair of plausible trajectories from the one state to the other: from what is now usually described as 'simple' forager society, which most though not all writers would agree tends to be peaceful, interdependent and egalitarian, to 'complex', more differentiated, hierarchical and aggressive social structures. (As discussed in Chapter 2, 'simple' and 'complex' should probably be reversed in these descriptions – in ecological terms domesticated cultures are radically simpler than wild ones.)

Interestingly, one of these trajectories is about scarcity and the other is about abundance. It appears that a shift towards *either* sustained scarcity *or* sustained surplus can knock a culture out of a stable cooperative stance – what complexity theory describes as a jump from one attractor to another. Scarcity sets off this shift by forcing people to compete in order to survive; surplus, by opening up the space for competition around status rather than survival, for some people's labour feeding others, for emergent social roles – priests, warriors, clerks – which are not directly productive of food. The scarcity scenario is associated with deserts; the abundance scenario, with coastal environments and fishing-based economies. It has further been suggested (Barker, 2006: 402) that a society based on abundance which then hits a patch of scarcity will be strongly motivated to increase food production through experimenting with agriculture.

One of the primary motors of cultural change is change in childrearing practices, and Sarah Blaffer Hrdy (2009) highlights the way in which the shift to sedentary agricultural society degrades childrearing, identifying two aspects of forager society which, while in themselves problematic, actually lead to good nurturing. In most forager cultures, the relative shortage of high-grade nutrition means that the average age of menstruation is sixteen; so mothers tend to be considerably more mature than in agricultural societies. 'Among foragers, any girl sufficiently well-fed to ovulate in her early teens was, almost by definition, a girl surrounded by supportive kin, people who ... were likely to be willing to help her rear her young' (Hrdy, 2009: 287). A further consequence of limited nutrition, that mothers need to devote considerable time to survival needs, means that successful childrearing is necessarily a collective enterprise involving at the very least grandmothers and often many more group members. The hard fact is that poorly parented children don't grow up at all:

> Back in the Pleistocene [i.e. the Ice Ages], any child who was fortunate enough to grow up acquired a sense of emotional security by default. Those without committed mothers and also lacking allomothers [maternal substitutes] responsive to their needs would rarely have survived long enough for the emotional sequelae of neglect to matter.
>
> (Hrdy, 2009: 290)

By contrast, in agricultural society, because of a relative abundance of high-grade protein the age of puberty steeply declines and more infants survive; but the shift to patrilocal and patriarchal structures also means that younger mothers have less support from their own mothers and other kinswomen – as well as increasingly removing fathers from the 'women's work' of childcare (Hrdy, 2009: 287–8). These factors, combined with the rise of competitive, dominance-based structures, set up a context for insecure and disorganised attachment leading to potentially even worse childrearing in the next generation.

> The end of the Pleistocene marked a consequential divide in the way children were raised as people began to settle in one place, build walled houses, grow and store food. While predation rates declined, malnutrition remained a problem, and deaths from diseases like malaria and cholera even increased. Nevertheless, child survival became increasingly decoupled from the need to be

> in constant physical contact with another person, or surrounded by responsive, protective caretakers in order to pull through. Many other things began to change as well. ... After the Pleistocene, and increasingly over the ensuing centuries, even young women still psychologically immature and woefully lacking in sympathy or social support could nevertheless be well-fed enough to ovulate and conceive while still in their early teens.
>
> (Hrdy, 2009: 286–7)

Like almost all thinking about Neolithic society, all this is speculative; not enough is known for us to be certain. It strongly suggests, though, that what Rianne Eisler (1996) calls 'dominator culture' may have arisen repeatedly all over the world in response to specific environmental factors. There is, perhaps, nothing in 'human nature' which intrinsically favours either peace or war, cooperation or domination; everything depends on circumstance. As Marx said, we make our own history but we do not choose the circumstances under which we do so. But Sorenson's work suggests that once dominator culture arises it spreads like a plague: cooperative, liminal, wild humans are profoundly vulnerable to humans who are closed and aggressive. They literally cannot bear to be around them.

We should imagine this sort of traumatic impact happening over and over again through prehistory and history, so that by now virtually the whole of humanity is locked in a post-traumatic-stress-disordered culture centred on domestication and control. And although domestication and hierarchy are very much bound up with and amplified by the adoption of agriculture, they are not directly its result, and may even to some degree be its cause. It seems likely that human domestication was greatly facilitated by the tranquillising effects of opioids contained in grains and milk. 'Civilisation arose', Wadley and Martin argue, 'because reliable, on-demand availability of dietary opioids to individuals changed their behaviour, reducing aggression, and allowed them to become tolerant of sedentary life in crowded groups, to perform regular work, and to be more easily subjugated by rulers' (Wadley & Martin, 2000: 6). Yet this picture, though convincing, is not the whole story: the most recent archaeological evidence clearly suggests that urbanisation began *before* agriculture. Hard though it is to conceive, there were once towns of hunter-gatherers. Hence Peter Wilson argues that 'architecture preceded cultivation. People domesticated themselves first. They made themselves at home' (Wilson, 2007: 107).

Like other writers, Steckel and Wallis point out that:

> Urban living came at a substantial cost. ... Neolithic cities and towns were unhealthy. Their residents were smaller in stature

> than hunter-gatherers and their bones had more lesions indicating dental decay, infections and other signs of physiological stress.
> (Steckel & Wallis, 2007: 1)

They ask, and propose a convincing answer to, the obvious question:

> How were healthy hunter-gatherers convinced to live in villages and cities where their health was measurably lower? The answer is that they were safer. Town dwellers suffered a third to a quarter of the human induced violent trauma experienced by hunter-gatherers.
> (Steckel & Wallis, 2007: 31)

While what is known as 'simple' hunter-gatherer cultures were and are egalitarian and relatively peaceful, 'complex' hunter-gatherer cultures which develop out of abundance tend to be hierarchical, settled and violent (Kelly, 1995; we should bear in mind that most of the evidence for such cultures comes from just one area of the world, the west coast of North America). Given these conditions, what Steckel and Wallis (2007: 3) describe as 'a coalition of elites that simultaneously creates and enforces elite privileges (including property rights) and reduces the level of violence in society' – basically a monopoly protection racket, otherwise known as a State – might be an attractive proposition. Individuals could be drawn to swap freedom (and health) for safety; wildness for domestication.

And this Neolithic bargain is basically still where we are up to as a civilisation; except for the vast multiplication of comforts, luxuries and indulgences which we have accumulated in an attempt to make up for what we have lost. But violence, poverty and danger are never eradicated, only exported, pushed further and further away, like garbage sent from Europe or North America to Africa or China – or like dangerous thoughts and feelings pushed into the unconscious or projected onto other people and groups; and what is repressed always returns in one form or another, just as the garbage returns as pollution released into the global environment, and as resentment towards the exporters from the receivers.There is another important aspect to the Neolithic bargain, however: it was also undertaken between humans and other-than-human species, a bargain initially of value to both parties:

> People did not take sheep into domestication; rather, people and sheep entered into a particular interaction by behavioural adaptation on the part of both species. The new relationship succeeded precisely because it benefited both species.
> (O'Connor, 1997: 152)

Groves puts it pithily: 'Humans domesticated dogs, and dogs domesticated humans' (Groves, 1999: 11). In exchange for using them for our sustenance, or to assist us in finding sustenance, humans took on in turn the sustenance, protection and reproduction of many species of plants and animals. The last of these, reproduction, is particularly important, having led to two interlocking practices: domesticated species become *unable to reproduce without human intervention*, while humans have *intervened in reproduction for purposes of genetic manipulation.*

Our genetic manipulation of other species has primarily been directed towards increased yield, improved flavour, ease of cultivation, biddable disposition and so on. But there are more subtle and darker aspects. Domesticated animals have been consistently both bred and conditioned towards a state of 'neoteny' – a behaviourally and physically arrested childhood which makes them both more attractive to us (big eyes, rounded heads) and easier to control because less aggressive and more attention-seeking (Price, 1999; Trut, 1999): think of how cats make kitten-sounds to us when they want food or stroking. It has even been suggested that neoteny as the result of environmental factors actually predisposed certain species for domestication (Coppinger & Smith, 1983).

> Domesticated animals are by their nature permanent juveniles, dependent upon us for care, for the protection from predators that they can no longer provide themselves; for the food that they no longer know how to find for themselves.
>
> (Budiansky, 1997: 110)

At the very least, such massive intervention in the very nature of other-than-human species surely calls for a corresponding respect and gratitude on our part. But things seem to have worked in the other direction: the greater our power over other species, the greater our alienation from them and contempt for them, our sense of (literally) god-given right to dominate and control – often justified by a 'nature red in tooth and claw' ideology. Budiansky's book *The Covenant of the Wild* (1997) makes very plain how much humans have manipulated, and still do manipulate, domesticated species, but at the same time strikes an oddly aggressive-defensive posture (Budiansky is himself a farmer), mocking the bleeding-heart liberals who question domestication, which he characterises as the result of evolution and hence 'natural'. Yet his use of terms like 'covenant' strikes a very different note of covert theology, harking back to the Judaeo-Christian idea that it was not only our privilege but also our *duty* to dominate and control other-than-human species.

As I have repeatedly emphasised in this chapter, at the same time as domesticating other creatures, we have also domesticated ourselves.

> In the early 17th century ... the word 'domesticate' was applied only to humans, in the sense of civilizing or becoming part of a household ... From the end of the 18th century animals were included; the use of the term in relation to plants was uncommon until the second half of the 20th century. By the 1970s, its scientific application was to a process driven by humans and culminating in the modification of certain plants and animal species for human benefit.
>
> (Leach, 2003: 356)

More than one author has pointed out that some of the traits developed in other-than-human domesticated species can also be seen in humans (Groves, 1999; Leach, 2003, and references therein). Perhaps the most important of these for our purposes is what Colin Groves calls 'a reduction in environmental awareness', which humans have undergone 'in parallel to domestic species and for exactly the same reason' (Groves, 1999: 11): domesticated species have no practical need of the keen senses of wild creatures.

> Most domestic animals, including even recently domesticated trout, have smaller brains and less acute sense organs than do their wild ancestors. Good brains and keen eyes are essential to survival in the wild, but represent a quantitatively important waste of energy in the barnyard, as far as humans are concerned.
>
> (Diamond, 2002: 701)

Like other domesticated species, that is, we no longer need to know where we are and what is going on.

Domestication was not a covenant, blessed by patriarchal deities – though this made and continues to make a good cover story; but it was a bargain. And we must ask whether it is a bargain which still benefits either humans or other-than-humans; in particular, whether we have kept our side of the deal. By breeding many species into something quite different from their original character – so much so that, without our constant intervention, they would either quickly revert to type or else become extinct – and by treating them so often with vicious unconcern for their welfare, we have surely broken our bargain with them.

It is fair to say that many of the problems we deal with every day in therapy have their origins in the Neolithic bargain. Both infant attachment and the social bond were transformed by the social and economic changes that took place. The newly degraded status of women, together with the changes in subsistence levels described above, gave rise to insecure and disorganised attachment patterns which must have been previously rare or unknown – as I have pointed out, in Ice Age forager bands any infant who survived would necessarily be securely attached (Hrdy, 2009: 290) – and hence to disturbed and dangerous adults, whose aggression and need for dependent attachment was harnessed by the newly arising state, as continues to happen in every army up to the present. The social bond, partly influenced by these new attachment patterns, shifted from a free partnership of equals to a patriarchal hierarchy underwritten by theism, a state of affairs damaging to every child, woman and man. These changes are the psychological equivalent of major meteor strikes; their effects are still with us.

BEYOND THE PALE

> Hunter-gatherer societies are marked by an emphasis on 'focus' in contrast to domesticated societies, which are distinguished by an emphasis on the boundary.
>
> (Wilson, 1988: 5)

> Something there is that doesn't love a wall.
>
> (Robert Frost, *Mending Wall,* 1995: 39)

In this book I return again and again to the question of boundaries, borders, separating lines of all kinds. Boundaries are a key factor in domestication: as Peter J. Wilson points out in his classic book *The Domestication of the Human Species* (1988), domestication is quite literally about building walls.

> The development of domestication 'meant', among other things, the construction of a technology that simultaneously enhanced the opportunities for concentration by erecting physical barriers against intrusion and interruption; reduced the chances of distraction; and hindered the free-flow capacity of people to pay attention to one another as an undifferentiated feature of the routine of everyday life.
>
> (Wilson, 1988: 176)

Since 'in a very real and literal sense the adoption of architecture is an acceptance of structure and constraint' (ibid: 78), Wilson places considerable emphasis on the way that living in houses gives rise to the ensemble of socially normative behaviours:

> It seems that day-to-day activity, the intimate, affective interaction between individuals, is encroached on by the various forms of structure that impose on a community. It means also that the social structure of a community, the formal, institutional arrangements, activities and relationships, are affected by, as they affect, the informal routines and emotions of people. The result ... is the growth of certain beliefs and practices that occupy a region between informal behavior and institutional behavior.
> (Ibid: 78)

Ian Hodder in *The Domestication of Europe: Structure and Contingency in Neolithic Societies* (Hodder, 1990) suggests that the Neolithic bargain was sealed through a set of concepts around the house and home – the 'domus' – which provided a ruling metaphor for social and economic transformation, 'a story about the domination and domestication of nature, used as a metaphor for the domination and domestication of people' (Hodder, 1993: 269). As the wild was brought in and domesticated through ideas and practices surrounding the domus, people were brought in and settled into the social and economic group of the village – thus defining, of course, a remainder of incorrigible 'outsideness' beyond the village wall.

Domestication carries with it the whole realm of *propriety*, the drawing of boundaries between acceptable and unacceptable behaviour. Again, Sorenson describes the impact of this on preconquest cultures (speaking not in general speculative terms, but of a shift he actually observed in a specific culture):

> Only when awareness shifted from liminal to supraliminal did the notion of correctness become a matter of concern – e.g., behaving 'properly,' having 'right' answers, wearing 'appropriate' clothes, etc. 'Improper' aspirations, inclinations, and desires were then masked as people tried to measure up to the 'proper' rule and standard. They used rhetoric and logic argumentatively with reference to norms, precedents, and agreements to gain and maintain dignity, status, and position. It was an altogether different world from that of the preconquest era where people freely spread their interests, feelings, and delights out for all to see and grasp as they lurched toward whatever delightful patterns of response they found attractive.
> (Sorenson, 1998: 83)

Perhaps it is not quite coincidental that Sorenson's preconquest people sound so much like hippies on weed or acid – nor that hippies so often describe their affinity groups as 'tribes'.

These issues of correctness and propriety can be summed up in the familiar phrase 'beyond the pale'. The Pale is a term which has been applied to a variety of territories 'within determined bounds, or subject to a particular jurisdiction', as the Oxford English Dictionary puts it – for example areas of France, of Scotland or of Ireland administered at different times by the English, or specified districts of Russia within which Jews were required to live. By extension, to be 'beyond the pale' is to act in ways which contravene the dictates of polite society, and hence to be banished to the wilderness, to the savage places (the coincidence that 'pale' also applies to skin colour adds bite to the phrase).

Contrariwise, the colonisation of the savage wilderness by civilisation entails the imposition of both property and propriety, cultivation of both the land and the individual. Gill and Anderson (2005: 1) quote an oddly Austenesque passage from Arthur Phillip, an early Governor of New South Wales:

> There are few things more pleasing than the contemplation of order and useful arrangement on the land arising gradually out of tumult and confusion; and perhaps this satisfaction cannot anywhere be more fully enjoyed than where a settlement of civilised people is fixing itself upon a newly discovered and savage coast.
>
> (Phillip, 1789/1988: 122)

They continue:

> Over the course of the subsequent century, the enactment of this ideal of settled cultivation, enshrined in John Locke's influential notion of property rights, discredited and eradicated other, more nomadic modes of relation to land. More than a cultural ideal, however, settled cultivation materialised a specific humanist ontology of human distinction from the nonhuman world, according to which cultivation would not only release the land's potential, but signal the passage of a universalised human out of a 'state of nature' and ultimately into a space of civilised accommodation with other humans and nonhumans.
>
> (Gill & Anderson, 2005: 1)

These themes are central to Daniel Defoe's *Robinson Crusoe*. They also appear clearly in the traditional account of the Romanisation of Britain – not wholly dissimilar to what was still taught in British schools until quite recently:

> The WALL, the most renowned workes of the Romans, which was the bound in times past of the Romane province; raised of purpose to seclude and keepe out the barbarous nations, that in this tract, were evermore *barking and baying* (as an ancient writer saith) *about the Roman Empire.*
>
> (Camden, 1586, quoted in Kelly, 2010: 15)

Civilisation requires a wall – or even a 'WALL' – to keep out the barbarians, who are here explicitly cast as animal-like ('barking and baying'). And barbarism is persistent, erupting through the veneer of civilisation. According to Francis Drake, an 18th century surgeon of York, Britons under Roman rule sometimes:

> divested themselves of their reason, as well as clothes, and run naked into the mountains, to starve among their few unconquered countrymen ... Like the Hottentots of Africa, who have thrown off the finest garments, and left the cosiest diet, to besmear their bodies with stinking grease, and fall to gnawing, again, of dirty guts and garbage.
>
> (Drake, 1736; quoted in Kelly, 2010: 16)

The fundamental boundary of domestication, which we have already repeatedly encountered from different angles, is that between the human and the other-than-human – thereby specified as the *non*-human, just as women are the non-male, children the non-adult, people of colour the non-white. This boundary can be understood as phobic, setting up a condition which we might term Cultural Obsessive-Compulsive Disorder. Mick Smith and Joyce Davidson bring this out in their analysis of 'phobias of "nature"', where they point out that most or all of the common phobias – spiders, mice, birds, etc – relate to the culture/nature boundary. They employ Kristeva's (1982) concept of the 'abject' to describe what is experienced as intolerably non-cultural:

> The threat is not a matter of poison or predation but is proportional to that thing's ability to stand in for – to symbolize – the differences that compose the predominant cultural logic upon which the maintenance of self-identity relies. This means that the things that are found disgusting, and the experience of disgust itself, are indicative of the abject's perceived ability to confound those norms, to cross the threshold between natural and cultural space, between categories of self and other. The abject is associated with that over which we seemingly have no personal or social control, that moves erratically, never stays fixed in vision, makes our skin crawl or darkens our doorsteps, that which escapes the

> classification that would exclude it altogether from a modern culture systematically cleansed of contaminating natural elements. ... [T]hese phobias might indeed crystallize something seriously wrong with modernity's cultural logic, with its relations to a nature that it believes it has suppressed and surpassed but which threatens to return in myriad uncontrollable ways.
>
> (Smith & Davidson, 2006: 63–4)

I would add to this the quality, real or imagined, of entering and disturbing our bodies – like mice, spiders, flies, microbes, airborne particles. Smith and Davidson draw on Mary Douglas's analysis of the relationship between bodily and social boundaries and her definition of impurity as the product of ambiguity or anomaly, 'matter out of place' (Douglas, 1970: 48, 53), and also on David Sibley's development of these ideas in a Lacanian context (Sibley, 1995). But they place at the centre of their discussion 'what we take to be *the* key feature of the modern Western symbolic order, namely, the all-pervasive boundary it constructs and relies upon between "culture" and "nature"' (Smith & Davidson, 2006: 47).

Kristeva's concept of abjection (Kristeva, 1982) refers specifically to those parts or products of the body which can be detached from it, and which therefore, she suggests, can fill us with alarm, disgust and anxiety: snot, blood, sperm, urine, faeces, hair, nails, and so on – all to a greater or less extent queasy and uncomfortable substances whose management is subject to rigorous rules. One might say that in detaching from the body, abjects cross the pale and move from the realm of 'nature' into that of 'culture', much as wild animals do when they enter human spaces. This is particularly clear, perhaps, with some animals which mimic or bring to mind uncontrollable aspects of our organic nature, as slugs resemble snot or faeces, and spiders remind us of genitals; more generally, many phobic objects mimic the movement of life energy in our own bodies – the writhing of maggots or snakes, the quick rush of mice or spiders which we fear will *run up our legs.* Gianna Williams describes a patient who was terrified of fleas penetrating her body through orifices or even through the pores of her skin (Williams, 1997: 104).

Paul Shepard in *The Others* shows how these various facets of phobia are interwoven, again referring to Douglas's work:

> Our society centers its aim of controlling organic nature on the 'natural' aspects of ourselves, sex, death, birth, defecation, growth, hedging them about with rites of cleaning and avoidance and projecting their dangerous qualities onto animals, which become a kind of code for them. This need 'to distance our social life from animal origins' is what anthropologist Mary Douglas calls

> 'the purity rule'. ... The tainted world of the flesh, above which our morality inspires us to rise, is more clearly seen in the animals than in our ambiguous selves.
>
> (Shepard, 1996: 274)

A continuous theme of domesticated culture is a repulsion against and superiority over humans who are too closely associated with animals and dirt – or conversely, the attachment of animal imagery to those over whom we feel superiority (see the quotation above about Roman Britons and Hottentots).

> Here, we find some of the most imaginative but also some of the most destructive stereotypical representations of others. ... To dehumanize through claiming animal attributes for others is one way of legitimating exploitation and exclusion from civilized society, so it is unsurprising that it is primarily peripheral minorities, indigenous and colonized peoples, who have been described in these terms.
>
> (Sibley, 1995: 28)

Sibley quotes examples relating to Gypsies, Jews, and Irish people, particularly associating them with rats.

One of the grounds for such accusations of animality (apart from convenience in justifying mistreatment) is that the human group concerned fails to observe 'natural' boundaries between domesticated and wild, human and animal, clean and unclean. But of course most of these boundaries are artefacts of culture rather than aspects of the world. The Kayapó, whom we met in Chapter 4, 'do not make a clear distinction between field and forest nor between wild and domesticated species. Gathered plants are transplanted, concentrated in spots near trails and campsites, to produce "forest fields". The sides of trails themselves are planting zones' (Posey, 2002: 10). As Posey is well aware, they do not make a clear distinction not through a failure of perception, but because there *is* no clear distinction. And the ability to tolerate such unclarity, to allow the world to be muddled and 'mixed up', is not a frequent property of domesticated humans.

THE DOMESTICATION OF CHILDREN

> The conflation of womanhood with the body (and its 'wild' energy) was also a powerful and enduring couplet, as was the idea that children's 'wild' behaviour should be subject to 'training' and discipline (as for animals).
>
> (Anderson, 1997: 473)

The 'always-already-happened' process of human domestication is in some sense repeated with each fresh generation. Sorenson (2006) lists the effects which he observed of compulsory school attendance on children brought up in wild/preconquest culture – effects which then spread out into their community as a whole.

> 1. As spontaneous liminal behavior of children was foreclosed most of the day by classrooms, it began declining outside the school as well.
> 2. Among these children awareness of and responsiveness to the concerns and feelings of others began to fade.
> 3. Mergings of individuality and solidarity were less often seen.
> 4. Uncertainty set in as to whether one should reveal what was really on one's mind.
> 5. Universal candor among these children vanished.
> 6. The once ubiquitous inquisitory and affirmatory dances of eye-contact gave way to aversion of eye-contact.
> 7. Open hearted comradeliness narrowed to a few close personal friends.
> 8. Open interest in novelty declined.
>
> (Sorenson, 2006: 5)

Many parents will experience something horribly familiar about this list: changes which we would perhaps dearly like to attribute to 'just growing up', but which can be more realistically understood as a deliberate process of taming imposed on children in our own society when they come to be schooled. Though few of our own children are fully wild before they start school, they are all partially so; but much of their liminal awareness, and the freedom and wellbeing that go with it, are stripped away in a systematic disciplining of the child's bodymind. Perhaps the core element here is restriction of the child's free movement and bodily expression, causing them to lose their embodied sense of self-in-contact-with-the-world: Sit still! Be quiet! Don't fidget! This suppression of ideomotor activity, as it is called (Spitz, 1997), is profoundly damaging to our embodiment: as Barrett Dorko describes it, 'being able to sit or stand "at attention" for prolonged periods, while largely impossible without tremendous effort or discomfort, becomes an unattainable but constantly desired goal' (Dorko, nd). He believes that this is the root of many physical and psychological difficulties in later life: wild mind prevented from natural homeostatic rebalancing.

Until recent times the explicit foundation of the process of child-taming was the threat or reality of punishment with physical pain; now in most Western schools this has been replaced by shaming and the withdrawal of approval, more subtle but equally hurtful sanctions. The fundamental notion, it appears, is still that children are 'animals' who need to be trained to be human – and that the mark of humanity is a loss of spontaneity and aliveness. If, as Chris Philo writes, 'the tendency has been to consider animals as marginal "thing-like" beings devoid of inner lives, apprehensions or sensibilities' (Philo, 1995: 656–7), then is the same not to some extent true of the way adults have traditionally viewed children? The point is made rather wonderfully in a passage discovered by Philo and Wilbert (2000: 22) in a 1920s text on *Secrets of the Zoo*:

> For their own sake, you have to make the Zoo's animals behave themselves ... For example, they must take their food decently and allow their cages to be cleaned, and if they have any little tricks or peculiarities they are encouraged to show them off ... Of course there are a certain number of 'hard cases' ... which are permanent mutineers against any form of restraint. Broadly speaking, however, discipline is enforced just as much as in any other place where the inmates are kept against their will, from a school for small boys, to Dartmoor Prison.
>
> (Mainland, 1927: 31)

The parallel between children and animals is constantly reinvented as if it was a new and alarming development:

> More than 50 percent of Britons think the country's children are beginning to behave like animals and many believe they are increasingly a danger to adults and each other, according to a poll released on Monday.
>
> A report by charity Barnardo's, which commissioned the survey, said the findings were shocking and showed a disturbing intolerance of children.
>
> 'It is appalling that words like "animal", "feral" and "vermin" are used daily in reference to children,' said Martin Narey, Barnardo's chief executive.
>
> 'These are not references to a small minority of children but represent the public view of all children.'
>
> (*Reuters*, 2008)

This popular view is largely created and maintained by the constantly repeated media trope of 'wild kids'. Many of the stories are blown up out of very little, to feed a moral panic (Cohen, 1972): the notion of 'wild kids' is itself an expression of the children-as-animals metaphor which is part of the domesticated world-view. Where there is a real problem, it is not about children or young people who are wild in the sense I am developing in this book, but about their being chaotic, lost, full of pain and inchoate aggression: consequences of civilisation, not of wildness.

WAS THERE EVER AN ALTERNATIVE?

The picture of the Neolithic bargain which emerges from all the evidence so far available suggests that farming and sedentary life in towns developed from a coming together of several disparate factors. 'The appearance of farming about 10,000 years ago is ... the consequence of a chance coincidence of events, in which a species with novel forms of behaviour first encounters a rare climatic event' (Layton, 1999: 114): that is, a global warming event, breaking the usual cyclical expansion and contraction of populations, was responded to by people who (partly as a result of Pleistocene conditions of hardship) had evolved complex social relations mediated by language.

It seems likely that prehistoric societies, like several contemporary ones, drifted in and out of what in hindsight looks like agriculture, perhaps more than once, before a settled pattern emerged. Subsistence systems incorporating animal and/or plant husbandry 'could well have been widespread in appropriate environmental contexts in the late Pleistocene and early Holocene in many parts of the world, and had no necessary trajectory in the direction of agriculture in any particular case' (Spriggs, 1996: 534). Graeme Barker, whose work I have quoted several times, is similarly emphatic:

> [T]here was no inexorable path to agriculture, no unstoppable progress along an evolutionary spectrum from low-input mobile foraging to intensive sedentary farming. Hunting-and-horticulture and hunting-and-herding did not lead automatically to agriculture. The archaeological record has in fact examples of societies that 'reverted' to less intensive methods of subsistence.
>
> (Barker, 2006: 397)

Nor is it clear that a sedentary lifestyle, even in towns, necessarily involves a cultural break. There are clear examples of sedentary forager societies, not all of which were hierarchical in nature. The Kayapó, living before contact with Westerners in a town of around 5,000 people, seem to have been an urban forager-gardener society still living in wild mind, and there appear to have been other such societies in the Amazon basin; there may have been many more in the prehistoric Old World.

But does this imply that another path could have been taken? This question is not only of abstract interest: it has significance for our possible future. To create the omelette of complex technological society, a large number of precious eggs have been broken; and while they clearly cannot be put back together again, it might be possible to envisage a future society which combines the best features of forager and post-agricultural consciousness.

The crucial issue, I have suggested in this chapter, is the break with the other-than-human. From this, everything else follows, including what Martin (1993: 145) describes as 'the anxiety over cosmic disorder that seems to lie at the core of all the agrarian religions'; including also the distortions of infant attachment and of the social bond, accompanied by and accompanying a changed perception of the world, no longer 'a giving environment' (Bird-David, 1990, 1993) but a recalcitrant resource to be dominated and wrenched into submission.

> It was indeed a revolution, but one which was as much about human imagination and psychology as economic and social behaviour. Alongside transformations in humans' relationships with animals and plants, and with each other, foragers' animistic notions of the world as an unconditionally giving parent were commonly transformed ... into a new theism. That theism usually appears to have involved new concepts of human destiny being in the lap of the gods, of sexuality being a threatening force, and of land as something to be controlled and pacified, an ancestor which only gave its wealth in return for favours rendered. In many respects [these cosmologies] were the forerunners of the agrarian-based Graeco-Roman, Judaeo-Christian-Muslim, and eastern religions of our own world, all of which have asserted the primacy of humans over the natural world, a primacy that is proving increasingly dangerous to sustain.
>
> (Barker, 2006: 414)

Whether we think that something different could have happened, then, depends in part on our idea of the relationship between material and psychological factors. If the Neolithic revolution was an imaginative one, then we could, at least in theory, have imagined something else. And what is going on at the moment – in this book as well as in many other places – is an attempt, triggered by the material factor of the collapse of the biosystem, to imagine something different, a way to live which is in some sense a return to forager culture, but using our technological skills to enable a far higher population density to be sustained while re-creating a way of life which corresponds to our bodily and psychological needs:

> Over the millions of years of our evolution, we grew bodies and minds that crave certain kinds of experiences – walking, throwing things, contemplating fire, dancing, sex, talking, spending most of everyday outdoors, etc. etc. Only in the last part of our long history have we shifted away from lives that gave us these satisfactions, and the 'sublimated' pleasures of industrial existence cannot replace them.
>
> (Robinson, 1994: 10)

Whatever might have been theoretically possible, what happened did happen – in several parts of the world at more or less the same time; and as I have already said, liminal or preconquest cultures are appallingly vulnerable to dominator ones, which seem as infectious and destructive to those with no inbuilt resistance as the smallpox and measles which decimated Native Americans. Perhaps an even better analogy is that of cancer, where a random mutation sparks off uncontrollable growth. Should we succeed in creating a new liminal culture, will it manifest the same vulnerability to any reappearance of dominator behaviour, or is it possible for undomesticated human existence to be more robust in the face of aggressive competition?

6

Wildness Under Control

> In a world of uncontrolled forces, conservatives sought to impose complete control, whether by pursuing technological fixes (like the nuclear missile shield) or treating US security as if it were something that could simply be willed.
>
> (Power, 2008: 68)

A domesticated/domesticating culture is founded upon an ideal of control: control of its environment, control of its population, control against accident, failure and unpredictability of all kinds. In fact, control becomes its identity; so that the ever-recurring spectacle of loss of control – since there can be no such thing as continuous centralised control – feels like a threat of annihilation which must be fought by all means possible. These means include violence on every level, of course, from the physical punishment of children to the threat of nuclear war; but they also include more subtle, if equally contradictory, strategies.

Karl Popper sums up some of these strategies and contradictions:

> The holistic [that is, totalising] planner overlooks the fact that it is easy to centralize power but impossible to centralize all that knowledge which is distributed over many individual minds ... [H]is attempt to exercise power over minds must destroy the last possibility of finding out what people really think, for it is clearly incompatible with the free expression of thought, especially of critical thought. Ultimately, it must destroy knowledge; and the greater the gain in power, the greater will be the loss of knowledge.
>
> (Popper, 1974: 89)

And, of course, knowledge and power must go together to succeed. We can see the same strategy, and the same contradiction, in action on a microscale in the American town of Wild Rose, Wisconsin, where in 1974 a district administrator removed from the town library the book *Bury My Heart at Wounded Knee,* by Dee Brown, which describes the ethnic cleansing of Native Americans. What distinguishes this from thousands of similar acts of censorship is the unusually direct explanation which the administrator gave for their actions. 'If there's a possibility that something might be controversial', she or he said, 'then why not eliminate it' (Dangerous Pages, 2009).

RUMBLE IN THE JUNGLE

One striking example of the failure of ongoing centralised control can stand for many others: Fordlandia, the vast rubber plantation complete with company town which Henry Ford built in the Amazon jungle in 1928 (Grandin, 2009). As James C. Scott writes in his review of Grandin's book, 'Ford fought two battles ... The first was with the workers of the Brazilian frontier, the second with tropical nature. Ford lost both' (Scott, 2009: 31). Ford tried to impose the plantation model on cultivating rubber trees, which naturally grow in mixed jungle where pests and diseases have many other available hosts (ibid: 32). Grown as a sitting target in artificial isolation, the rubber trees were wiped out; while at the same time, the jungle put mould on the office paper supplies and rusted the typewriters even before they had been unpacked (ibid).

Equally disastrously, Ford tried to impose a North American model of central control on his freewheeling Amazonian workers. While the imported US managers lived in splendid isolation in a replica of a Midwestern small town with 'cottages with front lawns and porches; sidewalks, streetlamps, a clubhouse where the men played cards, a pool, a tennis court, a movie theatre, a golf course and an ice-cream parlour', the local workers were subjected to a regime of 'civilisation':

> There were rigorous standards of sanitation and hygiene, and these were strictly enforced. Stray dogs were killed. Officials periodically inspected houses and compounds to make sure food was stored properly, corrals were tidy and well drained, laundry was properly hung on lines to dry, latrines were clean and well maintained, families were using company-provided toilet paper, and waste was properly disposed of. Employees were given physical examinations to check for sexually transmitted diseases; they were vaccinated and required to take anti-malarial pills (much detested for their side effects), which were dispensed when workers clocked out.
>
> (Scott, 2009: 31)

As Scott points out, 'the regimentation was only slightly more extreme than in Ford's many enterprises in Michigan'; but in Michigan his workers had been trained into domestication since birth. Scott also emphasises that 'Ford believed the measures constituted a noble effort to raise the nutritional, hygienic and moral well-being of his benighted workforce' (ibid). The workers experienced it differently, however;

and one day in 1930, an apparently 'trivial' incident – the introduction of a cafeteria system for the workers, with queuing, while managers were waited on at table – exploded into a riot.

> Everything in the dining-hall was smashed by the rioters: furniture, crockery, pots, glasses. Other workers came with knives, rocks, pipes, hammers, machetes and clubs and destroyed everything they could reach: the power house, the office building, the garage, the sawmill, the radio station, the receiving building. They burned the company records and tried to remove the pilings from the pier; company vehicles were looted and burned, and the time-clocks smashed. Then they went looking for liquor – and for the North American bosses. ... Most of the Americans escaped on a launch kept at the ready for just such an emergency, while provincial troops were summoned to put down the insurrection. Fordlandia staggered on, but it never really recovered.
> (Ibid)

CONTROLLING SOCIETY

James C. Scott is also author of *Seeing like a State: How Certain Schemes to Improve the Human Condition Have Failed* (Scott, 1998), which starts out from a wish 'to understand why the state has always seemed to be the enemy of "people who move around" ... nomads, hunter-gatherers, gypsies, vagrants, homeless people, itinerants, runaway slaves, and serfs' (Scott, 1998: 1); the freewheeling migrant workers of Ford's Amazon plantation are another such group. This leads Scott to study what he terms 'sedentarisation ... a state's attempt to make a society legible, to arrange the population in ways that simplified the classic state functions of taxation, conscription, and prevention of rebellion' (Scott, 1998: 2).

Scott identifies 'legibility' in this sense as 'a central problem in statecraft' (ibid). In essence, the state has two avenues: on the one hand to develop new techniques for deciphering the characteristics and activities of society, and on the other hand to construct a society which is intrinsically easier to decipher. The modern state has pursued both of these options to a high degree. However, history is full of ambitious plans for social engineering which have failed abjectly; and Scott's aim is to account for this repeated pattern of failure. His explanation is in effect an expanded version of Popper's analysis: that for the State, power and knowledge are mutually exclusive goals.

Scott continuously draws parallels between controlled societies and controlled ecosystems, both of which attempt to simplify complexity:

> Radically simplified designs for social organization seem to court the same risks of failure courted by radically simplified designs for natural environments. The failures and vulnerability of monocrop commercial forests and genetically engineered, mechanized monocropping mimic the failures of collective farms and planned cities. I am making a case for the resilience of both social and natural diversity and a strong case about the limits, in principle, of what we are likely to know about complex, functioning order.
> (Scott, 1998: 7)

As De Landa (2000: 60–70) points out, hierarchy is an effective way (whether desirable or otherwise) of organising a simple, homogeneous group of entities; complex, heterogeneous groups, however, naturally organise themselves into 'meshworks', of which ecosystems are the prime example. Hence an incipient hierarchy *must* either homogenise its population, learn to identify its homogeneous elements, or both. From this point of view, Scott and Popper are pointing out the essentially heterogeneous nature of human populations.

Both Scott and Popper identify what amounts to a social version of Heisenberg's uncertainty principle: the more one tries to know about any social network, the less one can control it, while the more one tries to control it, the less one can know about it (because people don't tell their controllers the truth). As Ursula Le Guin puts it:

> A chain of command is easy to describe; a network of response isn't. To those who live by mutual empowerment, 'thick' description, complex and open-ended, is normal and comprehensible, but to those whose only model is hierarchic control, such description seems a muddle, a mess, along with what it describes. Who's in charge here? Get rid of all these petty details. How many cooks spoil a soup? Let's get this perfectly clear now. Take me to your leader.
> (Le Guin, 1996: 88)

When a state or a scientific agriculturalist tries to clear away all the 'petty details', the local complexity that makes it hard to turn what is going on into a unidirectional flow chart, they prevent what is going on from happening at all; because in complex Wild Mind systems the flow of causation is not single but multiple, it splits, loops, and doubles back on itself, creating the 'mess' which is life itself.

THE FINAL TURTLE

'Thick description' is a term borrowed by the anthropologist Clifford Geertz (1973) from the philosopher Gilbert Ryle (2009) to indicate the need for *contextuality* in any adequate account of human behaviour. And since context is in principle infinite, Geertz asserts the impossibility of ever *getting to the bottom of things*, quoting a version of the well-known story about a Westerner who, told by a native informant that the world rests on a platform which rests on the back of an elephant which rests in turn on the back of a turtle, asks what the turtle rests on? Another turtle. And that turtle? Well, after that it's turtles all the way down.

Domesticated culture, as expressed in phenomena like the state, is constantly trying to shorten the informational food chain, to get to the final turtle (or as Russell Hoban, 1993, calls it, for reasons that only his book can make clear, the Last Visible Dog). This attempt is distilled in the concept and practice of *expertise*, which is:

> formulated on a global level, that is, within the abstract 'synthetic nature' constructed by science. And the terms it is built on are to be highly standardized, quantifiable and not subject to subjective interpretations. It is through such a model, its language and its terms that the necessary control, manipulation and supervision ... is established.
>
> (Van der Ploeg, 1993: 219)

Expertise occupies the opposite pole to *local knowledge* (Geertz, 1983): a term developed in anthropology and the new field of science studies to describe what James C. Scott calls 'the indispensable role of practical knowledge, informal processes, and improvisation in the face of unpredictability' (Scott, 1998: 6).

Van der Ploeg's illuminating paper 'Potatoes and knowledge' (1993) studies the vexed relationship between agrarian science and local farmers in the Andes. It describes how, from the scientists' point of view, it is 'only logical' to model the needs and procedures of agriculture in a standardised way, with so much nitrogen required equalling such and such a dose of chemical fertiliser, and so on. The practical reality of farming is very different for someone who knows the intricacies of their environment and follows what van der Ploeg calls *'art de la localité'*, growing perhaps a dozen varieties of potato each in their appropriate micro-climate and soil. But because the procedures and outcome of such an approach cannot be precisely specified, they simply do not register on the screen of the expert approach. 'Local knowledge ... is, under these conditions, rapidly becoming not just a marginal, but more than anything, a superfluous or even a counter-productive element' (van der Ploeg, 1993: 219–20; for another rich account of an agricultural local knowledge system, see Syse, 2010).

Wynne (1995) characterises local knowledges – which he argues are always necessarily plural – as:

> interwoven with *practices* ... highly dynamic systems of knowledge involving continuous negotiation between 'mental' and 'manual' labour, and continual interpretation of production experiences. ... However because it is so multidimensional and adaptive, experience is rarely expressed in a univocal, clear form. This is frequently mistaken for lack of theoretical content ... [But] there is indeed systematic theory, even though this is in a syntax linked to the local labour process and does not presuppose a universal and impersonal world.
>
> (Wynne, 1995: 67, italics added)

Stephen Marglin (1990a, b) describes a very similar polarity under the terms *techne* (equivalent to local knowledge) and *episteme* (expert knowledge), arguing that 'the accommodation of labour to capital owes much to the systematic subordination of *techne* to *episteme* in Western culture' (Marglin, 1990a: 24).

A famous early proponent of expert systems was Frederick Winslow Taylor, who introduced the concept of 'scientific management' which explicitly studied and co-opted local knowledge:

> Under scientific management ... the managers assume ... the burden of gathering together all the traditional knowledge which in the past has been possessed by the workmen and then of classifying, tabulating, and reducing this knowledge to rules, laws and formulae. ... These replace the judgment of the individual workman. ... Thus all of the planning which under the old system was done by the workman, as a result of his personal experience, must of necessity under the new system be done by management in accordance with the laws of science.
>
> (Taylor, 1911/1967, quoted in Marglin, 1990b: 224)

It is striking how much this passage reads like a critique of 'Taylorism' rather than support for it; striking also how directly it parallels other themes of control which we are exploring in this book, for example the ego's desire to believe itself in control of essentially autonomous bodily and psychological processes. Scientific management seems actually to have originated in the military administration of various enterprises like mines, railways and armaments (De Landa, 2000: 82–5).

It is no accident that practices related to the land and to plants are so often cited in discussions of expertise versus local knowledge. Agriculture is an ancient and profound example of a core human activity which involves working *with* natural processes, rather than cutting across them. To grow food and raise animals, one must relate to an Other, and to some minimal extent respect its needs and wishes – while also of course, as I have discussed, to some extent fighting those needs and wishes. Once agriculture parts company from local knowledge, the stage is set for disaster; and Scott devotes a chapter (Scott, 1998: Chapter 8) to detailing how expert agriculture has repeatedly failed to produce results in the developing world, particularly in Africa.

> It is the systematic, cyclopean short-sightedness of high-modernist agriculture that courts certain forms of failure. Its rigorous attention to productionist goals casts into relative obscurity all the outcomes lying outside the immediate relationship between farm inputs and yields. This means that both long-term outcomes (soil structure, water quality, land-tenure relations) and third-party effects, or what welfare economists call 'externalities', receive little attention until they begin to affect production.
>
> (Scott, 1998: 264)

This economists' concept of 'externalities' is one of the most egregious ways in which the illusion of control is maintained in our society. Any costs of a particular activity that are not borne by the commercial interests directly concerned can be written off as 'external', and therefore ignored, allowing the continuing appearance of benefit; often the state ends up picking up the tab. This splitting off process (similar in form to the splitting and projection studied by psychotherapy) has been applied to pollution, environmental degradation, and carbon emissions, though this is now coming under increasing challenge (Martinez-Alier, 1995; Stern, 2006); it is a major factor in the maintenance of expert systems agribusiness in the developed as well as the developing world (Pew Commission, 2008). Laura and Dana Jackson in their book *The Farm as Natural Habitat: Reconnecting Food Systems with Ecosystems* (2002) describe how:

> Many people are only vaguely aware that their food is not produced on Old MacDonald's Farm but in a sterile landscape of row crops drained by ramrod-straight, silt-laden streams and interspersed with meat factories housing thousands or millions of animals. A

> few consumers are concerned about the rising numbers of genetically altered crops, about the treatment of animals, and about the effects of farm chemicals in drinking water. But for most, farm country is not where you find nature anyway.
> (Jackson & Jackson, 2002: 2)

But 'nature' cannot be corralled into parks and left there. Farming is a major cause of habitat destruction for 38% of the species on the US endangered species list – above commercial development, grazing, logging and dams. Defining this destruction and other disastrous effects as an 'externality' allows agribusiness to continue unchecked, and maintains a crazy splitting in our society's perception of the world. The Jacksons' book and others like it (Scher & McNeeley, 2007; Shrestha & Clements, 2004) are trying to bridge the split and put agriculture back in its ecological context, as it is, for example, in Andean farming: 'To raise a *chacra* [cultivated land] is not merely to domesticate plants and animals; it is to nurture lovingly and respectfully, in other words, to nurture ritually, together with plants and animals, the soils, waters, micro-climates, and in general, the whole land' (Apffel-Marglin & Rivera, 1995: 24).

CONTROL GONE OUT OF CONTROL

> No general or politician will ever state: 'Relax, nothing is under control'.
> (Prince Constantijn of the Netherlands, 2005)

According to Stephen Marglin, 'development' and 'modernization' mean in practice:

> On the economic side, industrialization and urbanization, as well as the technological transformation of agriculture; on the political side, rationalization of authority and the growth of a rationalizing bureaucracy; on the social side, the weakening of ascriptive ties and the rise of achievement as the basis for personal advancement; culturally, the 'disenchantment' of the world (to use Max Weber's terminology), the growth of science and secularization based on increasing literacy and numeracy.
> (Marglin, 1990a: 2)

'In a word', he sums up, 'development means Westernization' (ibid).

The more rationalised and bureaucracy-driven our society becomes, the less controllable everything becomes; so the striving for control becomes less and less sane, more and more a matter of simplifying not *reality*, but *appearance*. The rise of the contemporary 'neo-liberal state' heightens this situation: through an ideological conviction that the free market will magically solve all problems, the state resigns many of its traditional functions, leaving a frightening vacuum.

> Political authority, and the system of values and relationships which political authority rests upon ... has been replaced by the vast and complex system of regulation, inspection, performance management and audit which has bred the new quasiprofession of auditors, regulators and inspectors to administer and manage it. ... [W]here government once willed the means to health and welfare, now it tends to prescribe the ends while others are increasingly left to supply the means, and these people must be watched, regulated; and as with all instrumentally oriented practices, the logic governing the attainment of these ends is the logic of rules. In short where government was, now regulation, inspection, performance management, audit and quality assurance is.
> (Cooper, 2001: 352–3)

Belief in the power of the 'free market' to resolve all problems is a distorted parody of the Wild Mind consciousness which I discussed in the last chapter. Wild Mind recognises that things work best if we surrender control – or rather, admit that we *have* no control: as the *Tao Te Ching* says:

> The world is ruled by letting things take their course.
> It cannot be ruled by interfering.
> (Feng & English, 1972: Section 48)

Neo-liberalism bears a superficial resemblance to this recognition – neo-liberal gurus are in a sense twisted mystics, trusting in the spontaneous wisdom of the market. In practice, though, neo-liberalism applies the concept only as a glamour cast over the exploitative self-interest of global enterprise, inviting us to give up our control, not to the natural course of things, but to late industrial capitalism. The basic mechanisms are splitting and projection, the definition of all negative consequences as 'externalities', buttressed by an audit culture which cannot accept the inevitability of imperfection and at least occasional failure. Translated into the realm of international affairs, for example, this produces the 'War Against Terror' and the disasters of Iraq and Afghanistan. Zygmunt Bauman warned prophetically in 1992 that 'catastrophes most horrid are born ... out of the war against catastrophes' (Bauman, 1992: 25; see his development of this position in e.g. Bauman, 1991).

Andrew Cooper highlights the irreality which results from neo-liberal ideology, and the ways in which this relates to deeper psychosocial issues – issues which psychotherapy has traditionally tasked itself with exposing:

> [A]ll these practices and methodologies which are supposedly devoted to transparency, and the exposure of failure, poor practice and so on may serve in fact to disguise and distort fundamental and painful truths which we seem no longer to be able to face as a society. ... However capable we may be of improving on past performance, in the domain of health, welfare and mental health practice there always will be mistakes, there will be failures and deaths, there will be guilt, anxiety and the wish to blame. These things will not and cannot go away.
>
> (Cooper, 2002: 360–1)

If this picture is correct, how can psychotherapy allow itself to be captured by audit culture without betraying its own nature? Cooper also writes:

> It is not simply that we are all being subjected to something unpleasant. We are all to one degree or another implicated in the collective state of mind I want to discuss, because we have all bought into it, have allowed it to occupy our thinking; at the political level we are deeply implicated in its development by virtue of our activity or passivity as citizens.
>
> (Cooper, 2002: 350)

THE SURVEILLANCE SPIRAL

The neo-liberal state provides the context for the disturbing developments charted by Anna Minton in *Ground Control: Fear and Happiness in the Twenty-First Century City* (Minton, 2009). She demonstrates how control of city streets and public places has increasingly been ceded by local government to corporate entities, giving rise to gated estates on the one hand, and massive shopping/leisure/housing complexes like Liverpool One or Stratford City on the other. These areas, often in the form of 'Business Improvement Districts', masquerade as public spaces but are actually either privately owned or privately managed and controlled through unaccountable security firms.

> The absolute minimum level of security on every private estate I've visited has been round-the-clock private guards and blanket

> CCTV coverage. ... It has seemed like a natural extension for today's open-air malls without walls to expand their CCTV networks to 'cover every inch of the site', as I was proudly told in Liverpool One. Similarly, the uniformed private-security guards who have long patrolled commercial property premises have emerged into daylight and are now on the streets of the new private estates ....
>
> (Minton, 2009: 32)

The mantra of the order which these methods police is 'Clean and Safe' (Minton, 2009: 44ff). This translates into controlling all forms of spontaneous activity, particularly by young people, homeless people and other non-mainstream groups, including remnant political activity like demonstrations (Minton, 2009: 48–52). Unfortunately this leaves a space which is empty and lifeless, leading to a further strategy, articulated to Minton by the manager of a Business Improvement District:

> We audition our buskers ... but I'm afraid we control all that – they have to book into our diary. I don't think we'd ever apologise for wanting that control because it would reduce quality and safety. We prefer planned creativity. There's a trade-off between public safety and spontaneity. What you want is a few surprises, I agree with that, so we add in unpredictability with lighting schemes and water features, anything that adds to the quirkiness of what happens when you walk around as a consumer. We make huge efforts to import vitality.
>
> (Minton, 2009: 54)

There could hardly be a clearer description of the replacement of heterogeneity with homogeneity *disguised as* heterogeneity, 'importing vitality' as one might import oxygen to Mars. And alongside this is the growth of fear as a continuous aspect of our existence: 'all around the country security is becoming an ever increasing part of the physical environment, fuelled by property, insurance and risk, and the role of the police in urban design' (Minton, 2009: 140). As Minton also points out: 'There is now a growing body of research ... which shows that taking more precautions against crime and strengthening security can increase levels of fear and social isolation' (ibid) – leading to the demand for yet more security! The ever-visible symbol of this inflationary surveillance spiral is the CCTV camera: Britain has the most CCTV of any country in the world, more than the rest of Europe put together (Minton, 2009: 47). As William Gibson neatly puts it, CCTV cameras are:

> a symptom of auto-immune disease, the state's protective mechanisms 'roiding up into something actively destructive, chronic, watchful eyes, eroding the healthy function of what they ostensibly protected.
>
> (Gibson, 2010: 57)

DOMESTICATED PHILOSOPHY

> To show that a category mistake has been committed one must typically show that once the phenomenon in question is properly understood, it becomes clear that the claim being made about it could not possibly be true.
>
> (Wikipedia, 'Category mistake')

It is in this chapter and the previous one, perhaps, that I find it most difficult to avoid being gripped by a partisan dualism which pits wildness and domestication horizontally against each other. We need to step back and remind ourselves that at its simplest and least emotionally charged, the problem with domestication is a philosophical one: it constitutes and produces a *category mistake* (Ryle, 2002). That is, domestication implicitly claims properties that by definition it cannot have. It identifies itself as the *opposite* of wildness, rather than as a modified and in some ways damaged version of it. However the material ground of domestication is wildness – the ensemble of complex systems, beyond prediction and control, which constitute the biosphere.

As Anthony Wilden rigorously argues (Wilden, 1987a: Ch. 1; see also 1987b: Ch. 1), 'society' and 'nature' – equivalent to domestication and wildness – represent different levels in a logical hierarchy; and 'a relationship between levels ... in a hierarchy, whether or not it involves conflict, does not constitute an opposition' (Wilden, 1987a: 26). Hence, to treat wildness and domestication as equivalent and opposite forces is what Wilden calls an 'error of symmetrization' (ibid): 'symmetrical relations can exist only between items of the same level of reality, or of the same level of logical type' (1987a: 21–2). In terms Wilden also uses, wildness forms the 'environment' for domestication (Wilden, 1987a: 63; see also Wilden, 1972: 220–5) – it surrounds it in all directions. As we can see throughout this book, if we open domestication up, so to speak, we always find wildness within, underneath, around and behind it, like grass sprouting between the pavement cracks. But if we open wildness up, we find more wildness.

To avoid dualisms, to do without them, we need to ask ourselves what function they serve and why they so easily arise. There is a recursiveness built into dualism that can easily make critiques of dualism seem absurd: as soon as we suggest that splitting is a bad thing, we seem to have created a split between splitting and non-splitting! However, Wilden shows us that, like domestication and wildness, non-splitting and splitting are not symmetrical concepts: non-splitting – wholeness – is more fundamental than splitting, occupying a different level of logical hierarchy. Wholeness is the environment for splitting, the context in which splitting takes place.

The human mind spontaneously creates (or recognises) dualities, in indigenous cultures as much as in domesticated ones (Levi-Strauss, 1963, 1966); indeed, the bodymind itself is inherently polarised (or seems to us to be inherently polarised) between left and right. *Dualities*, however, are very different from *dualism*; the difference being that, like other 'isms', dualism places different values on the polarised pairs – starting with left and right themselves, which in many cultures are seen as respectively at least to some extent 'bad' and 'good'. This *difference of value*, as opposed to the *valuing of difference*, is the most objectionable property of the List – philosophically as well as politically.

There are also some specific propositions implicit in domestication which are philosophically unsound. For example, domestication asserts that life can be brought under control and made safe. An immediate way in which this is plainly impossible is that living creatures unpredictably and unavoidably die; but death is only the most evident form in which uncontrollability is inherent to life. As I have been arguing throughout, life is a property of certain complex systems, and complexity is beyond prediction and control.

As part of its campaign for control, domesticated thinking also tries to restrict what can be counted as knowledge. Local knowledge is generally dismissed as not really proper knowledge at all. Van der Ploeg counters this:

> *Art de la localité* has been characterized as a kind of knowledge that goes directly 'from practice to practice' ... It does not pass through a theoretical stage in which discourse is developed; there are, so the argument goes, 'no theoretical expressions'. ... This image ... is, in my opinion, fundamentally wrong.
>
> There is, of course, 'theory' in *art de la localité*, but this theory is organized in a way that markedly differs from scientific discourse. ... [T]he scope is not a presupposed universe but one specific to the localized labour process itself. Legitimation is not sought in the construction of laws, but in the coincidence with perspectives and interest, which again are perceived as part of the locality. ... Perceived through the matrix of scientific criteria *art de la localité* becomes indeed nearly invisible, ignorance of the people involved being one of the most common assessments.
>
> (Van der Ploeg, 1993: 210–11)

The primary form of knowledge validated by domesticated thinking is 'objective' and non-personal. As Banuri puts it, 'I see a particular assumption – "that impersonal relations are inherently superior to personal relations" – to be the distinguishing element of the modernizers' world view' (Banuri, 1990: 74). This rejection of subjectivity leads into a wider rejection of nature itself. The category mistakes I discussed above are problems of *epistemology* – that is, they relate to how we know things; but we now see that domestication also creates problems of *ontology* – that is, problems about what things are. Nicholas Gill and Kay Anderson summarise this as 'the ontological distinction of human/nonhuman that turns nature into an object for "improvement"' (Gill & Anderson, 2005: np; see also Glendinning, 2000). The feminist philosopher Kay Barad further argues that the very existence of ontology as a separate category – the separation of being from knowing – is symptomatic of domestication:

> The separation of epistemology from ontology is a reverberation of a metaphysics that assumes an inherent difference between human and nonhuman, subject and object, mind and body, matter and discourse. *Onto-epistem-ology* – the study of practices of knowing in being – is probably a better way to think about the kind of understandings that are needed to come to terms with how specific intra-actions matter.
>
> (Barad, 2003: 829)

These are complex and rarefied arguments; but they have enormous practical implications – for example, the way that the development of factory farming has been virtually unexamined from an ethical viewpoint by mainstream culture. Or take the suppression by the British colonial administration in India of variolation – the worldwide local knowledge practice of inoculation with fluid from someone suffering from smallpox – and the forced substitution of vaccination, using cowpox serum (Apffel-Marglin, 1990). Variolation was practised by Polish, Greek, French and Welsh peasants, but the Royal Society had to find out about it from China and Constantinople (Apffel-Marglin, 1990: 106, quoting Hopkins, 1983); it had considerably better results than vaccination, but no scientific status.

A third example is the reaction to the establishment of rabbits in Australia – a subset of the enormous theme of attempts to root out the 'foreign' in many parts of the world. It is certainly true that the arrival of non-native species can sometimes be a disastrous side effect of globalisation. But the disaster can also be much exaggerated, indeed assumed: 'many of the pastoralists [in Australia] blame the rabbit for damage for which they themselves are responsible, through their stock' (Ratcliffe, 1947: 218). Aborigines have a clear grasp of this, related to their rejection of abstract categories of native/non-native: Rose (1995) found that not only has the rabbit been adopted by aborigines as an important food source, but many see the rabbit as now 'belonging' to the country, similarly to what we call native animals. Most did not see the rabbit as causing damage to land, one respondent saying if the rabbit was to be eradicated on the grounds it was not native and caused land degradation, then cattle, with 'bigger mouths than rabbits' (Rose, 1995: 116) should also be removed. So much for the Rabbit-Proof Fence! Australian whites often also express fear and repulsion towards non-white human immigrants, which may be not unrelated; there is also a link in the UK, where 'balsam bashing', a common expression for rooting out one non-native species, *Impatiens glandulifera*, is eerily parallel to 'Paki bashing'.

What these three very different issues – along with many others mentioned in this chapter – have in common is a privileging of abstraction over concreteness, theory over practice, the impersonal over the subjective. They are based on an epistemology and ontology that are both essentially *instrumental* – what matters is what is useful to white Western humans – but which also undermine instrumentality by their rejection of practice in favour of theory, leading to a system of bad decisions.

DOMESTICATED PSYCHOTHERAPY

> The analyst roams.
> (Leo Rangell, 1979: 95)

Hopefully the general relevance of this wide-ranging discussion to psychotherapy and counselling will be apparent. The therapy field is already experiencing a ferocious struggle between the 'expert systems' approach and the 'local knowledge' approach: a struggle in which expertise always has the debating advantage, because it can speak simply and with one voice – simplification and univocality being two of its essential characteristics.

This struggle is not a new one for the field of therapy, which has always held a tension between local knowledge and expertise, between thickness and thinness, art and science, wildness and domestication. I looked at some historical aspects of this tension in Chapter 1; here I want to identify its role in the clinical practice of psychotherapy and counselling, and in particular, the ways in which domestication installs a self-censorship or 'therapy police' in practitioners – primarily through an insufficiently examined notion of *boundaries.*

Many supervisors have noticed that their supervisees inhibit their own responses, and in fact their own best judgement, in line with an internal modelling of what they believe is expected of them by their profession. This is natural, and in some ways appropriate for trainees or newly qualified practitioners who need to develop an 'internal supervisor', though even here it can be unhelpfully exaggerated; but for experienced therapists or counsellors it acts as a block to authentic relationship with their clients. Joseph Sandler, an elder of psychoanalysis, wrote in 1983 that 'the conviction of many analysts [is] that they do not do "proper" analysis ... that what is actually done in the analytic consulting room is not "kosher," that colleagues would criticize it if they knew about it' (Sandler, 1983: 38). He goes on to say:

> Any analyst worth his [*sic*] salt will adapt to specific patients on the basis of his interaction with those patients. He will modify his approach so that he can get as good as possible a working analytic situation developing. I believe that the many adjustments one makes in one's analytic work, including the so-called parameters that one introduces, often lead to or reflect a better fit of the analyst's developing intrinsic private preconscious theory with the material of the patient than the official public theories to which the analyst may consciously subscribe.
> (Sandler, 1983: 38)

There are aspects of the training and culture of psychotherapy and counselling, though, which militate against these adaptations and adjustments – or at any rate, make the practitioner guilty and secretive about them. Gifted and well-established – and courageous – practitioners may be able to speak openly about the ways in which they have stepped outside the conventional framework – as when Brian Thorne writes about working naked with a client (Thorne, 1987), or Peter Lomas about taking a session out of doors (Lomas, 1974/1994: 146), or Mario Jacoby about physical contact with a client (Jacoby, 1986) – but they are partially protected by the exceptionalism which attaches to celebrity: 'It's all right for *them*'. And even therapeutic celebrities have kept silent about some of their actions: Winnicott, for example, never revealed that he too touched some of his clients (Little, 1990). Indeed, one should mention that Brian Thorne's account was resurrected and held up to scandal over twenty years later as a way of discrediting his opposition to state regulation of psychotherapy and counselling (Newman, 2010).

Sanford Shapiro gives a good description of how the young practitioner's spontaneity can be systematically inhibited.

> My first lesson in being 'proper' was in 1959 during my first year of psychiatric residency at Detroit Receiving Hospital. ... I was pleased that my supervisor was psychoanalyst Frank Parcells, a wise, kindly man with an excellent reputation.
>
> I had detailed process notes for our first supervisory meeting, and I described how the patient came in to a session and said: 'Hello, how are you?' 'I'm fine,' I answered, 'And how are you?' Parcells interrupted me: 'Why did you say that?' he asked. 'Well,' I said, 'It seemed the natural thing to do.' Parcells gently explained that it would be natural in a social situation, but this was therapy, not a social situation. Thus I learned my first rule of proper technique. Each rule that I subsequently learned acted as a restraint and led to an increasing rigidity in my style of working.
>
> (Shapiro, 1995: 4)

Shapiro traces the rigidity of psychoanalysis back to Freud:

> Freud said: 'The doctor should be opaque to his patients and, like a mirror, should show them nothing but what is shown to him' (Freud, 1912, p. 118), and analysts should 'model themselves during psychoanalytic treatment on the surgeon who puts aside all his feelings, even his human sympathy ...' ... Although Freud trusted himself to be spontaneous, and could feed the Rat Man when he was hungry and organize financial support for the Wolf Man when he was destitute, he did not trust his students nor did he write down guidelines for being spontaneous or using intuition. So in the beginning, Freud determined what was proper analysis and what was not.
>
> (Shapiro, 1995: 5)

It comes across very clearly, however, from the book *Unorthodox Freud: The View from the Couch* (Lohser & Newton, 1996), which collects together accounts by Freud's patients of their analyses with him, that Freud worked in a way very different from that which he recommended to young students of analysis. As well as the examples of generosity given by Shapiro, Freud at times revealed himself to his patients. After little more than a week of daily sessions with the poet HD (Hilda Doolittle):

> I veer round, uncanonically seated stark upright with my feet on the floor. The Professor himself is uncanonical enough; he is beating with his hand, with his fist, on the headpiece of the old-fashioned horsehair sofa ... The Professor said, 'The trouble is – I am an old man – you do not think it worth your while to love me.'
>
> (HD, 1985: 15–16)

Later in the analysis, when HD revealed her maternal transference onto him, he responded, according to her report, '"But – to be perfectly frank with YOU – I do not like it – I feel so very, very, very MASCULINE." He says he always feels hurt when his analysands have a maternal transference. I asked if it happened often, he said sadly, "O, very often"' (quoted from a letter in Lohser & Newton, 1996: 49, with original capitals; the version in HD, 1985: 146–7 is considerably watered-down).

These events are filtered through HD's preoccupations and projections, but together with the other reports collected by Lohser and Newton they strongly suggest a much more spontaneous and relational way of working than Freud recommended to others. And this is very much the general situation in the therapy world: do what I say, not what I do. I have more than once had the experience, when speaking at a conference about my use of touch in therapy, of being told privately by some elderly and experienced figure: 'Well, I'm happy for *you* to work in this way, I can see you know what you're doing, and I might do some of it myself – but I would never publicly condone it.'

THERAPEUTIC BOUNDARIES

> Hunter-gatherer societies are marked by an emphasis on 'focus' in contrast to domesticated societies, which are distinguished by an emphasis on the boundary.
>
> (Wilson, 1988: 5)

Touch is a useful example, because it so clearly constellates anxieties about 'wild' and out-of-control feelings and behaviour. These anxieties – both within the therapy profession and in the wider society – have intensified over recent decades, and become condensed into the quintessentially domesticated concept of 'appropriate therapeutic boundaries'. Younger practitioners are so familiar with the notion of boundaries that it may come as quite a surprise to find out that they are a very recent introduction. A literature search shows that before the 1990s, therapists did not speak of 'boundaries' in this specific sense, meaning 'lines of behaviour which must not be crossed, by the therapist, by the client, or both'. Of course issues of acceptable behaviour were discussed long before then, but under a variety of different headings; and there is something very significant about the way in which all these themes were gathered together under a single rubric which seems to have been borrowed originally from the discourse of sexual abuse.

In saying this I am intending no criticism whatever of the theory of boundaries which has grown up around work with survivors of sexual abuse. It is enormously helpful and clarifying – *within that context*. But its appropriation as a way of thinking about issues like fees, telephone contact or session times has had the effect of installing a subliminal notion of what both its advocates (e.g. Simon, 1989) and its opponents (e.g. Zur, 2004) have called the 'slippery slope' theory: that any flexibility or inventiveness around the usual ways of doing therapy – a single toke on the spliff of adaptability, so to speak – leads to the hard stuff, to sexual abuse of clients. It has been claimed in all seriousness by proponents of the 'slippery slope' theory – writing not in the 1920s but in the 1990s – that the use of first names between practitioner and client is a predictor of sexual abuse further down the line (Epstein & Simon, 1990; Gutheil & Gabbard, 1993).

Freud is very often blamed for this state of affairs, because of the technical papers on psychoanalysis which he wrote to guide young practitioners (Freud, 1912, 1913, 1914, 1915b). Whatever one feels about his recommendations (and that is explicitly what they were), it is interesting to find that Freud very often explains them not as a protection for the *analysand*, but as for the benefit or convenience of the *practitioner*.

> The psycho-analyst who is asked to undertake the treatment of the wife or child of a friend must be prepared for it to cost him that friendship, no matter what the outcome of the treatment may be: nevertheless he must make the sacrifice if he cannot find a trustworthy substitute.
>
> (Freud, 1913: 125)

And a little later in the same paper:

> [H]e should also refrain from giving treatment free, and make no exceptions to this in favour of his colleagues or their families. This last recommendation will seem to offend against professional amenities. It must be remembered, however, that a gratuitous treatment means much more to a psycho-analyst than to any other medical man; it means the sacrifice of a considerable portion – an eighth or a seventh part, perhaps – of the working time available to him for earning his living, over a period of many months.
>
> (Ibid: 132)

Freud is mainly thinking practically, flexibly, locally; he might have been quite surprised to find Robert Langs arguing that these local arrangements match the unconscious needs of *every single patient.* Langs' follower David L. Smith lists a set of twenty-one 'fundamental ground rules' including such matters as a set time, a set fee, and no gifts being accepted, which he claims all psychotherapy clients 'unconsciously want their therapists to follow irrespective of their conscious preferences. They appear to be *universal* rules' (Smith, 1999: 139, original italics). In a note he continues, ludicrously but quite logically, 'this implies that patients' unconscious secured-frame criteria are the product of hominid evolution' (ibid: 140).

The idea that we have evolved as a species to require a set time and fee in therapy is not widely held; but it *is* now widely held that all clients at all times should be treated within the same set of boundaries. Over something like twenty years, the idea that boundaries are a key element in therapy has become more and more dominant, to the extent that for many practitioners it is now part of their conceptual wallpaper, an axiom which they have perhaps never questioned. The emphasis on boundaries has been read back into earlier therapeutic formulations, and is now understood as universally present. But is this really the case?

The humanistic therapies, and in a different sense behavioural therapy, developed partly in reaction to what was seen as the rigid structure of psychodynamic work. Humanistic therapy stresses the importance of offering warm, genuine contact; while behavioural therapists, at least originally, saw their work as avoiding all the apparatus of transference and projection and simply applying expert techniques, so that the relationship is one between equals, equivalent to that with one's accountant or architect: 'The resulting relationship is one in which I have felt quite comfortable having good friends as clients and good clients as friends' (Marquis, 1972: 48–49; see also Lazarus, 1994).

But the developing concept of appropriate boundaries, and in particular its codification in legal and quasi-legal structures, increasingly forces all therapists and counsellors into defensive practice – that is, working in ways which are based not on giving the client the therapeutic environment best suited to them, but on avoiding vulnerability to malpractice hearings. In a crucial contribution to the theory of therapeutic boundaries, Gutheil and Gabbard (1993) developed a distinction between 'boundary violations', which they saw as always harmful, and 'boundary crossings', which may be neutral or beneficial. However, they also argued that even boundary crossings which are justified and consistent with good care should be avoided, on the basis of their possible adverse appearance in court. This process of avoiding behaviours not because they are wrong, but only because they might *appear* wrong, is known as 'risk management'. It is clearly similar to the Wild Rose, Wisconsin approach described earlier in this chapter: 'If there's a possibility that something might be controversial then why not eliminate it.'

According to Gutheil and Gabbard, 'the risk-management value of avoiding even the appearance of boundary violations should be self-evident'. But there are other values central to therapy that may occasionally demand 'the *appearance* of boundary violations', or at least that we certainly do not '*avoid*' that appearance. Therapy is as much about questioning boundaries as it is about asserting them; as much about supporting clients to break out of the rules as it is about teaching them to observe the rules. For some clients at some times, it is crucial to know that the therapist will act within a defined frame. For others, or for the same clients at other times, it is equally crucial that the therapist dances outside the frame, and that a trust can be established which is based on authenticity rather than on predictability.

Therapy based on authenticity may reasonably be characterised as 'undefensive practice', as opposed to the 'defensive practice' which is becoming more and more the norm of contemporary therapy. Defensive practitioners, in the extreme, neither like nor trust their clients; they see them as a potential threat, a danger to be negotiated. On one level this threat is to the practitioner's standing and income, should a complaint be made; but more deeply, one feels that the real threat is to the practitioner's insecure self-image and self-esteem.

A more positive and realistic picture of the situation is put forward by Johnston and Farber (1996), who surveyed what practitioners think and do around 'everyday' boundaries in psychotherapy – starting and ending sessions on time, payment of fees, changing session times, and so on. They found that:

> Patients make relatively few demands and psychotherapists accommodate them most of the time. This finding stands in opposition to the generally accepted image of the psychotherapist standing firm in the face of persistent attempts by the patient to challenge existing boundaries and suggests a spirit of cooperation and good faith under-emphasized in theoretical writings.
> (Johnston & Farber, 1996: 397)

Jodie Messler Davies (2004) describes the extreme difficulty of working, while having a heavy cold, with a client she refers to as Karen who seems to use Davies' illness to confirm her negative picture of their relationship, and calls her 'such a bitch ... cold and unfeeling', leaving Davies 'stunned' (2004: 715). However, (after some great self-supervision on Davies' part) something transformative happens in the next session:

> On Friday afternoon I am still sick ... I brace myself for Karen's entrance. ... But I notice, almost immediately that something feels

> palpably different. The air feels warmer, her eyes look softer and more searching, my own body seems to relax even before I can formulate the experience. ... 'You really do look lousy,' she says, with an uncharacteristically warm and playful smile. 'I feel lousy,' say I. But I smile.
>
> ...
>
> Karen reaches down into her book bag and pulls out a large silver thermos and mug. As she opens the thermos and begins to pour, the warm smells of honey, vanilla and cinnamon fill my office. I am mesmerized as I watch Karen, intrigued with her swift and competent movements. 'This will be good for you,' she says. 'My grandmother used to make it for me when I was sick. It is a combination of hot tea and hot milk with a lot of other wonderful stuff.'
>
> (Davies, 2004: 725)

At this point, alerted by CCTV, the Therapy Police smash down the door and storm into the consulting room. All of the familiar objections to 'gratifying' the client flash through Davies' mind, and all of the ways in which an 'interpretation' could maintain the therapist's control of the situation. 'I try to will myself to think, despite the feverish "buzz" in my head. My patient is attempting to feed me warm milk! There must be an incredible interpretation in this somewhere!' (Davies, 2004: 725). For paragraphs of text, though probably only a few microseconds of real time, she wrestles with her internal judges, with her intellectual process. Then she takes the milk.

> She holds the mug out to me, an expression of intense pleasure and hopefulness suffusing her face. As I reach for the mug our fingers touch for an instant and I recall that my own grandmother brought a similar recipe with her from Russia; one she would prepare for us when someone in the family was sick with a cold.
>
> ...
>
> I take Karen's mug in my own hands, breathing in its healing, aromatic warmth. ... the intoxicating smells and moist heat penetrate and soothe. ... I take a long, deep, healing gulp of Karen's milk ... I smile at Karen through the steam, and she smiles back.
>
> (Davies, 2004: 725–7)

We can take this as an example of undefensive practice – informed and guided as of course it should be by a critical understanding of the many levels involved, but not *controlled* by that understanding; and, like hunter-gatherer societies, with an emphasis on focus, not on boundaries (Wilson, 1988: 5). The focus is a deeply *embodied* interaction (see Chapter 4, this volume). There is a lot about touch, taste, smell; Karen brings a 'palpably different' atmosphere when she arrives, the air feels warmer, her eyes softer, her smile warmer and evoking an answering smile from the therapist. The mug of milky tea, the 'wonderful stuff', is described in highly sensuous terms; as it is passed over, 'our fingers touch for an instant', and both client and therapist recall their grandmother. This is a multisensory, multidimensional, psychosomatic interaction, bringing with it an abundance of positive memories and associations for both people. It is a moment of healing.

Of course, it is only the beginning of a long process of coming to understand a very difficult relationship. But it seems clear that this undefensive embodied interaction, where so much is both communicated and expressed, through so many sensory channels, creates a bridge of intersubjectivity over which other communications can then pass. Embodied relationship, in fact, is 'wonderful stuff': the milk of human kindness! And sometimes we must take the risk that the milk *might* be poisoned, the client might be seeking to manipulate us in some way. The risk we take is the authentic expression of our wish for contact with the other.

7

Wild/Human

> We must begin to develop the idea that everything has equal rights because existence itself is equal. In other words, we are all here: trees, people, snakes, alike.
>
> (Alice Walker, 1983/2005)

> After she had lived a year in Sinshan she said to me one day, 'It's easy to live in Sinshan. It's easy to live here. In Sai it was hard; everything was hard; being was hard. Here it's soft.'
>
> I said, 'The work here is hard.' ...
>
> 'Not that kind of hard and soft,' she said. 'Animals live softly. They don't make it hard to live. Here people are animals. ... Here everybody belongs to everybody. A Dayao man [in Sai] belongs to himself. He thinks everyone else belongs to him, women, animals, things, the world.'
>
> I said, 'We call that living outside the world.'
>
> (Ursula Le Guin, 1988: 366–7)

To sum up points that I made in the previous chapters, a key boundary for domestication is that between humans and other animals – or between 'human' and 'animal', a description that itself enacts the boundary. This distinction is an important component of the wider, and equally artificial, distinction between male rational civilisation and female irrational wildness which is an ongoing theme of this book. As always, though, what is pushed away returns with added force; the wild or animal (or female) side of human beings is a constant shadow presence, becoming more and more frightening and intolerable the more it is suppressed: the vampire, the lamia, the werewolf, the beast, the savage, the serial killer.

There is no single solid criterion, however, for drawing this boundary between humans and others – apart from the circular criterion of being human. Each supposedly unique human trait which is proposed turns out not to be unique after all. Language? Tool use? Self-recognition? There is a queue of other species able to meet the entry requirements. There are already humans campaigning for equal rights to be given to apes, or to all mammals: they may sound crazy now, but after all, so did the early feminists and abolitionists.

As an example of these dissolving boundaries between 'Us' and 'the Others', self-awareness (as demonstrated by the ability to recognise oneself in a mirror) was once thought to be a purely human characteristic. Gradually we have had to admit that four other kinds of primate share this capacity; then dolphins and Asian elephants were added; but now the first non-mammal has been found capable of self-recognition – the magpie! (Primates: Taylor Parker et al, 2006; dolphins: Janik et al, 2006; elephants: Plotnik et al, 2006; magpies: Prior et al, 2008.)

As Bertrand Russell pointed out:

> One may say broadly that all the animals that have been carefully observed have behaved so as to confirm the philosophy in which the observer believed before his observations began.
> (Russell, 1995: 23)

Researchers find what they look for, in other words, and fashions change: the list of supposedly exclusive human traits and skills identified in various other-than-human species is suddenly growing by the day. Fungus-growing ants use antibiotic-producing bacteria to control garden parasites (Currie et al, 1999). Hierarchical syntax has been identified in the songs of humpback whales (Suzuki et al, 2006). New Caledonian crows solve physical problems through causal reasoning (Taylor et al, 2009). Chimpanzees use spears to hunt other animals (Pruetz & Bertolani, 2007). Elephants and rhesus monkeys can count (Irie-Sugimoto et al, 2009 for elephants; Brannon & Terrace, 2000 for monkeys). And, although this was denied by orthodoxy for decades, individuals from many species are homosexual (Bagemihl, 1999; Roughgarden, 2004: Ch 8); two male flamingos in Gloucestershire, partners for six years, 'adopted' an abandoned egg and successfully reared the chick, feeding it by producing milk in their throats – which flamingo parents of both sexes routinely do for the first few weeks (*Guardian*, 2007). Monkeys (Brosnan & de Waal, 2003; de Waal & Brosnan, 2006) and dogs (Range et al, 2009) expect to be treated fairly, monkeys, like most humans, being more tolerant of unfairness in those with whom they have close relationships; and animals in general exhibit a moral sense and a commitment to 'wild justice' (Bekoff, 2009; Bekoff & Pearce, 2010).

Other-than-humans also frequently form cross-species friendships, as can be seen in many excellent video clips on YouTube, though I recommend turning off the sound of human beings going 'Aaahh' (e.g. http://www.youtube.com/watch?v=iHj82otCi7U; http://www.

youtube.com/watch?v=ULlsVcW5bRI), and at the Interspecies Friends website (http://interspeciesfriends.blogspot.com/). They – mammals, certainly – also form lasting friendships with humans (e.g. http://www.youtube.com/watch?v=rkglYMYbyeo), and warm and tender friendships within their own species (e.g. http://www.youtube.com/watch?v=epUk3T2Kfno).

But the whole discussion of criteria for admission to the club – of how *similar to humans* various animals might or might not be – misses the radical point made by Alice Walker in her epigraph to this chapter: that all beings have equal rights not because we are all 'the same', but because *we are all here.* The differences between humans and other animals are not marks of the others' inferiority, but only of diversity. Indeed, Deena Metzger suggests: 'Perhaps it is not that we need to see that humans are also animals. Perhaps we also need to see that some animals, at least, are more than human' (Metzger, 2009: 4). Our assumption of qualitative difference and qualitative superiority prevents us from actually encountering the other-than-human. Metzger again:

> For a long time, I have been contemplating what the etiquette might be between human and animal if we ever enter into reciprocal relationships with each other. It will require, in the deepest sense, a change of mind. ... Coming into some recognition of the true face of the others we call animals, what will be the polite and respectful conventions, the procedures, ceremonies, formalities, unwritten codes of honor by which we will approach these beings?
> (Metzger, 2009: 4)

Some of the ways in which we have so far 'approached' other-than-human beings on this planet will, if we survive environmental disaster, come to be perceived as shocking in the way that the slave trade is now perceived. The violence and objectification to which humans have subjected other species is dreadful not only in its effects on the others, but in its effects on ourselves. Rejecting and abusing other-than-human animals, we are also rejecting and abusing the animal in ourselves.

HUMAN ANIMALS

> Not until man [*sic*] acknowledges that he is fundamentally an animal, will he be able to create a genuine culture.
> (Wilhelm Reich, 1946/1975: 376)

When we talk of humans 'behaving like animals', the animal we mean is generally the human one. We frequently project onto animals our most characteristically human negative traits. Equally (and rather contradictorily), we talk about people being 'treated like animals' when they are being abused and degraded. The following passage from a review of a book about the Palestinian–Israeli conflict illustrates some of these themes and the confusions that arise around them:

> Avnery clearly believes that he has performed his patriotic duty in combat. Yet an incident during an assault on the Arab village of Nebi Musa early in the war troubles him:
>
> > I am running with the squad, my rifle in my hand. I feel that I have to shoot. A movement in front of me. A little Arab dog running away. I raise my rifle and shoot. The dog howls.
> >
> > The howling wakes me up. What have I done? Have I become an animal? Shlomo, running behind me, raises his rifle and shoots. The howling stops.
> >
> > That incident makes me feel sick. I want to get away.
>
> Ari Folman's recent animated film *Waltz with Bashir* was an attempt by another Israeli combat veteran to make sense of his experience. Folman took part in the 1982 invasion of Lebanon, which culminated in the massacre by Israel's Christian Phalangist allies of Palestinian refugees in the Beirut camps of Sabra and Shatila. Twenty years after the invasion, Boaz Rein Buskila, who fought with Folman, told him about his nightmare in which 26 wild dogs were racing through the streets baying for his blood. It was only after he had had the nightmare many times that he remembered a night-time assault on a Lebanese village during which he shot 26 dogs to prevent them giving away his unit's position. The story helped Folman recover his own memory of that summer-long invasion in which at least 20,000 Palestinians and Lebanese were killed. For Buskila, as for Avnery, the shooting of a dog forced him to reckon with what was really going on: the shooting of people, not all of whom could shoot back.
>
> (Glass, 2009: 16)

Here the association is rightly made between the abuse of animals and the abuse of humans – and we see the typical way, which I will discuss in Chapter 8, in which animals can announce in our dreams difficult themes which have been forgotten by the conscious self. But the human supremacist assumption still comes through, that what *really* matters is not the killing of the dogs (also unable to shoot back), but the killing of the people – and also, that violence is an 'animal' quality not a human one ('Have I become an animal?'). In Buskila's dream, and in Avnery's metaphor, the animal victims become the aggressors – an idea which is frequently used to justify their extermination.

Wilhelm Reich, who is quoted at the head of this section, wrote at length about how humans project our own traits onto animals:

> 'Away from the animals; away from sexuality!' are the guiding principles of the formation of all human ideology. ... The animal has no intelligence, but only 'wicked instincts'; no culture, but only 'base drives'; no sense of values, but only 'material needs'. It is precisely the human type who sees the whole of life in the making of money who likes to stress these 'differences'. ... Man [*sic*] would have good reason to be happy if he were as free from sadism, perversions and meanness, and as filled with a natural spontaneity, as any one of the animals, whether an ant or an elephant.
>
> (Reich, 1946/1975: 370–1)

TWO MEETINGS WITH THE OTHER-THAN-HUMAN

> The animal scrutinises [humans] across a narrow abyss of non-comprehension ... The man too is looking across a similar, but not identical, abyss of non-comprehension. And this is so wherever he looks. He is always looking across ignorance and fear.
>
> (Berger, 1980: 24)

> we direct them
> and manage them and herd them and train them and follow
> them and map them and collect them and make specimens
> of them and butcher them and move them here and move
> them there and we place them on lists and we take
> them off lists and we stare at them and stare
> at them and stare at them
>
> (Rogers, 1998: xx)

Below are two summary descriptions, out of many others, of situations in which it seems that animals, the despised, abused and feared and projected-onto victims and possessions of humanity, have actually become the teachers, the elders, in animal–human relationships. The first story also focuses on an other-than-human *individual*, rather than a group or species – an important corrective to what Owain Jones rightly identifies as 'the ethical invisibility of the individual non-human other' (Jones, 2000: 279).

Billy Jo the chimp

Jane Goodall is famous for her tireless work with chimpanzees. In public talks she has described one of her regular visits to see chimps being used in medical research (Rust, 2009a: 11). There she met Billy, or Billy Jo, a chimp living in a cage measuring 5′x 5′, with no light, and simply a car tyre. Billy Jo had lived in this cage for ten years, having spent his early years in a circus (where his teeth were bashed out with an iron bar, to make him less aggressive). When she met his gaze she saw how happy he was that someone had relieved the grinding monotony of the day, for the only time he had any stimulation was when he was taken out to have liver biopsies or other tests. Tears welled up in her eyes and started to trickle down her face at the sight of this animal so deprived of his freedom and dignity.

Billy Jo then reached out through the bars and caught the tear on her cheek, while he carried on grooming her wrist.

While this story is shocking and upsetting on many levels, what often disturbs people the most is Billy Jo's capacity to relate, and to *feel with* a human being, despite all those years of maltreatment.

Eventually Billy Jo was rescued from his captivity and spent the last years of his life living with other rescued and damaged chimps at the Fauna Foundation in Canada, where he became a destination for something approaching pilgrimage. Gloria Grow, the director of the Foundation, describes Billy Jo as follows:

> You meet people in your life that are so magnetic that you never forget them. Billy was that kind of chimpanzee. He had a way of making people fall in love with him. ... Maybe it's because he was this amazing contradiction – a majestic, incredibly powerful male who could instantly become intuitive, compassionate, and kind and interact with some humans and chimpanzees in the gentlest ways. ... I get so mad when I think about this incredible, majestic force of nature confined to that windowless cage. There, they trashed his body. He was repeatedly 'challenged' with various strains of HIV and hepatitis. He was meant to die. They used him and used him, pushed and pushed until he lost his identity. How could he treat people with any respect? He would shake in his 5′x 5′x 7′cage trying desperately to prevent anyone from approaching. ... After being betrayed by humans in both the entertainment world and in the research laboratory, he was somehow able to let himself love again ... let himself give again to humans. He was somehow able to use his power to surpass all that had been done to him. He became someone we relied on. With new people, he would have his guard up, but he always

> seemed to have a second sense about people he could trust. He had this ability to sense people's pain.
>
> (Project R&R, 2006; see also the interesting account in Bradshaw et al, 2009)

Deborah Straw also wrote about Billy Jo when he was still alive, describing how while held in the research lab he 'was sedated more than 289 times, 65 times by four or five men surrounding his cage, throwing tranquilizer darts into his body ... Today, Billy Jo ... still cannot bear to have strangers grouped in front of him. When he first arrived at Fauna, he used to bang on his cage, scream, rock and stare into space when left alone. Even today, he sometimes chokes, gags and convulses as a result of his traumas' (Straw, 2000: np). She focuses in particular on Billy Jo's ability to forgive. On first arriving at the Fauna Foundation, he was attacked by other chimps who almost entirely bit off one of his fingers, which had to be amputated. The only available people with the appropriate skills were from the lab where Billy Jo had been held, and Billy Jo recognised them.

> Explains Grow, 'He was screaming, frightened ... They went up to Billy. ... He was so scared of the dart gun.' ... The techs [from the lab] told Pat [at Fauna] that he would have to stick Billy with the dart gun as the chimpanzee had begun to trust Pat enough to allow him to do so. However, Pat felt this would be a betrayal, a reinforcement of what humans had done repeatedly to the chimpanzee. Gloria went over to Billy, and held one of his hands. Pat held the other. They talked soothingly to him. In the end, Pat did give him the needle. 'We were telling him we loved him,' recalls Grow. 'He could see empathy and compassion. We do not lie to them. Then he started to drop asleep ...'

Straw adds:

> According to Grow, that day, Billy Jo made 'such a leap of faith. ... He wasn't angry with Pat. He had forgiven us. They learn to forgive because they have faith in someone, faith that they will not be betrayed. This is part of their healing process,' explains Grow. Despite his close to 30 years in service to humans, in service surely not chosen by him, Billy Jo still likes us. He is willing to give us the benefit of the doubt. He is willing to open his heart.
>
> (Straw, 2000: np)

She continues:

> Billy Jo is but one example of chimpanzee forgiveness. As Sheila Siddle, co-director of Chimfunshi Wildlife Orphanage, a non-profit refuge in Zambia which cares for more than 70 orphaned chimpanzees, writes, 'Chimpanzees have suffered so much pain and trauma at the hands of humans ... yet they still have the grace to forgive us.'
>
> (Straw, 2000: np)

The idea that chimps or other species forgive us (mentioned not only by Straw but by several other writers, e.g. Bekoff, 2009; Bradshaw et al, 2009) is perhaps not so much a precise description of what is going on for them, as an expression of our need to be forgiven.

Deena Metzger and the elephants

The feminist writer Deena Metzger begins her account of an extraordinary encounter with elephants like this:

> I never expected to enter into an alliance with elephants and it has only been a few years since I have begun to imagine what an alliance with an animal might mean. One cannot enter into such a relationship unless one's entire world of assumptions and beliefs has changed radically.
>
> (Metzger, 2009: 1)

She goes on to describe a trip in 1998 with her husband Michael Ortiz Hill to Zimbabwe, where they met with Augustine Kandemwa, the Zimbabwean *nganga* with whom Hill works (Hill & Kandemwa, 2007). As the result of a series of dreams and synchronicities, she arrived in Zimbabwe with the intention – the meaning of which was unclear even to herself – to 'sit in Council with the elephants'.

Before visiting Chobe National Park with Hill, Kandemwa and two friends, Metzger prepares herself:

> What I do know is what I don't know: what my dreams have meant; why the elephants have become so important to me; what it can possibly mean to sit in Council with the elephants or with other animals; why I imagine that I who have lived a fairly urban life and who have never fully lived among the animals, might come into such a relationship with them.
>
> ... There is a great longing in me for the restoration of the natural world. ... I have a passion for a world truly based upon a council of all beings.
>
> (Metzger, 2009: 2)

In the park they see a large bull elephant, and stop some distance away.

> I begin chanting aloud ... I know the elephant can hear it. Slowly the elephant lifts his head from the grasses and begins walking along the river. He does not stop to graze nor does he look around but walks with clear determination and intention. ... The elephant has raised his trunk and is curving it over itself and under itself and up and over again. That is, he ties his trunk into an impossible knot. I have never even seen photographs of such a movement, of such a mudra. ...
>
> Then the elephant bows his head. There is no other way of describing it. He bows his head and unfurls his trunk.
>
> In my mind, I am speaking to him. ... Then, I silence my mind. I have said enough. Humans have said enough. I want to be empty and to listen. The elephant moves toward me with the same grace and determination as he moved down the river. ... He can, if he wishes, wrap his trunk about me without moving closer. Later Augustine will tell me that his hand moved twice to start the car but each time he stopped. He decided even if it came to it to allow me my chosen death.
>
> (Metzger, 2009: 2)

The elephant comes to Metzger and makes eye contact, which continues for many minutes, then leaves.

> When I have words, I ask what must be asked. Did you see this? Did this happen? So on and so forth. Recounting the moments, verifying them, remaining astonished.
>
> Then we quiet down. We do not explain or understand anything except that Amanda says: 'You are an ambassador and they sent their ambassador and you have made a covenant with each other.'
>
> (Metzger, 2009: 2)

As they begin to leave the park, something even more extraordinary happens:

> Elephants are coming down the hill and crossing the road to the river. At first only a few females and their babies, but now more of them are coming. Waves of elephants. Waves upon waves. Augustine stops the car and we jump out and kneel again. I can hear Amanda sobbing behind me. ... There are dozens of them lined up alongside the river and still more are coming. Bulls and cows, old ones and young ones, babies and adolescents. It is like

> ... I do not know ... I think ... it is like the world ended and then it was saved and the animals are coming forth into the new dawn.
>
> ... Augustine drives very slowly and very carefully along the river. The elephants are lined up for at least a quarter of a mile, as if for a parade. Now it is Amanda and Michele and myself in the back of the truck. We are passing by them. They are bowing their heads and flapping their ears at us. And we are bowing and waving and saying, 'Thank you. And bless you. And thank you. And bless you.'
>
> (Metzger, 2009: 2)

Metzger adds:

> I do not think I called the elephants to me. I think they are coming to us, calling us. I think they are consciously transmitting cries of anguish and grief, and some of us are hearing them and are responding.
>
> (Metzger, 2009: 4)

Originally I presented these two stories – which I find profoundly moving – without comment, feeling that they spoke for themselves. Several readers expressed confusion and dissatisfaction, asking me to provide some sort of context or explanation. I'm still not sure that I understand why; but I wonder whether it is hard for us to let the other-than-human express *itself*, even (and necessarily) through the words of humans. Alerted by this reaction from readers, I looked again at the stories and noticed how much of what could be seen as projection, how much reading-in of human responses, they contain: 'forgiveness', 'alliance', 'sitting in council', 'willing to open his heart'. I think we have to recognise that, like transference and countertransference in the therapy room, this is unavoidable and in fact represents our best attempt to bridge what Berger (1980: 24) calls the 'abyss of non-comprehension' between humans and other species, replacing Berger's 'ignorance and fear' with love and the need to make amends.

WILD HUMANS IN THE MIDDLE AGES

One way in which European culture has tried to deal with the impossible boundary between human and animal, wild and domesticated, is through the medieval figure of the Wild Man:

> A hairy man curiously compounded of human and animal traits, without, however, sinking [*sic*] to the level of the ape. It exhibits

> upon its naked human anatomy a growth of fur, leaving bare only its face, feet, and hands, at times its knees and elbows, or the breasts of the female of the species. Frequently the creature is shown wielding a heavy club or mace, or the trunk of a tree.
> (Bernheimer, 1952: 1)

The Wild Man was not literally part ape, or any other species (though it had strong connections with that anciently sacred creature, the bear: Bernheimer, 1952: 53–5), but precisely what the name implies: a wild version of the human.

The Wild Man in this passage is 'curiously compounded' not only in terms of species but also of gender: 'a hairy man ... it ... its ... the female of the species'. Although these creatures are always referred to as Wild *Men*, there are many depictions of both male and female versions, and of family scenes with wild men, women and children; there are also specifically female versions of the animal–human hybrid such as Melusine (Yamamoto, 2000: 212–24). I shall refer to them therefore as Wild Humans, which brings out even more clearly their essentially paradoxical and transgressive nature from the point of view of medieval civilisation.

> The wild man was the abstract concept of 'noncivilisation' rendered as a fearful physical reality ... Sublimated in the wild man were the preeminent phobias of medieval society – chaos, insanity, and ungodliness.
> (Husband, 1980: 5)

Husband emphasises only one side of the complex valuation given to Wild Humans. They were also known as 'orcs' – the same word which Tolkien appropriated in *Lord of the Rings* for his evil and degenerate blend of human and animal, something which from his patriarchal viewpoint is necessarily an abomination; in the film version, Orcs are shown being 'born' from muddy earth. But the word is also cognate with Orcus, the ancient Italian god of death and the underworld (Bernheimer, 1952: 42ff). This has been linked with 'the dual role of the wild man as a harbinger of fertility and as an embodiment of the returning dead' (ibid: 56). The Wild Man was sometimes identified as leader or member of the Wild Hunt or Wild Horde (ibid: 28, 50, 54ff) – the same group with which, as we saw in Chapter 1, Freud identified himself and other psychoanalysts!

From one point of view, as Dorothy Yamamoto points out (2000: 170–6), the Wild Human forms a complementary polarity with the figure of the chivalric knight – the smooth, armoured, polite body of the knight and the hairy, erupting, energetic, uncontained body of the wild man. This complementary opposition is strongly expressed in the medieval poem *Sir Gawain and the Green Knight*. At the same time, however, the Wild Human holds within a single image the opposition of domesticated (human) and wild (animal). In the later medieval/early modern period an idealisation of wildness develops, with depictions of Wild Humans lounging courteously in bowers.

> Wild men now turned into conspicuously gentler creatures. ... The stereotypes of wild men munching on infants or doing unpleasant things with animals were replaced by paragons of family life: a hairy hand-holding between demure couples, or snub-nosed little wild things having their heads patted by their proud parents.
>
> (Schama, 1995: 96)

Further, Le Goff argues that for medieval culture, 'the "wild" is not what is beyond the reach of man, but what is on the fringes of human activity' (Le Goff, 1988). Wild Humans can be viewed not as oppositional but as liminal figures, inhabitants of the forest which, as well as being in one sense the wild polarity of the world, was also much used by hunters, charcoal burners, swineherds (Yamamoto, 2000: 150) – and, of course, outlaws.

One of the most fascinating versions of the medieval Wild Human, though, portrays them not as an alien creature but as ordinary humans who have *become* wild through experiencing intolerable aspects of civilisation – specifically, the horrors of war. There are many versions of this story, in which someone crazed by the violence of battle becomes mad, throws off their clothes, and runs wild in the forest, where they often grow hair or feathers over their body. Two of the most famous of these figures are Merlin and Mad Sweeney (*Suibhne Geilt*); a female and lesser known equivalent is Mis, whom I discuss below.

Merlin, or Myrddin, or Lailoken, is not only a figure in the Arthurian cycle, but appears in a number of other medieval contexts, notably as a *Fer Caille* or Man of the Woods. Driven mad by the Battle of Arfderydd in 573, Merlin is said to have seen a fearful vision in the sky over the battlefield accusing him of responsibility for the slaughter, whereupon he lost his mind and fled into the woods. Although his life in the forest is hard, Merlin is befriended by his 'dear companion', a wolf, and hidden from human searchers by a wild apple tree (Dames, 2002: 39–48).

There is a subtext in these stories about the supplanting of paganism by Christianity. The Battle of Arfderydd which drove Merlin wild saw the defeat of a pagan Celtic king by a Christian one. And the Irish King Sweeney is driven wild at least in part by the curse of a

Christian cleric at whom he has shot an arrow, smashing the bell on his chest. The curse tells him 'That bell which thou hast wounded / will send thee among branches, / so that thou shalt be one with the birds' (O'Keeffe, 1904: 13). When Sweeney hears the uproar of the clashing armies:

> turbulence, ... and darkness, and fury, and giddiness, and frenzy, and flight, unsteadiness, restlessness, and unquiet filled him, likewise disgust with every place in which he uséd to be and desire for every place which he had not reached. His fingers were palsied, his feet trembled, his heart beat quick, his senses were overcome, his sight was distorted, his weapons fell naked from his hands, so that through Ronan's curse he went, like any bird of the air, in madness and imbecility.
> (O'Keeffe, 1904: 15)

Sweeney (who later became a character in works by Flann O'Brien, 1939/1967, and T.S. Eliot, 1932, among others) grows feathers on his body and becomes so light that he can run through the treetops.

The adjective which Sweeney and Merlin share, *'Gelt'* or *'Geilt'* in Irish Gaelic and *'Gwyllt'* in Welsh, is ambiguous: on the one hand it means mad from terror, on the other hand it means 'wild', with implications of inspiration (Goodrich, 2003: 113). In their revulsion from battle and from Christianity, and through their suffering in the outdoors, these Wild Humans are transforming their consciousness. In some ways they are a blend of the Green Man and the Fool, who often share with them feathers and a lighter-than-air quality. Although Merlin complains of cold and hunger, he also celebrates the more-than-human world and the mystery of change: 'Are not the buds of thorn very green, the mountain beautiful, and beautiful the earth?' 'How wonderful it is that the world is never long in the same condition' (Dames, 2002: 47); just as Sweeney praises birdsong, the different trees, and the red deer, 'antlered one, belling one, you of the musical cry' (Dames, 2002: 45). In one version of Merlin's story, finally his sister Gwendydd builds him an observatory in the forest where he spends his time 'watch[ing] fire-breathing Phoebus, and Venus and the stars gliding from the heavens by night, all of whom shall show me what is going to happen to the people of the kingdom' (Parry, 1920/2008: 16–17).

A parallel narrative is the story of Mis (Ó Cuiv, 1952–1954), who goes mad after her father Dáire Dóidgheal dies in battle; she drinks his blood, and runs away into the wilderness. She grows long hair and nails and a coat of fur or feathers, and gains the ability to run like the wind and levitate, all in parallel with Mad Sweeney; unlike that timorous figure, though, Mis becomes a terrifying menace, killing animals and humans and turning the area where she lives into a wasteland. Dubh Ruis, harper to the King of Munster, decides to tame her. He attracts her with his music, and reawakens memories of her father and past life. They make love, and gradually Dubh Ruis reintroduces her to domesticated ways of eating, sleeping, and bathing, scrubbing and scraping her body vigorously until in two months her reason is restored, her coat of fur or feathers falls away, and she goes home with Dubh Ruis and marries him. When Dubh Ruis is later killed, Mis responds in a measured and civilised fashion by composing a song over his body.

Although the extant text of the story dates only from the late 18th century, and clearly shows many modern features, Cameron (1997) argues that it also illustrates many aspects of shamanic initiatory illness; he demonstrates a number of precise correspondences between the events of the Mis narrative and the initiatory journey of a Kwakiutl shaman from the American North West Coast – which underlines the point that the medieval Wild Human, like the shaman, is a liminal figure who joins together the wild and the domesticated. In the story of Mis as it is preserved for us, the shaman's return to the human world has been overlaid with patriarchal themes of the domestication of the woman through sex and marriage.

WILD WOMEN

> Bone by bone, hair by hair, Wild Woman comes back.
> (Pinkola Estes, 1992: 26)

It may be that Mis's destructiveness and Sweeney's gentleness represent parallel reversals of the social norm, where men were conventionally aggressive and women passive. Certainly, besides Wild Humans of whatever gender, there is a distinct category of Wild Women whose femaleness is an important aspect of their identity. As I have discussed in Chapter 1 and Chapter 2, the dualistic List at the basis of Western culture identifies women with wildness, nature and the body – as an inferior polarity compared with men, domestication, civilisation and the mind.

When stereotyped in this way, one recourse is to adopt the label one has been given as a badge of identity, to reverse its valuation and find positive meaning in it. This is what has been done by homosexuals with words like 'queer' and 'dyke', and by feminists with words like 'virago' and 'shrew'. Similarly, as we have already seen in Chapter 3, women can identify with the label of 'wild' which is assigned to them pejoratively by patriarchy, and align themselves positively with the earth and the other-than-human. Because their 'wildness' is feared, women have been domesticated, restricted to the *domus*, the home; to identify as wild is to reject this restriction.

This is the strategy, for example, of Susan Griffin's great classic, *Woman and Nature: The Roaring Inside Her*:

> He says that woman speaks with nature. That she hears voices from under the earth. That wind blows in her ears and trees whisper to her. ... But for him this dialogue is over. He says he is not part of this world, that he was set on this world as a stranger. He sets himself apart from woman and nature.
>
> ...
>
> *We are the bird's eggs. Bird's eggs, flowers, butterflies, rabbits, cows, sheep; we are caterpillars, we are leaves of ivy and sprigs of wallflower. We are women. We rise from the wave. We are gazelle and doe, elephant and whale, lilies and roses and peach, we are air, we are flame, we are oyster and pearl, we are girls. We are woman and nature. And he says he cannot hear us speak.*
>
> (Griffin, 1984: 1, original italics)

It is also the strategy of Clarissa Pinkola Estes in her well-known book *Women Who Run with the Wolves: Contacting the Power of the Wild Woman*, where she celebrates:

> An old, old memory ... of our absolute, undeniable and irrevocable kinship with the wild feminine, a relationship which may have become ghosty [*sic*] from neglect, buried by overdomestication, outlawed by the surrounding culture, no longer understood anymore. We may have forgotten her names, we may not answer when she calls ours, but in our bones we know her, we yearn toward her; we know she belongs to us and we to her.
>
> (Pinkola Estes, 1992: 7)

The risk, though, with such subversive reframings of 'women = wild', is that they offer legitimation to much more dubious conceptualisations of Wild Men, such as those offered by Robert Bly in *Iron John* (1992), where personal/cultural preferences about how men should be are portrayed as gendered absolutes. It is an easy slide from there to the territory of *Men Are from Mars, Women Are from Venus* (Gray, 1993), in which – paralleling evolutionary psychology – elements of contemporary mainstream gender behaviour are enthroned as universal truths. Gender essentialism is a core element of the List that underpins domestication.

WILD HUMANS AROUND THE WORLD

> The Yeti inhabits that nebulous area of zoology where the Beast of Linnaean classification meets the Beast of the Imagination.
>
> (Chatwin, 1990: 271)

Medieval Wild Humans, alongside their powerful mythic and symbolic roles, were also widely regarded as literally real, physically existing creatures. Similar large hairy wild beings of both sexes are reported all over the world, from the Yetis of the Himalayas and the Sasquatch or Bigfoot of North America to many other lesser known creatures inhabiting for example Russia, China, Vietnam, Czechoslovakia, Scotland, Malaysia, Spain, Panama and New Zealand (for these and many more see http://www.bigfootencounters.com/creatures.htm).

Such beings are often referred to by the Western media as the 'Missing Link', which seems to me an extraordinarily appropriate title: although it originates in an outdated archaeological theory about the supposed 'missing link' between proto-human apes and homo sapiens, it also exactly captures one of the primary symbolic functions of the Wild Human, remaking the broken link between humans and the rest of the ecosystem. Richard Dawkins suggests that our ability to split human from animal rests precariously on the accidental non-existence of breeding intermediaries between us and the chimps, giving the impression of a natural boundary:

> We need only discover a single survivor, say a relic *Australopithecus* in the Budongo Forest, and our precious system of norms and ethics would come crashing about our ears. The boundaries with which we segregate our world would be shot to pieces.
>
> (Dawkins, 1993: 85)

But even in the absence of such a survivor, the archetype of a being simultaneously human and other-than-human survives and holds power. As Peter Steeves writes, Bigfoot 'represents a crisis in our categorisation of the world' (Steeves, 2002: 256). And just as Wild Humans hold ambiguity between human and other-than-human, they also hold ambiguity between material and psychic reality.

It is fascinating to trace the shifting boundaries and connections between human and animal, physical and symbolic, in different accounts of Wild Humans. In Native North American cultures, the emphasis varies as regards the physicality or otherwise of what is often called the 'Big Man' (again, there are female Bigfoots, but patriarchal cultures identify maleness as the norm). According to Gayle Highpine:

> Special being as he is, I have never heard anyone from a Northwestern tribe suggest that Bigfoot is anything other than a physical being, living in the same physical dimensions as humans and other animals. He eats, he sleeps, he poops, he cares for his family members. However, among many Indians elsewhere in North America ... Bigfoot is seen more as a sort of supernatural or spirit being, whose appearance to humans is always meant to convey some kind of message.
>
> (Highpine, 1992: np)

In his book *In the Spirit of Crazy Horse,* Peter Matthiessen records some statements about Bigfoot from Sioux informants. Joe Flying By, a Hunkpapa Lakota, said:

> I think the Big Man is a kind of husband of Unk-ksa, the earth, who is wise in the way of anything with its own natural wisdom. Sometimes we say that this One is a kind of reptile from the ancient times who can take a big hairy form; I also think he can change into a coyote. Some of the people who saw him did not respect what they were seeing, and they are already gone.
>
> (Matthiessen, 1991: xxix–xxx)

Oglala Lakota Medicine Man Pete Catches spoke of him as follows:

> There is your Big Man standing there, ever waiting, ever present, like the coming of a new day. He is both spirit and real being, but he can also glide through the forest, like a moose with big antlers, as though the trees weren't there ... I know him as my brother ... I want him to touch me, just a touch, a blessing, something I could bring home to my sons and grandchildren, that I was there, that I approached him, and he touched me.
>
> (Matthiessen, 1991: xxxviii)

Highpine offers statements from other Native Americans which develop the idea of Bigfoot as a spiritual figure:

> Ray Owen, son of a Dakota spiritual leader from Prairie Island Reservation in Minnesota, told a reporter ... 'They exist in another dimension from us, but can appear in this dimension whenever they have a reason to. ...'
>
> Ralph Gray Wolf, a visiting Athapaskan Indian from Alaska, told the reporter, 'In our way of beliefs, they make appearances at troubled times', to help troubled Indian communities 'get more in

> tune with Mother Earth'. Bigfoot brings 'signs or messages that there is a need to change, a need to cleanse.'
>
> (Highpine, 1992: np)

This idea that Bigfoot appears as a sign that something needs to be rebalanced (see also Matthiessen, 1991: xxiii) is shared by many tribes in different parts of North America, including the Hopi, the Ojibway, and the Iroquois (who also, like so many other cultures, speak of 'little people' alongside the 'big people'). As we saw in Chapter 4, rebalancing is a core function of wild mind.

The Wild Human as a meaningful archetype or a spiritual reality makes a great deal of sense. Yet there is also sufficient evidence for their physical existence to lead the distinguished physical anthropologist George W. Gill to the conclusion that:

> The following alternate hypotheses must be listed as the two possible explanations for our results:
>
> that the most complex and sophisticated hoax in the history of anthropology has continued for centuries without being exposed;
>
> that the most manlike (and largest) nonhuman primate on earth ... remains undiscovered by modern science.
>
> Either conclusion appears totally preposterous ... yet one ... must be true.
>
> (Quoted in Halpin & Ames, 1980: 289)

But Gill, naturally enough, does not even consider a further alternative: that something which is psychically real and meaningful may at times take on all the elements of material reality. This is the conclusion which those who study anomalies, for example UFOs, often come to: the distinction between 'real' and 'symbolic' is as unsound as that between 'human' and 'animal'. Kaledon Naddair explores this viewpoint in his excellent discussion of Celtic Wild Humans – the Gruagach, the Fynoderee and others (Naddair, 1987: 136–68).

In his wonderful tall story *Boomer Flats,* R.A. Lafferty describes a version of the 'missing link' who turn out to be always already living among us – we just don't notice them much.

> 'There used to be a bunch of them on the edge of my hometown,' Willy McGilly said. 'Come to think of it, there used to be a bunch of them on the edge of every hometown. Now they're more likely to be found in the middle of every hometown.'
>
> (Lafferty, 1974/1994: 54)

Later we find out more about these wild humans:

> 'They're born without much shape. Most of them never do get much shape. When they have any, well actually their mothers lick them into shape, give them their appearance.'
>
> 'It's an old folktale that bears do that.'
>
> 'Maybe they learned it from the bears, then, young fellow.'
>
> (Lafferty, 1974/1994: 55)

The informant turns out to be one of 'the creatures' himself – as does one of the investigators.

WHAT IS IT WE NEED FROM ANIMALS?

> In a Tewa Pueblo narrative from the Southwest, people and animals lived together beneath a lake in darkness. The first Mothers – powerful women – sent one man to find the way to the surface world, the one we now inhabit. When he reached this world he saw the wolves, mountain lions, and coyotes. On seeing him, they ran to him and wounded him, then they told him, 'We are your friends,' and healed him, showing him the special abilities they possessed, their abilities to harm and their equal abilities to heal. When the Tewa man returned to the Mothers, he said to them, 'We have been accepted.'
>
> (Hogan, 1998: 8–9)

Earlier in this chapter, I mentioned inter-species friendships, and gave details of some internet examples. There are in fact hundreds of such video clips on the internet: there is something that profoundly fascinates many people about other-than-human creatures' ability to extend friendship. It seems to me that this fascination is based in a deep desire to return to the Peaceable Kingdom, where 'the lion lay down with the lamb', and where humans and animals were not master and slave, not persecutor and victim, but friends – even kin.

'We have been accepted', the Tewa man tells his people, after the predator animals have harmed him and then healed him; and several people who work with other-than-humans speak of their miraculous ability to forgive us. And according to a North Cheyenne leader of ceremonies:

> After years recovering from removals and genocide, indigenous peoples are learning their lost songs back from the wolves who retained them during the grief-filled times, as if the wolves, even though threatened in their own numbers, have had compassion for the people.
>
> (Hogan, 1998: 12)

There is a particular safety and healing, it seems, in the wilderness and the wild creatures – the wild creatures who are most dangerous, yet compassionate. Without effective natural predators, Western humans are cut off from a direct experience of this. How are we to understand and deeply know that animals are our friends, that our own wildness is our friend? As we will see in the next chapter, forms of therapy are developing to address these questions.

8

Wild Therapies

> The exterior landscape and its creatures are an inseparable part of the interior landscape, the landscape of the spirit and the heart.
> (Caswell, 2007: 609)

There are many ways in which and levels on which therapy can draw from the energy of wildness. I now explore three approaches to this: therapy in wild places; the wild and the other-than-human as it expresses itself in the therapy room; and therapy with the help of other-than-human animals.

For some years now a number of practitioners have been taking clients out of the therapy room and into the more-than-human world; while other practitioners and organisations have vehemently opposed some such practices as 'unboundaried' and dangerous. At the same time, the wild and other-than-human comes to meet us *within* the therapy room: I will describe some of the many ways in which dreams, fantasies and synchronicities use – or are used by? – other-than-human beings as means to explore psychological issues.

Looking from this point of view, we are able to see how many of the issues clients bring to therapy actually have to do on a fundamental level with the wild/domesticated axis. As a simple example, many clients struggle with self-assertion and healthy aggression, which feel to them violent, savage, and ultimately 'animal'; a similar conflict often arises around sexuality. In order to assert their needs and wants they will have to make friends with their own 'animal' nature.

LEAVING THE THERAPY ROOM

> Psychotherapists are by and large indoor people.
> (Linden & Grut, 2002: 28)

One fundamental move into wild therapy is the move out of doors. This can be as simple (though not necessarily easy) as taking a client to sit in the garden; or as complex (though not necessarily difficult) as taking a group into a 'real wilderness', perhaps with the intention that each person will spend a substantial time alone there. Although these two directions are in many ways very different, the first step – out of the therapy room – is perhaps the crucial one: once we have left the room, we can potentially move anywhere.

It is possible, though, to take the therapy room with us, or at any rate to take the old, comforting, restrictive frame which corresponds to the therapy room. Some 'wilderness therapy' does all it can to stay essentially domesticated, creating a rigid framework of rules to keep things both physically and emotionally 'safe'. This sort of model is based on the paradigm of nature as something for us to *use*, which I discussed in Chapter 3: as Robert Greenway suggests, 'a wilderness that must heal us is surely a commodity, just as when we can only look at wilderness as a source of endless wealth' (Greenway, 1995: 135). The opposite polarity is around letting the other-than-human itself *perform* the therapy, if it chooses to, rather than simply being a setting for the therapy to take place: it treats the other-than-human as sacred and approaches it in awe and gratitude.

Operating in the field between, around and including these two models are an enormous variety of different practices using a variety of names, including 'horticultural therapy' (Diehl, 2009; Linden & Grut, 2002), 'wilderness therapy' (Greenway, 1995, 2009; Harper, 1995), 'outdoor therapy' or 'adventure therapy' (Gass, 1993), 'nature therapy' (Scull, 2009), and more. None of these terms are interchangeable, and some refer to very different theories and practices. I propose to roam briefly through this field, starting out from the unobtrusive, generally unnamed practice of wandering out of the therapy room with our clients.

Getting out of the house more

This practice is unobtrusive and unnamed partly through fear that it will be condemned as transgressing boundaries – the traditional 'therapeutic frame', where both parties sit in chairs in a room and talk. In some circles this frame is idealised and dogmatically enforced as the only good way to work (see Chapter 6). However as they grow more experienced many practitioners quietly introduce their own variations, though few of them announce these publicly; and accompanying clients into the garden, the field or the woods is quite widespread among therapists who have easy access to such spaces. In workshops on ecopsychological themes, even during conventional conferences, I find that a large proportion of participants usually admit to having at least tried this out, and many of them have been doing it for years.

There are many possible reasons for moving outside. Some clients, for example some survivors of sexual abuse, are overwhelmed with anxiety when shut in a room with a stranger; they may feel a lot safer out of doors, and it is usually possible to build up sufficient trust to come back inside when the weather changes – simply responding to their anxiety itself helps to induce trust. Other clients are naturally drawn to and in touch with the outdoors, spending a lot of their time there anyway, and accompanying them to their comfort zone can be an important way to develop relationship. Others again come with an agenda – perhaps arising from environmental concerns – which includes exploring and deepening their connection with the outdoors. Sometimes the initial suggestion will come from the client, sometimes from the therapist (usually responding to something in the client's material or self-presentation). It can be a one-off experiment; or it can become the primary way of working for a particular therapeutic dyad.

When two people regularly work out of doors, it is common for the other-than-human to take part in the therapy in a whole range of ways. Synchronicities abound, often involving other animal beings:

> I remember a very moving moment in a session when my client was unable to speak for some time. I could tell she was feeling distressed and cut off, and I had tried several times to build a bridge with words, but the gap between us remained. Then, in the same moment, we both glanced down to see the tiniest of spiders weaving a web between our arms. We grinned at each other, speechless with wonder, making a deep connection without the need for words. In subsequent sessions we spoke of how the spider's web was an affirmation about trusting the connecting processes of life in that most difficult moment.
>
> (Rust, 2009b: 43)

Synchronicities can also involve plants, trees, weather, even encounters with other humans; often they are clearly a matter of what catches our attention because we are thinking about something similar, rather than dramatic enactments like the example above. This is especially true if the session is conducted walking rather than sitting on a spot – even more of a departure from the usual frame, but sometimes a very useful one, introducing the sense of a quest for meaning (see the discussion of medicine walks, below).

Growth work

Once we venture into the garden, the path out of doors then forks. One direction is *further* outdoors, towards the wild; the other direction is *down*, into the soil, into an active relationship with the garden itself.

Like many of the so-called 'active therapies', therapeutic gardening has historically been seen as appropriate for 'special' groups – children, the mentally ill, asylum seekers, substance abusers, those with learning difficulties. But why should they have all the fun? As with dance movement therapy or art therapy, therapeutic gardening seems suitable for pretty much anyone who would like to experience it.

Generally, however, it requires some sort of institutional or organisational setting to provide the garden in which to work. Once this is in place, one can proceed in a number of different ways; the therapeutic content can range between simply an opportunity to benefit from exercise and the calming and grounding effects of working in a garden, with individual or group therapy happening alongside this and often indoors, and much more radical fusions of the two. The Natural Growth Project, a trailblazing scheme set up by Jenny Grut and the Medical Foundation for the Victims of Torture, was established on thirty allotments and in a large garden (for those too disabled by torture to manage an allotment). Those on the allotments are visited weekly by a psychotherapist and a gardener.

> The role of the garden and the allotments is not only to provide a place of peace but to offer a space where the client is able to re-enact his or her trauma and start to lay it to rest. The therapist's role is not to co-ordinate activities but rather to reflect on the experience of the client through the contact with nature. Using nature as a metaphor, it is possible very quickly to access deeply traumatic events and to work on the most difficult feelings, and the life cycle embodied in nature carries the promise of healing.
> (Linden & Grut, 2002: 12)

As one example of how gardening can act as a metaphorical container for traumatic feelings, Linden and Grut (2002: 61–6) describe an Iraqi Kurd man, subject to intense anger and frustration as a result of his torture, who retaught himself patience by removing every last scrap of couch grass and other weeds from his allotment site. At the same time, the weeds he removed stood for 'bad memories, bad feeling, bad thoughts' (ibid: 63). In the process of removing the weeds, he turned his allotment temporarily into a wasteland – but this enabled him to grow both patience and, in due course, a garden of fruits and vegetables, flowers and herbs. A relevant aspect of the story is that this client, like many others from Iraq in the project, refused to use chemicals to control weeds and pests: despite the fact that artificial fertilisers and weedkillers are routinely used on the land they come from, they:

> made the link between chemicals used on the soil, which can contaminate the produce grown, and chemicals used against them by Saddam Hussein. 'How can we do the same to plants, to the food we eat?' Shortly after that, the clients voted not to use chemicals on the project, and thus at their instigation a commitment was made to organic gardening.
> (Linden & Grut, 2002: 50)

This Medical Foundation project has given rise to several others around the country and elsewhere.

Walking on the wild side

Having escaped the house, some therapists make a break for the hills. However various their approaches, they share the belief that 'wilderness holds the potential for transformative experiences' (Harper, 1995: 185). Different practices emphasise different aspects of this potential for transformation: for some it is primarily about how humans learn to bond and cooperate, and how individuals confront their fears and develop their survival skills and self-esteem in the face of 'nature' (e.g. Gillis & Ringer, 1999). Although this approach – which tends to be called 'adventure therapy' – has been justifiably criticised for not paying sufficient attention to the role of the other-than-human world (Beringer & Martin, 2003), it is nonetheless implicitly about bringing humans into a position where the other-than-human world impacts them, and has to be negotiated rather than ignored; in that sense it is to a degree necessarily ecopsychological.

For others, the main focus is on opening and surrendering to the other-than-human and more-than-human, and allowing oneself to be moved and changed by the encounter. This tends to be called 'wilderness therapy'. These different emphases have probably always been present in human interactions with the wild (simply put, the difference between going for food and going for visions), and once again I want to avoid a dualistic contest between them and suggest that there is a place for each, and also for various blends of the two (Russell & Farnum, 2004). Some practitioners have indeed started out as 'adventure therapists' and developed into 'wilderness therapists' through transformative personal experiences (Key, 2003).

A core element of both wilderness and adventure therapy is the 'solo': a period of time spent in the wild outdoors on one's own. Clearly an irreducible aspect of the solo is *survival*, physical and psychological – testing oneself against the wild; there may or may not also be an aspect of *encounter*, opening oneself to being touched and changed by the wild. Jean Angell (1994), writing about women's solo wilderness trips, identifies four styles or flavours; she describes them as the vision quest, the reflective solo, the survival skills solo, and an informal, self-chosen and self-organised period of time alone in the wilderness.

Wilderness therapy programs are widespread; in 1998 there were estimated to be over 700 in the United States alone (Friese et al, 1998). However, an increasing proportion of these are now 'boot camps', intended to instil discipline into unruly young people, or slimness into obese young people.

> The philosophy of wilderness therapy is to allow children to experience the force of nature as their teacher and to avoid staff use of force and restraint. Boot camp programs are designed and run with a high degree of interpersonal confrontation as well as physical and psychological aggression toward students. ... Obtaining control and compliance through the use of intimidation and coercion is characteristic of a boot camp program. Wilderness therapy and boot camps are distinctly different and incompatible approaches to working with youth.
>
> (Conner, 2007)

Boot camps, in other words, impose domestication on the wilderness, which becomes simply a conveniently sequestered space in which to confine and control unwilling young people (see the gothically comic novel *Holes*, by Louis Sachar, 2000). However well intentioned, they are about domestication rather than wild mind. Wilderness therapy proper is still quite a mixed bag, sometimes with elements of boot camp discipline and/or athletic machismo about it. A key question, as I have already suggested, is to what degree the other-than-human and more-than-human are put at the centre of the practice. According to Almut Beringer and Peter Martin:

> Even when adventure therapy relies on particular natural environments to achieve its objectives, some conceptualizations ... remain silent on the outdoor setting as a therapeutic medium, instead highlighting 'adventure' as the healing factor. Wilderness in a therapeutic process seems mostly valued because it provides distance from and a contrast to the clients' urban base; the fact that wilderness may have healing qualities due to its 'naturalness' remains largely unexamined in adventure therapy theory and practice.
>
> (Beringer & Martin, 2003: 30)

Beringer and Martin identify 'a conceptual insensitivity toward the powers of the natural worlds', and suggest that 'adventure therapy ignorant of the healing powers of nature may well be a part of the environmental problem rather than contributing to its solution' (both from Beringer & Martin, 2003: 32). They argue that:

> The power of wilderness/outdoor adventure therapy programs may lie neither, or not solely, with the therapist and her/his therapeutic skills, nor with the carefully designed program, nor even with the adventure clients undergo. Rather, what may be equally critical, if not more so, in bringing about change for the better may be due to 'nature' – being in and interacting with the natural worlds. This potency of nature, although not highly rated in the profession, has been supporting adventure therapy and, we would argue, is in large part responsible for the growth and alleged effectiveness of the field.
>
> (Ibid: 33)

Emphasising the role of the other-than-human in wilderness therapy by no means involves discounting the role of the human community. Kerr and Key (2010: 6) suggest that 'the most complete setting for us to encounter and heal our psychological wounds combines an accepting, holding, human presence with wild nature', pointing out the millennia-long tradition behind this combination, which sets up a creative tension between our aloneness in the face of the more-than-human, and our solidarity as human beings: 'time in the wilderness can equip us to return to our communities and take compassionate action from an increased sense of inner security' (Kerr & Key, 2010: 6). Most solo work, including the vision quest which I discuss in the next section, embeds time alone in the wild within a structure of sharing and story-making.

Vision quests and medicine walks

> I died a number of times during those thirty days, but I learned and found what can be found and learned only in the silence, away from the multitude, in the depths. I heard the voice of nature itself speak to me, and it spoke with the voice of a gentle motherly solicitude and affection. Or it sounded sometimes like children's voices, or sometimes like falling snow, and what it said was, 'Do not be afraid of the universe'.
>
> (The Inuit shaman Najagneq describing his initiation: Osterman, 1927: 128)

The 'solo' structure is also central to spiritual practices of the wild, like the Native American vision quest; and there has been a fruitful interplay between these approaches and wilderness therapy (Foster & Little, 1988, 1989). The original vision quest (the Lakota name for it translates literally as 'crying for a vision') was a profoundly demanding experience, involving going naked and fasting into the wild for four days, taking only a blanket and sacred pipe: 'empty the mind, listen to the spirits of the wind and clouds, try not to sleep, and wait for an answer or a vision concerning one's life purpose' (Angell, 1994: 87). Contemporary Western versions tend to be somewhat moderate in comparison, but still serious undertakings.

Some stay close to the original, though often with a psychological rather than shamanic emphasis. Kurt Caswell (2007) describes his experience of a vision quest in Death Valley organised by the Californian School of Lost Borders, which consisted four days of preparation ('severance'), four days of fasting alone in a wild landscape (the 'threshold'), and four days of group work to interpret and understand the threshold experience ('incorporation'). He emphasises that 'the vision quest is a self-made ceremony (no one is here to interpret anything for me)' (Caswell, 2007: 613): in the altered state induced by fasting and solitude and the process of 'severance', every event takes on meaning, as the other-than-human is set free to speak to us and we are set free to listen. 'The exterior landscape and its creatures are an inseparable part of the interior landscape, the landscape of the spirit and the heart' (ibid: 609). Caswell ends his account:

> You want to know if the vision quest changed my life. You want to know if a vision quest will change yours. You will have to walk that road for yourself, of course. I can tell you that my story in the desert is now part of everything I do, everything I say, everything I see. I can't now imagine my life without it.
> (Ibid: 624)

Caswell also describes the often hostile scepticism or simple incomprehension with which many people react to hearing about the vision quest. The mother of one of his fellow participants simply said, '"And you won't be able to shower for how many days?"' (ibid: 609). This is another meaning of going out into the wilderness – leaving behind consensus reality and its view of what makes sense and what matters; and it isn't easy to bring back anything that will be understood. One can only trust that one's experience, with that of other like-minded people, will somehow affect and become a part of shared reality.

A variation on the vision quest is the medicine walk, also derived from Native American practices. Instead of sitting on one spot, the task is to move through a territory holding a question about one's life, and attend to what one encounters. A full-scale medicine walk lasts at least from dawn to sunset, but can be longer; it will involve an alternation of walking and resting. Those who undertake it are encouraged to fast.

> The walk is a mirror that reflects the signs and symbols of your inward quest. ... As you wander, become aware of Nature's awareness of you. Signs and symbols indicating your life purpose, inherent gifts, personal values or fears, will present themselves. As you discern the beauty of life and the reality of death in the world around you, ask yourself: 'Who are my people?' Pay attention to who you think about, worry about, wish was with you, and so forth.
>
> (Foster & Little, 1988: 35)

The medicine walk can be used as part of the preparation for a vision quest or some other rite of passage.

Rites of passage

I have once or twice mentioned rites of passage; what does this mean? Many indigenous peoples mark – in a sense, create – transitions from one stage of life to another through ceremony of some sort. Often they are modelled on symbolic death and rebirth, these being the most fundamental life transitions, which shape our understanding of the other ones. Many people involved with growth work feel that we in the West suffer from a shortage of meaningful rites of passage, in particular marking the transition to adulthood; and they have tried in various ways to create such events.

Malidoma Somé, an African shaman, has worked extensively with Westerners on such initiatory events. He writes:

> It has to have a moment of separation from the family and the community. It has to happen in nature and be a genuinely challenging ordeal. Whatever the initiates feel before entering this cycle must be deepened to the point of transcendence, giving them the opportunity to feel whole. Finally, and most importantly, there has to be a strong community ready to welcome the survivors of the ordeal. This welcoming must be massive, not like a simple ceremony of giving a diploma, but a recognizable, wholehearted embrace and valuing of the initiates' power to contribute to the community. In other words, this last stage must make the returning men and women want to maintain the pride of their community. This will fuel a continued sense of belonging, which is so much lacking in the heart of the modern youth.
>
> (Somé, 1994: 68)

Unfortunately, there is a chicken-and-egg factor here: when Western society is able to provide something like this, the need for it will be far less urgent – and conversely, we need people who have been through this sort of initiation to set up the conditions for providing it. Currently in the West there is no single shared vision of society and cosmos; so a unifying vision quest which affirms society's values is not a possibility.

Identifying key features

Several people have explored various models of what the 'active ingredients' of outdoor experience might be. Margaret Boniface (2000), for example, uses Csikszentmihalyi's (1990) concept of Flow and Maslow's (1971) concept of Peak Experience. Kaplan and Kaplan (1989; also Kaplan, 1995) develop the subtle and helpful concept of 'soft fascination':

> Soft fascination occurs when involuntary attention – the opposite of stressful, directed attention – is engaged. Clouds, sunsets, and moving river water capture attention but do not require directed attention, allowing room for cognitive reflection. Because demands upon directed attention are diminished, psychological restoration becomes possible. Kaplan and Kaplan argue that these types of natural phenomenon – clouds, sunsets, etc. – are prime types of stimuli to induce cognitive rest. Attention is captured by an interesting and aesthetically pleasing environment that does not necessitate a high degree of cognitive processing. Thus, soft fascination allows for release from stressors that cause mental fatigue, easing away from cognitive strain and relaxing.
> (Russell & Farnum, 2004: 42)

This seems to me a very good account of *how* being outdoors relaxes us, as most people know it does. And as I have already indicated, relaxation is at the heart of psychotherapy. Margaret Kerr and Dave Key point out that a part of what may relax is the rigid boundary between self and environment, and suggest that this offers 'a deeper understanding of how experiences of wild and green spaces can heal the self as part of our larger ecology'. They suggest that wilderness activates 'our capacity to open up both *ecologically*, as we become aware of our biological interdependence with the rest of nature and *metaphysically*, as we go beyond our narrow egoic sense of self' (Kerr & Key, 2010: 1). Hence 'in wilderness, the metaphysical and the physical may become inseparable' (ibid: 3).

> For us, wilderness describes places where we can experience 'wildness' – our self as part of the 'primordial gestalt'. Being part

> of that wild pattern changes our sense of self. 'I' as a 'part' becomes different because of the whole. Previously frozen self-constructs can start to thaw, and the possibility of transformation and greater authenticity naturally arises. It is here that we can experience a wider, deeper, reality where phenomena that we have never encountered before emerge and present themselves to our conscious mind. Our journey into wilderness becomes a journey into the unconscious.
>
> (Kerr & Key, 2010: 2)

Adaptations

Making these sorts of events part of therapy in the ordinary sense is not easy. (Of course, there is nothing that says they need to be part of therapy, but that is what this book is ultimately about.) A key element of the traditional vision quest or medicine walk is that one undertakes it *alone* – not accompanied by a friendly shrink! The same is obviously true of solos in general. A solo, up to and including a vision quest, can certainly be the centre of a group therapy event – as are the School of Lost Borders events like the one described above by Kurt Caswell, or the workshops led by Key and Kerr and Rust and Key (Rust & Key, 2007): facilitation is very helpful in preparing for and integrating this sort of experience.

There does seem to be a valuable role, also, for smaller scale 'micro-versions' of wilderness practices, both in a workshop context and within outdoor one-to-one therapy sessions. Therapist and client together can explore the meaning of synchronistic experiences, and discuss the feeling evoked by the setting in which they are working. In this context, the therapeutic relationship frequently becomes a significant part of the work – as in the experience with the spider quoted above from Mary-Jayne Rust: in a sense, the relationship can become the 'question' which is being asked in the micro vision quest of the session.

The power of place

I have experimented with a different kind of micro vision quest, asking workshop members to undertake a brief 'zoom-in' to their immediate outdoor context. Standing in an outdoor spot, close your eyes, turn round several times, take a step; open your eyes and experience *where you are*, using all your senses; sit down and explore the local vegetation and insect life; listen to the birds. Then connect with another participant, share and explore your experience. Something like this is less likely than four days and nights alone in the wilderness to be a life-changing experience. But who knows? The power of an experience lies as much in its timing as in its content.

And there is something very powerful simply in the realisation that the ground right under our feet is full of its own life, energy and significance. As I discussed in Chapter 4, indigenous knowledge is intensely local, and the relationship of indigenous peoples to the place where they live is intensely spiritual and intensely emotional. And as we also saw in Chapter 6, there is a huge difference between the sort of knowledge which can be abstracted and generalised from place, time and person, and the knowledge that is inextricable from local, embodied, energetic experience.

This sort of therapeutic work, then, and all its variants, are not about asking wild places to answer questions or to solve our problems, but about letting ourselves become open to what Swan (1991) calls 'the power of place'; we might then be drawn to some sort of action which expresses that power. Here therapy crosses with ecology, geography, architecture, art, and environmental practices of all kinds – with what seems like an innate human drive to interact with special places, some of the earliest known expressions of which can be seen in cave paintings and stone circles. A potentially important tool here is Goethean Observation, a method of comparatively non-dualist interaction with the world which can be powerfully adapted to exploration of place (Brook, 1998).

ANIMALS IN THE THERAPY ROOM

> A psychotherapist whom I supervise opened our supervisory session with the following: 'So what's with the animals out there? Everyone in my practice is coming in and talking about animals. What's going on?'
>
> (Bernstein, 2005: xv)

Creatures are everywhere in therapy. They throng in the consulting room: lurking under the sofa, scuttling across the carpet, buzzing and flapping around our heads, fluttering and knocking at the window. They peer from our clients' eyes, and from our own; gather in the jungles and savannahs of our inner worlds. Then there are our clients' pets, past and present, that can hold so much of their emotional life; and *our* pets, to which our clients attach so many of their feelings about us. And, of course, there is always that elephant in the corner of the room ....

Increasingly over the years I have noticed the presence of these beings, 'the Others', as Paul Shepard calls them (1996); noticed the myriad ways in which I and my clients make use of them, press them into service as symbols and metaphors for many different experiences and issues; noticed also how sometimes they refuse to serve, take on a fierce, independent life of their own, insist on their own wild meaning: that what they mean *is* wildness itself, in which, says Thoreau (1862: para 18), 'is the preservation of the World'.

For example: a young man explores how he holds his body, and discovers there what he calls a 'monster', a ravening, tearing beast. 'It wants to be free,' he says; 'it just wants to be free.' Over the course of the session he moves from a principled determination to keep it imprisoned, to a tentative exploration of how it might be released.

For example: a woman client who was sexually abused as a child dreams of a unicorn in a field, and of a stallion which wants to join the unicorn there, but waits politely to be invited. She identifies herself with the unicorn (with its connotations around virginity and untouchability), and identifies me with the stallion that wants to 'come in', but only if I am asked.

For example: on a workshop, participants are asked to form pairs and share a memory of someone in their lives who unconditionally supported and accepted them. As I move round the room, I find one group member in tears: she can't think of anyone. Ten painful minutes later, supported by her partner and by me, she remembers someone: her childhood pet cat.

Each of these vignettes reflects the profound significance for our psychology of other-than-human beings. Paul Shepard says that 'the human species emerged enacting, dreaming and thinking animals and cannot be fully itself without them' (Shepard, 1996: 4); he describes 'the animals as Others in a world where otherness of all kinds is in danger, and in which otherness is essential to the discovery of the true self' (ibid: 5). This is certainly borne out by my experience as a therapist, where animal imagery appears spontaneously over and over and over again as a transformative element in the work. I am of course not the first therapist to notice this; in particular, Jung and many Jungian analysts have contributed the observation of synchronistic appearances of animals in the 'real world' alongside their psychological appearance in the client's material.

But what to do with all these animals? How are we to understand them and work with them? Therapists take many different approaches, often contradicting each other – suggesting that, as one might expect, there is no *one* function that animals fulfil in our psyche.

Animals as instinct

Jung saw a critical task of therapy as that of 'becoming animal' (Shamdasani, 2003: 253). He had a helpfully paradoxical way of talking about this:

> People don't understand when I tell them they should become acquainted with their animals or assimilate their animals. They think the animal is always jumping over walls and raising hell all over town. Yet in nature the animal is a well-behaved citizen. It is pious, it follows the path, with great regularity, it does nothing extravagant. Only man is extravagant. So if you assimilate the character of the animal you become a peculiarly law-abiding citizen, you go very slowly, and you become very reasonable in your ways, in as much as you can afford it.
>
> (Jung, 1930–1934/1998: 168)

Without using the word, Jung is in effect playing with the two senses of 'wild' which I discussed at the start of this book: 'wild' as that which stands outside human culture, and 'wild' as the disorderedness which is uniquely found *inside* human culture. According to this second sense, animals are not wild, because they 'follow the path' of their own nature. Hence Jung identifies animals with the instinctual (Shamdasani, 2003: 253); and, like a Taoist master, enjoins human people to come into harmony with their instincts. Jungians have developed a complex and detailed taxonomy of the psychological significance of different animals, studying the mythology and folklore associated with them and their use in art and literature (Hannah, 2005).

However, Jung also argued that the repression of the animal in humans means that when it resurfaces it does so in an uncontrolled and catastrophic explosion (Shamdasani, 2003: 251). This part of his thinking is conventional for the earlier 20th century, and similar to the way in which Freud also associated animals with instinct:

> Wild beasts are as a rule employed by the dream-work to represent passionate impulses of which the dreamer is afraid, whether they are his own or those of other people. ... It might be said that the wild beasts are used to represent the libido, a force dreaded by the ego and combated by means of repression.
>
> (Freud, 1900: 410)

And again: 'Wild animals mean people in an excited sensual state, and further, evil instincts or passions' (1916–1917: 158). A disappointingly trite and domesticated perspective, projecting onto the other-than-human what humans cannot accept about themselves.

In his book *The Dream and the Underworld* James Hillman breaks with the whole 'animals represent instinct' approach: 'I prefer to consider animals in dreams as Gods, as divine, intelligent, autochthonous powers, demanding respect' (Hillman, 1979: 147). This is in line with his whole approach to dreams, focusing not on interpretation but on a respectful acceptance and inhabitation of the dreamworld. He says further of animals:

> Let us remember that the animal kingdom is bigger than ours. We are members of it and subject to it, so that we may pass only a few cautiously respectful remarks about their images, as one of their fellow citizens with whom we human animals have fallen on rather bad terms.
>
> (Hillman, 1979: 147)

He applies this approach in the beautiful book of words and images, *Dream Animals* (Hillman & McLean, 1997).

Animals as spirit

Animals often manifest as representatives of spirit and of the paranormal in our dreams and synchronistic experiences (Totton, 2003b: 12). Spiegelman (2003) describes several such experiences involving other-than-human creatures, of which this is one example:

> I was working with an Asian man, religious in orientation ... Some months into the work I dreamed that he had the mark of a fox on his face, and that this mark suggested he should become a healer. The next day I received a copy of a journal which described an ancient cult in his country, called the Fox cult, which trained in shamanic healing. The following evening, during my drive home from my office, I caught sight of a fox in the headlights of my car. ... When I informed my analysand of these experiences at our next meeting, he told me that he had indeed been thinking about becoming a healer, but had thought it presumptuous. ... Subsequently, his own dreams suggested this path, and ultimately he became a healer.
>
> (Spiegelman, 2003: 146)

Particularly common is the presence of a bird as a symbol or embodiment of psychic experience (Spiegelman, 2003: 144; Peerbolte, 2003: 55; Totton, 2003b: 5–6).

Animals in the bodymind

Wilhelm Reich, the founder of body psychotherapy, was extremely sensitive to the appearance of animal figures in his work with clients.

> The total expression of the body can usually be condensed in a word or formula which, sooner or later in the course of the character-analytic treatment, suggests itself. Strangely enough,

> they are usually formulas and names derived from the animal kingdom, such as 'fox', 'pig', 'snake', 'worm', etc.
> (Reich, 1942/1983: 302)

For example, he describes working with someone whose intellectual skills functioned as 'an extremely cunning way of avoiding deep insights' (Reich, 1933/1972: 307). 'One day a term occurred to me for his behavior. I told him that it reminded me of *a cunning fox or lynx*' (ibid, original italics). Soon afterwards, the patient remembered an incident from his third year: he badly injured his left arm in a fall, and as he was being carried to hospital saw a shop selling stuffed animals, including a fox and a reindeer.

He then remembered lying, tied to the operating table, momentarily hallucinated the smell of chloroform, and saw the chloroform mask about to be placed over his face – a mask which strongly resembled a fox's head. At that moment he thought 'This is a fox's face which I am getting here!'

> Even as a child, he knew that foxes are caught in traps; in his native country, they were caught in steel traps with spikes that fasten upon one of the animal's legs and 'break its bones'. On the way to the hospital, the boy had strained his intellect to see how he might elude this catastrophe. This was perhaps the first time that his intellect had served the purpose of warding off a great and imminent danger. And the analytic treatment was warded off in the same way, cunningly, 'like a fox'. ... He had been a fox in the trap his whole life.
> (Reich, 1933/1972: 307–8)

The fish and the ape

In *The Function of the Orgasm* (Reich, 1942/1983: 309–29), Reich gives a detailed narrative of an analysis carried out probably in the early 1930s, when his technique of body psychotherapy was quite gentle and non-interventionist. (The following summary draws on my earlier account in Totton, 1998: 107–12. All quotations are from Reich, 1942/1983, as above.) This case history illustrates a therapeutic approach which focuses deeply on surrender and spontaneity. It also shows how, as Reich suggests, animal figures can begin to manifest in such a process, and what sort of role they play.

Using a version of Sandor Ferenczi's 'relaxation technique' (Ferenczi, 1929/1999a), over six and a half months of six or seven sessions a week Reich patiently and repeatedly encouraged his analysand just to breathe and 'give in to every impulse', let go to any spontaneous bodily phenomena – trembling, jerking, or whatever manifested itself. The person in question, who had come because of his alcoholism, presented with two striking features: what Reich calls his 'psychic reserve' – extreme superficiality, politeness, and inability to express aggression; and his 'very striking facial expression', empty and masklike with a small tight mouth which 'hardly moved in the act of speaking'.

Reich decides to focus on the latter, and repeatedly draws the patient's attention to it. 'Following the consistent description of the rigid attitude of his mouth, a twitching of his lips set in, weak at first but growing gradually stronger.' Reich encourages the client to give in to the twitching, and:

> his lips began to protrude and retract rhythmically and to hold the protruded position for several seconds ... In the course of these movements, his face took on the unmistakeable expression of an infant. The patient was startled, grew fearful, and asked me what this might lead to. I allayed his fears and asked him to continue to give in to every impulse, and to tell me whenever he sensed an inhibition of an impulse.

As the sessions continued, 'the various manifestations in his face ... gradually aroused the patient's interest. This must have some special meaning, he said.' Pulling gently on this thread, Reich and his patient gradually unravel the whole structure of his defences. For a long while the facial expressions, even when they quite plainly portray grief or anger, are not accompanied by any felt emotion. This is common in psychotherapeutic bodywork: even when the emotional significance is plain, it is often some time before the client themselves can feel it.

Reich realises that the muscle tensions in the face represent 'not only the warded-off affect but also the defence': that is, the muscle spasticity contains both the unconscious impulse and its repression. The patient's small, tight mouth represented a continuous suppression of the urge to move his lips and to cry. 'Several weeks passed' – that is, twenty or more sessions of patient, repetitive work with the facial twitch – before the crying and anger began to express themselves more fully as a state of 'impotent rage, as is often experienced by children with adults' – still without emotional involvement, but with the patient having 'an immediate grasp of the meaning of his action, without any explanation on my part. He knew that he was expressing an overwhelming anger which he had kept locked up in himself for decades.' He became more emotionally aroused when he thought of 'his older brother, who had very much dominated and mistreated him as a child'.

As the work continues, Reich follows the patient's emotional charge as it shifts between bodily and psychic focus. While the patient *speaks* with detachment of his experience, his *body* reacts emotionally, and Reich stays with the body expression until the emotion comes into the words. The spasms and twitchings spread gradually into the chest and belly, and then jump to the legs. The 'gap between his muscular actions and the patient's perception of them ... remained unchanged' – in other words, there was still no emotional *experience* even in these dramatic bodily expressions.

To progress further, Reich has to step back, as it were, and consider the client's character.

> We both knew that he was very cautious. ... This 'caution' was also contained in his muscular activity ... I pointed out again and again that, while it was true he revealed his anger in his muscular actions, he never followed through, never really struck with his raised and clenched fist. ... After consistently working on the defence against the muscular action for a number of sessions, the following episode from his fifth year of life suddenly occurred to him.

The patient describes a betrayal by his mother: seeing him playing near the edge of a cliff, she became frightened, 'lured him to her in a sweet voice,' but then gave him a terrible beating. He spontaneously connects this memory with both 'his defensive attitude towards women' and his general character trait of caution.

However, the holding-back continues. One day, the patient begins to talk about his enthusiasm for trout fishing, and describes in detail the process of casting the line and so on.

> In the act of telling and demonstrating this to me, he had an enormously greedy, almost sadistic expression on his face. It struck me that ... he omitted one detail, namely the moment at which the trout bites into the hook.

However,

> Roughly four weeks elapsed before the following took place: ... strange twitchings appeared in the abdomen. ... The upper part of his body jerked forward, the middle of his abdomen remained still, and the lower part of his body jerked towards the upper part. The entire response was an organic unitary movement. There were sessions in which this movement was repeated continuously. ... In one such attack, his face had the unmistakeable expression of a fish. Without any prompting on my part, before I had drawn his attention to it, the patient said 'I feel like a primordial animal,' and shortly afterward, 'I feel like a fish'.

'His caution became understandable now,' Reich says: 'he did not trust anyone. He did not want to be caught' – hooked like a fish. The patient now starts to be able to let 'sweet', 'voluptuous' sensations of energy flow through his body when he breathes. And this is accompanied by a real emotional shift:

> In the process of working through this connection, his personality underwent a conspicuous change. His superficiality disappeared; he became serious. The seriousness appeared very suddenly during one of the sessions. The patient said literally: 'I don't understand; everything has become so deadly serious all of a sudden.'

As his body continues to surrender more deeply to energy flow, the patient recovers a memory from about two years old:

> He was alone with his mother at a summer resort. It was a clear starry night. His mother was asleep and breathing deeply; outside he could hear the steady pounding of the waves on the beach. The mood he had felt then was the same deeply serious, somewhat sad and melancholy mood which he experienced now. We can say that he remembered one of the situations from earliest childhood in which he had still allowed himself to experience his vegetative (orgastic) longing.

I believe that that this 'longing', this deep spiritual connection with the more-than-human world, is a central human trait which is suppressed and alienated by much of Western society. In a moving therapeutic encounter, Reich's patient re-experiences his innate capacity to feel connection with the universe; to do so, he has to surrender to his bodily impulses, and to meet the powerful image of an animal, rather like the animal 'ally' which shamans discover in trance.

Through this image of the hooked fish offered freely by the body, Reich and his patient discover the relationship with the mother; and later in the work, through a similar image of a gorilla they discover the relationship with the father.

> He jumped up, his mouth contorted with pain; beads of perspiration covered his forehead; his musculature was stiff as a board. He hallucinated an animal, an ape. In doing so, his hand had the bent attitude of an ape's paw, and he uttered sounds from the depth of his chest, 'as if without vocal cords,' he himself said afterward. It was as if someone had come very close to him and threatened him. Then, trance-like, he cried out, 'Don't be angry, I only want to suck.'

The 'fish' betrayed by the mother; the 'ape' threatened by the father 'who wanted to obstruct his sucking'. Once these two primordial figures have emerged from the body armouring, the work can be concluded, as the patient realises he believes – his body believes – that:

> 'a man is hard and unyielding; any form of surrender is feminine'. ... Immediately following this realisation, his infantile conflict with his father was resolved. On the one hand, he felt sheltered and protected by his father. ... At the same time, he strove to stand on his own feet and be independent of his father. ... When he finally experienced surrender in the reflex [the 'orgasm reflex', a soft yielding of the pelvis with the outbreath], he was deeply baffled by it. 'I would never have thought,' he said, 'that a man can surrender too.'

He encounters, in other words, the List and its binary opposition between masculine and feminine, as this is inscribed directly in his body. And only by transcending this rigorous opposition between protection and independence, hardness and softness, can he become a free person, a man who 'can surrender too'.

ANIMAL THERAPISTS

> The seemingly simple change in my perception of the horse from a dumb animal that needs to be defeated to an animal with a well-structured culture with wants, needs and a desire to be comfortable led to many other physical, mental, and spiritual transformations. I came to realise that many of the difficulties I had encountered during my younger years were the result of my ego-oriented perception of the world.
>
> (Powell, 1999: 103)

There has been interest for many years in the therapeutic potential of contact with real, physical other-than-human animals. At first the emphasis was on the *use* of these animals, as Winnicottian transitional objects, as 'a "Safe barrier" in the case of untrusting children who, for good reason, prefer animals to humans' (Schildkrout, quoted in Levinson, 1996: 39), or simply as a source of comfort and encouragement to relaxation. As that quotation indicates, like many other slightly 'wild' forms of practice – art therapy, play therapy – therapy with animals was primarily regarded, and widely still is regarded, as mainly suitable for working with children.

The role of animals in this therapy has often been treated in an extraordinarily contemptuous way. An article from 1990 describes the animal as 'a *prosthesis*' facilitating the establishment of a therapeutic relationship by the therapist (Draper et al, 1990, original italics). Bizarrely, researchers in Japan and the United States (Wada et al, 2005; Gatenby & Breazeal, 2005) are currently experimenting with using robots in the form of animals, seals or birds, presumably because they are more convenient and less troublesome than living animals – without considering that their aliveness might be an important part of their contribution to therapy.

Gradually, though, a majority of therapists have realised that it is not only a matter of using other-than-human animals as convenient proxies or aids to relaxation: that *the animal itself* can take an active part in the therapy – an interaction which has become known first as 'animal-assisted therapy', and then as 'animal-facilitated therapy'. Most of the work here has been done with dogs and with horses, both beings of particular sensitivity to human emotional fields. I have been told by therapists who work with clients and the clients' own dogs that these animals show clear relief when the therapy begins: someone else is sharing responsibility for the problems of which they are very much aware.

Jane Karol identifies some of the features of this work, specifically in relation to horses:

> Most communication with horses is carried out nonverbally. Because the horse's response is immediate, the rider must learn to be aware of how his or her body accomplishes that communication, and how to listen for and interpret the nonverbal cues the horse gives in response. ... Thus, the process of learning to ride can further the client's knowledge about how he or she communicates nonverbally and he or she will get immediate and clear feedback about the effectiveness of that communication from the horse.
>
> (Karol, 2007: 84)

Here is one of the examples she gives of how the process can work, a vignette of a nine-year-old boy diagnosed with ADHD. Initially, Karol invokes other animal beings as a way of communicating with the child and supporting him in trying out different styles of being in relation to the horse.

> Before he was able to ride, he needed to learn how to control his body. He was asked to copy and practice the style of movement of a turtle, a lion, and a sloth so that he could better control his

> hyperactive tendency while he rode. He learned quickly how to slow his body down and move like a turtle or allow himself to speed up and move like a lion.
>
> (Ibid)

This helped him learn to relate to the horse, but not sufficiently:

> [H]e still became angry when the horse didn't understand his cues (he felt as if the horse wasn't listening to him) and he kicked the horse with anger. The horse immediately stopped moving, swished his tail in anger in return, and became rigid in his body. I explained to the boy that the horse was trying to listen to him but was confused with his cues. ... In order for the client to get the horse to do what he wanted (i.e. to walk forward), he needed to control his anger and learn what the nonverbal cues were to ask the horse to walk. ... Finally, the client settled his body and began to ask the horse to move forward quietly. The horse listened and the client felt immediate success as he controlled his anger and his body and focused on more productive ways of communication.
>
> (Ibid: 84–5)

In brackets, Karol then makes a very significant point:

> I think one should note there that the full learning experience, whereby a more successful kind of communication immediately allowed the boy to move forward, was made possible by another wonderful quality horses have, namely their generosity of character and an ability to forgive quickly.
>
> (Ibid: 85)

Karol also emphasises that 'the interaction between client and horse can serve as a therapeutic change agent through *the actual body experience* in conjunction with the emotional and psychological connection between human and horse' (ibid: 81). As an example:

> A 13-year-old girl ... suffered from angry outbursts and long hours of depression. Not coincidentally, when she rode she had trouble getting the horse to move in an even rhythm. ... I worked on helping her develop a flowing consistent cadence in each of the horse's gaits. What was helpful therapeutically for this client was the comparison of the horse's need to move in a constant balanced rhythm with her own need to find a steady internal rhythm for herself and its expression externally.
>
> (Ibid: 87)

The importance of embodied experience is beautifully expressed in Linda Kohanov's *The Tao of Equus*:

> Some of the most exciting moments in my practice happen when a first-time equestrienne realizes that to liberate the horse's body from mirroring her own physical issues, she has to breathe into her abdomen, unclench her jaw, relax her shoulders, release her pelvis, and allow her upper torso to float quietly over hips that follow the naturally fluid pace of her mount. Tears of joy or wails of sorrow frequently accompany this seemingly minor breakthrough ...
>
> (Kohanov, 2001: 212)

Although embodied interaction is a powerful channel for change, for many equine-facilitated therapists it is not crucial for the client to ride the horse. As herd animals vulnerable to predators, horses have learned great sensitivity to mood and atmosphere; this is often particularly true of horses which have themselves suffered abuse, just as it is true of many human abuse survivors.

> These mindful creatures have developed a magnificent capacity for responding to subtle changes in the arousal of other horses as well as predators, a ... talent they easily transfer to interactions with people. ... Even the most secure horse knows that any two-legged creature conveying the gestures of one emotion in order to hide another is either up to no good or delusional enough to be dangerous to herself and others.
>
> (Kohanov, 2001: 105–6)

Horses, in other words, are truth-sensers. The same is no doubt true of all species which form emotional bonds with humans; and this makes them all potential therapists. Gerald Mallon entitles a paper 'Some of our best therapists are dogs' – 'because of their interactive, affectionate, non-judgmental, and social nature' (Mallon, 1994: 89). Very little has yet been published about feline-facilitated therapy, as distinct from companion cats, but a great deal of it seems to go on informally; I have heard from several therapists about the active role that their cats take, forming distinctly different relationships with particular clients – one therapist who has several cats has found that they each 'take on' different clients, who are then ignored by the others while 'their' cat turns up reliably for sessions. An interesting paper (Wells et al, 1997) suggests that feral cats make particularly valuable facilitators:

> In other therapeutic contexts, animals are generally introduced into the treatment situation by their handlers, and are quite clearly extensions of these humans. They are well-trained, civilized, often eager to please, and generally must meet a number of well-defined requirements designed to select those animals best suited to be good companions. In contrast, the feral cats contribute to the therapy how and when they choose, offering the many dimensions of their different character, preferences, pleasures and dislikes as enhancements to the therapeutic process.
>
> (Ibid: 125)

Feral cats, that is, provide wild rather than domesticated therapy!

Kohanov quotes equine-facilitated therapist Barbara Rector as saying:

> Every riding teacher giving a lesson sees it. When the person is unable to access what is going on in her own body and mind, the horse will express it behaviorally or actually even become locked up in his own body. ... The horse doesn't judge what they're feeling, or hold grudges. As soon as the person acknowledges his fear or anger, a horse with a talent for this work will walk over to him and lend support.
>
> (Kohanov, 2001: 202)

In other words, not only does the horse offer feedback by which the client and therapist can measure what is going on in the client; a horse 'with a talent for this work' can also become actively and deliberately engaged in helping the client. And horses which have themselves suffered abusive treatment are often the ones most able and willing to help troubled humans.

It is worth noting how the involvement of animals in therapy allows various non-mainstream practices to be smuggled in, as it were, because of the way animals are flagged culturally as associated with bodies, feelings, intuition, and naturalness. Levinson (1996; see also Wells et al, 1997) emphasises the importance of touch in animal-assisted therapy: in many cases therapists who would not touch or be touched by a client are happy to work alongside animals who will and do. Similarly, it is accepted that animals will use non-rational sensitivities in working with human clients; after all, what else could they be expected to do?

Working out of doors, working with animal imagery, and working with the help of actual animals, are just three examples of how the other-than-human and more-than-human are already involved in psychotherapy. 'Wild therapy' already exists in a number of concrete forms. However these various approaches have not yet been thought about together as aspects of a distinct therapeutic approach; nor have the wider implications of their 'wildness' yet been clarified – all of these ways of working can be used in what I would call 'wild' or 'domesticated' versions. In the next chapter, I will finally try to specify what I mean by wild therapy as a general approach.

9

Wild Therapy

> Out beyond ideas of wrongdoing and rightdoing
> there is a field. I'll meet you there.
>
> When the soul lies down in that grass,
> the world is too full to talk about.
> Ideas, language, even the phrase *each other*
> doesn't make any sense.
>
> (Jelaluddin Rumi, translated by Coleman Barks, 1999: 36)

In the previous chapter, I described several specific forms of therapeutic work which link with the concept of 'wildness', because they involve the outdoors, animals, or wild thinking or feeling of various kinds. In this chapter I want to ask: What would something called 'Wild Therapy' look like? What would constitute a general theory of wildness in psychotherapy and counselling? I think that I have already provided the materials for an answer, but in this chapter I want to bring those materials together.

To begin with, it seems to me that wild therapy might not *look* very different from a lot of therapy as it is already practised – for two reasons. First of all, a number of people are already working to a greater or lesser extent as wild therapists: what I am doing in this book is not inventing something completely new, but finding a way to talk about and connect up trends that already exist. And secondly, wild therapy does not require – though it may well include – exotic techniques and direct involvement with the outdoors, for example. It is an *attitude of mind*, rather than a bag of tricks, and this attitude may express itself in a great variety of ways, including sitting in a room and talking.

Like all approaches to therapy, wild therapy is based on a model of positive human functioning. This model describes a view of how people should be, and a related view of how therapists should be. Many therapies are uncomfortable with the idea that they incorporate 'shoulds', but I believe this is inescapably the case (Totton, 2005, 2008: 146–7), so I want to come clean about my values. My own model of positive human functioning is implicit, and sometime explicit, in what follows.

What should be clear is that I want therapy to be a force for change in our culture. The development of organisations and institutions to regulate therapy has been a two-edged process; at its most negative, it has sought to bring therapy – at first a deeply radical and even subversive activity – back within the walls of domestication. Freud had a profound ambivalence about this process, which can be explored, as I discussed in Chapter 1, through his use of terms like 'wild' in his writings, and also emerges in his rejection of attempts to restrict analytic training to medical doctors (Freud, 1926). Similarly, Jung said of psychotherapy that 'holding lectures, giving instruction, pumping in knowledge, all these ... procedures are of no use here' (Jung, 1976b: 534); while later Carl Rogers, an equally illustrious figure in the humanistic world, proposed that we '[do] away with "the expert", "the certified professional", "the licensed psychologist"' (Rogers, 1973/1980: 246). As I hope I have made apparent, I believe that there are core features of psychotherapy which render it impossible to domesticate without disempowering it: therapy is, in fact, inherently wild, and cannot be rendered safe in the way that regulation processes intend (Totton, in press).

Naturally enough, the characteristics of wild therapy shadow and at some points repeat what I identified in Chapter 4 as the qualities of Wild Mind. The project of wild therapy is to deepen and sustain contact with Wild Mind for both client and practitioner. Here are some of the key attributes I see in wild therapy:

- It recognises the interdependence of everything that exists.
- It is through-and-through relational.
- It identifies the role of the other-than-human and more-than-human in the therapeutic process.
- It supports, protects and defends liminality.
- It celebrates embodiment as a central aspect of our existence.
- It welcomes the spontaneous and the unknown, trusting what arises of its own accord.
- It seeks to transform fear-based defensive practice into undefensive, contact-based, adventurous practice.

I will look at these one by one – though they are of course deeply interconnected – and with each I will explore clinical aspects of the theme, how it manifests in real people in the therapy room. All of the examples from my own work are fictionalised.

THE INTERDEPENDENCE OF ALL BEINGS

Over and over in this book I have emphasised the importance of thinking *ecosystemically*. What does this mean in the context of the therapy session? Well it certainly contradicts treating the client as an isolated monad, whose experiences and problems relate purely or primarily to their internal reality. Most therapists would probably sign up to this, but its implications perhaps go further than many recognise.

A client or a therapist – a person – is part of several ecosystems. To begin with, there is the literal ecosystem of which the human species is part: a swollen yet at the same time drastically simplified global system where anything not directly devoted to serving humans is defined as a weed and liable to extermination, while even the client species on which we feed are also under constant environmental stress, as are we ourselves, and the entire top-heavy, rickety construction is in constantly increasing danger of unravelling. We are part of this; it affects us all the time, whether we know it or not, and therapy which ignores this context is a band playing on the deck of the Titanic.

Then there are the local ecosystems to which we may or may not consciously relate, but which still help shape our lives: the woods and waters and hills and valleys and gardens of our neighbourhood, along with all the beings that inhabit them, together with the buildings we spend time in, the roads we travel, the machines we use or which are used on us, the jobs we do, the air we breathe, the food we eat, the water we drink. All these help to form our *environment*, in a much deeper sense than we normally use the word: 'The conditions under which any person or thing lives or is developed: the sum-total of influences which modify and determine the development of life or character' (Oxford English Dictionary). Our context, our ground, our field of being. Also part of our field of being are the human social ecosystems to which we belong, and which encompass both the concrete and local, and the long-distance, or even abstract – our dead, for example, are also part of our social ecosystem, and the books we read or don't read, the TV we watch or don't watch, the ideas we take in or reject – and the system of power relations within which we exist.

As we have seen in Chapter 2, our relationship with all these features of our environment is a *mutual* one: we affect them as they affect us, in a condition of dependent co-arising. We are each an open system nested within other open systems, and with yet other open systems nested within us. This complex field of being is always present in the therapy room; when therapist and client meet, a new field is created from their relationship. And at any moment the action, the news, the creative spark of growth, can come from anywhere in the field. While I focus on the meaning of the client's words, the action can be taking place in their body sensation or in mine, in my 'random' memory or in theirs, in the weather or the bird at the window or the fly which insists on buzzing around our heads or the gurgle through which our bellies communicate with each other or the car door slamming in the street or the taste of something salty on the tongue. Whose tongue? Does it matter?

Many therapists are at least partially aware of this: it is a knowledge at the heart of therapy, though perhaps not always in its head. Projective identification, communicative countertransference, embodied countertransference, synchronicity – all these terms and more touch on what I am talking about, but at the same time often act to push away its full wild significance, to stick a label on something disturbing so that we can forget about it. Wild therapy does not forget, but nor does it 'get used to' it, preferring to remain in sacred awe. 'In your natural mind, there are no mysterious connections or synchronicities. There is no wilderness. Everything is part of you' (Mindell, 1993: 43).

A quite different way of talking about these things is in terms of 'the paranormal', or, to move even further away from acceptable labels, in terms of 'magic'. It is quite a relief to come out into the open like this! A related Freudian concept is 'the uncanny', which translates the German word *unheimlich*. In his essay on *The Uncanny*, Freud consults the dictionary, and discovers that *heimlich* – the word for what *unheimlich* is *not* – has two linked but opposed meanings: first of all, 'belonging to the house, not strange, familiar, tame, intimate, friendly, etc.'; but then also 'concealed, kept from sight, so that others do not get to know of or about it, withheld from others' (Freud, 1919: 222–3). The *unheimlich* is the undomesticated, that which is not concealed but out in the open: something which we would perhaps rather keep in the family, familiar, but which by its exposure is made strange and frightening. Something we all know goes on, but which domesticated people don't talk about. Even to themselves.

This is one way in which the issue of domestication enters into therapy (Totton, 2007: 394, see also Totton, 2003c). Clearly it is central to the therapeutic process to bring out into the open things which are generally kept private and secret. And equally clearly, a great deal of ambivalence surrounds this: as clients, we both want and don't want to reveal ourselves to the therapist, while as therapists we are also often equally unsure about being observed by the client. Freud talked of 'the feeling of repulsion in us which is undoubtedly connected with the barriers that rise between each single ego and the others' (Freud, 1908: 153). Wilfred Bion puts it like this: 'We all have to be aware that patients are frightened of us. They are afraid because they think we are ignorant, and they are possibly even more afraid that we are not ignorant' (Bion, 2000: 152).

Rather than papering over these fears – which, I want to emphasise, apply to the therapist as much as to the client – wild therapy tries to *engage with* them: to make them a consciously acknowledged part of the process, so it becomes apparent that they are only one version of a much wider anxiety which arises around the whole idea of interdependence. Through wild therapy our actions are revealed as details in a much larger pattern, steps in a collective dance in which we are partnered with the whole of existence (Totton, 2007: 398). This radical de-centring of our identity is terrifying, but ultimately exhilarating and awesome.

Clinical aspect

One sort of therapy situation to which this particularly applies is when we feel a pressure to be open about our own process. We are mostly trained to be extremely cautious about this – to protect ourselves, to ask internally 'where does this impulse come from?' What I have just said about interdependence, though, makes this sort of question a lot less relevant. The impulse has come from somewhere in the field; if it is a strong one that catches our attention, then it no doubt needs to be brought into expression – which will probably allow us to find out more about it.

As an example, a client saw me grimace slightly, and asked me what the matter was. Without going into detail I was open with them that I had been thinking about a situation with a friend which was upsetting me – and as I said this, I suddenly realised a connection with the client's issues which gave a helpful new angle on them. More important for the client, though, was that I had been thinking about someone else while listening to them, which replicated their continual sense of being tolerated but ignored.

A different sort of example is a client who, while sitting in the therapy room with me, set off car alarms in the street whenever they suppressed an anxious thought! We came to rely on this phenomenon to tell us what was going on in our work together. By the end of the therapy things had become a lot more peaceful for the neighbours.

RELATIONALITY

All the above implies a much deeper reading of the concept of relationality. 'It's the relationship, stupid' has been a motto of therapy for some time now, but this can often mean little more than the obvious platitude that therapy happens between two people, and how they get on makes a big difference. An ecosystemic approach to therapy means taking the view that each of us is *created by* the web of relationships that surrounds us, at the same time as we co-create that web. It is impossible to grasp an individual's issues and problems without a sense of their relational field – because their problems are problems of that field. So every client is the 'designated client' representing a relational field with a problem, a field which is having difficulties in growing.

In fact, the client is likely to be one of several 'designated clients' of that field who are seeking help in a variety of places, perhaps without realising that their individual problems are aspects of a larger issue, and everyone who is part of the field in question will be moved to try to do something about whatever is blocking it from growth. (Some of them may be moved to amplify the block as a way of helping it ultimately dissolve.) When we become someone's therapist, we become part of their relational field, part of the problem and part of the attempted solution; there is no possibility of, nor would there be any point in, our standing outside and observing in expert fashion. Even the systemic family therapists behind the one-way mirror are a part of the field, and if they are any good they know it. And in fact, since the nature of a field is that it has no actual edges, no point where its influence finally ceases, we are all to some extent part of each other's relational field even if we live on opposite sides of the planet.

This casts a different light on the work of therapy. Like everything else in the world, a therapy relationship is one detail of a huge collective process extending far in space and time, an open system in dependent co-arising with everything else. This allows us to relax in the knowledge that what happens between us – just like the rest of our lives – is in many ways conditioned by factors over which we have no control. What we can offer is our awareness and curiosity about what is happening in the room, as the visible tip of something much bigger.

Working with relationship is largely about tracking the action when it moves out of the client's location in space and into our own. It might move somewhere else altogether, but when it moves into our own being this is particularly wonderful and challenging. Wonderful because it allows us to directly *feel* and *taste* the quality of the client's experience, to know in our flesh and bones what their words are trying to tell us. Challenging, because it demands that we *use* ourselves and our experiences as resources in the therapy work, rather than simply identifying with them unquestioningly as one usually does – 'I feel irritated, so they must be irritating; I feel loving, so they must be loveable'. This requirement that we dis-identify from our own position is one of the reasons why doing therapy is good for the therapist.

But there is another and superficially opposite aspect of relationship in therapy, which is about simply committing to it. Freud said: 'The cure is effected through love' (Letter to Jung, 1906: Freud & Jung,

1974: 12), and he was right, though perhaps not in the way he intended: when we are able authentically to love a client, they become able to grow. However, often before we can love them, we need to hate them – or be angry, bored, indifferent, frightened, contemptuous. We don't necessarily need to express these feelings directly to them, and this would clearly often be destructive, but we do need to be able to own these feelings to *ourselves* (and our supervisors), and find some way to enable them to move and transform. And in doing this, of course, we will often find out how our feelings are an expression of the client's story. This applies also to some of the apparently loving feelings that we experience: they may be more about the client's story than about our actual heart connection with them.

Clinical aspect

Loving a client doesn't mean throwing oneself into intimacy with them. It means offering them heart contact, while at the same time holding a loving sense of what boundaries they need at any given moment. To illustrate this I will use the story of 'Angela', which I have partly told elsewhere (Totton, 2006).

Angela initially gave the impression of being enveloped in a force field labelled 'Keep away'. Over a three-year period of once-a-week therapy, what gradually emerged was an extreme psychological fragility which had been concealed under a fairly robust outer persona. Several times she hid from me behind a chair, or asked me to close my eyes because my gaze was too disturbing. Angela could be described, in fact, as a 'borderline personality', and as she very gradually came to trust me, she showed more and more of her fearful and rageful underlying experience.

As this developed, I started to sense more and more of an impulse in myself to hold her, and also a change in her own attitude. This crystallised decisively one day when she talked about a young boy who had turned up on her doorstep, and fantasised that he was 'looking for someone to adopt him'. I said spontaneously, 'I wonder whether you are looking to be adopted – maybe you want me to adopt you.' She said 'Yes, maybe – I'd like to be your daughter. What would it mean? Would I be able to be cuddled by you?' 'Yes, I guess you would,' I responded. 'We'll have to think about how that would work.'

Thinking about this interaction afterwards, I felt nervous about what I was embarking on, and whether I was promising more than I could deliver, but it also felt right. We spent the next ten or twelve sessions after this not touching, but exploring all the elements of this fantasy, and talking about what I could and could not offer, and what it would mean to us both. It would take much too long to describe the whole of this process, but eventually Angela was coming for two one-

and-a-half-hour sessions a week, and spending long parts of each session being held by me as we talked. The agreement was that on each occasion she could explicitly ask me to come and sit on the sofa with her, and ask for any touch she wanted – for example, holding her hand or putting my arm around her.

Looking back I see two main functions for this, in a sense, artificial approach. Firstly, it helped Angela be able to stay in therapy, while this deepened to the point where she could hardly endure the spaces between sessions, or the end point of each session, so powerfully restimulated was her experience of loneliness and deprivation. Touch offered her a literal and symbolic 'holding' which made it just barely possible for her to leave each time, and to come back despite her anger at the suffering she experienced in between. Secondly, it allowed her to explore her need for holding and her capacity to choose and control how and when it would happen. She had many early experiences of being overwhelmed and invaded by physical contact, and the contract which I have described made it possible for her to create a separation between comfort and invasion which had not previously been available to her.

I say more about the work with Angela below, when I discuss embodiment.

THE OTHER-THAN-HUMAN AND MORE-THAN-HUMAN

Human relationality is crucial to wild therapy, but in itself it doesn't go far enough. Therapy has so far tended to focus obsessively and autistically on human beings and their relationships with each other, to the exclusion of the rest of the universe. Many people – including many practitioners – would in fact assume that the entire subject matter of therapy is human relationship and our feelings about it. But we don't just have feelings about human beings. We have actual or potential relationships with animals, plants, trees, hills, rocks, rivers, winds, dreams, ghosts, fairies, spirits, and many other aspects of reality – and if we *don't* have such relationships, their absence will have a profound bearing on our states of difficulty and distress.

Jungian analysis is explicitly aware of this in a way that most other forms of therapy are not. In his memoir *Memories, Dreams, Reflections*, Jung writes:

> Because they are so closely akin to us, and share our unknowingness, I loved all warm-blooded animals, who have souls like ourselves and with whom ... we have an instinctive understanding. We experience joy and sorrow, love and hate, hunger and thirst, fear and trust in common – all the essential

features of existence with the exception of speech, sharpened consciousness, and science.

(Jung, 1963: 74)

And later:

> I could never free myself from the feeling that warm-blooded creatures were akin to us and not just cerebral automata. Consequently I cut demonstration classes [i.e. vivisections] whenever I could. ... My compassion for animals did not derive from ... philosophy, but rested on the deeper foundation of a primitive attitude of mind – on an unconscious identity with animals.
>
> (Ibid: 104)

We might argue with some of his formulations here, and wish that his sense of kinship could extend beyond mammals, but Jung goes a great deal further than most other therapists, and this has communicated itself to many of his followers (e.g. Hannah, 2005; Bernstein, 2005). Hence this aspect of wild therapy – a recognition of biophilia (Wilson, 1990), our inherent love of and need for the other-than-human – is strongly expressed in a lot of Jungian work.

Clinical aspect

Many people come to therapy at least partly because their connection with the other-than-human and the more-than-human has been weakened or damaged in some way. Sometimes they are conscious of this when they come, sometimes not. I have grown used to the emergence at some point in long-term therapy of two memories: one, of the client's childhood love for an older person, often a grandmother or grandfather; the other, of the client's childhood love for an other-than-human creature or a more-than-human reality. This will of course often be a pet, but sometimes it can be a horse, a sheep, or a cow, or even a zoo animal with whom they formed a loving connection, or it can be a tree, a pool, a waterfall, a hill, a rock, a view, the starry sky – some children are in love with the whole more-than-human world. Just like the relationship with the grandparent, these connections are experienced as *mutual*: the child felt *loved* as well as loving, the memory is deeply nurturing to them, and this often becomes part of what is re-experienced in therapy. If their childhood was difficult, they may well feel that their other-than-human carer protected them from despair (see also Wells et al, 1997: 127).

To recover this memory of biophilia if it has been forgotten or put to one side is often a profoundly moving event. It allows the person to 'find' and form relationships with the other-than-human and more-than-human in their current world – which may lead to major life changes. Recovering the memory may be accompanied by guilt for having abandoned these beings and this aspect of the world, as frequently happens in adolescence when human relationships become so urgent and demanding.

I am thinking in particular of a client who worked in IT and lived a highly urban lifestyle, going to the theatre and opera, eating out a lot, and frequently flying around the world with her female partner. During therapy she started talking about how, as a young woman, she had loved to walk alone in the mountains, loved to breathe the cold air and gaze into the endless spaces. As she grew up, she realised, she had transferred this exhilaration to the intellectual realm and used it in her work. But she discovered that she missed something profoundly important – the sense, as she put it, that the mountains were 'looking back at me', benignly and without judgement. She began to walk in the mountains again, and eventually took her partner with her; their relationship became deeper, and their lifestyle slowed down and became less consumption-focused.

The other main way in which the other-than-human features in therapy is of course the sense of loss and fear about environmental destruction which many clients bring – some consciously, many unconsciously. When this issue surfaces, it will certainly be 'overdetermined', as Freud puts it; in other words, an interpretation might validly go in a number of directions, for example finding childhood experiences or current personal matters related to this theme. The most useful approach is often to offer a 'thick description' of the various related meanings we perceive. But to leave out the direct connection to the environmental crisis would be a betrayal of both the client and the other-than-human itself.

Mary-Jayne Rust (2008b: 74–5) gives the example of a client with longstanding addiction to eating and other forms of consumption who brought the following dream:

> She is standing in the middle of lush rainforest as termites destroy the trees. Finally, she is left alone, all the forest has been consumed and its inhabitants are extinct.

The connections to the client's personal material are obvious. But Rust saw what was to her an equally obvious connection – unmentioned by the client – to the clear-cutting of the rainforest as part of the West's consumption of nature. When she raised this, the client became angry, accusing her of 'bringing her green agenda into the room'.

> I felt accused of bad therapy practice, of intruding upon 'her' world with 'my' concerns. I felt angry, and, in my swirl of intense feeling reactions, I could not find a satisfactory response. My thoughts ran along these lines: 'The green agenda belongs to all of us. What about our western cultural agenda that is in the room the whole time? It's this agenda that we really need to be concerned about ... this is the real *work against nature* ...'
> (Rust, 2008b: 75, original italics)

This was some years ago, and Mary-Jayne did not feel able at that time to find a way to insist on the relevance of her response: 'After all, I had been trained to interpret outer world issues in terms of the inner world' (ibid). But the rest of her paper makes clear that she would now stand firm for the environmental – and of course relational – significance of the dream and the interaction.

When we leave the therapy room and go out of doors with a client, or when we have a cat or dog with us in the therapy room, we are immediately opening the situation up to the other-than-human, as I discussed in Chapter 8.

LIMINALITY

In Chapter 4, we encountered the concept of 'liminal awareness', which exists 'on the threshold of consciousness ... focused on at-the-moment, point-blank sensory experience – as if the nub of life lay within that complex flux of collective sentient immediacy' (Sorenson, 1998: 82–3). In its openness to what surrounds it, liminal awareness is intensely vulnerable to toxic elements of its physical and psychological environment. 'When that openness gives way, empathy and rapport shrivel' (ibid: 83).

Sorenson initially believed that liminal awareness existed only in unconquered, undomesticated cultures – hence his original term, 'preconquest consciousness'. Gradually it became clear that elements of liminal awareness survive in every culture, including our own; as discussed in Chapter 4, individuals with strong liminal awareness have a hard time of it in Western culture, and many of them find their way to therapy – hence some of the responsibility that we bear as therapists for supporting, protecting and defending this awareness. It makes clients deeply vulnerable in two ways: because of what they pick up from their environment, and because the very fact of picking it up makes them get labelled as, and often feel, mad. Madness may be more tactfully described – 'over-sensitive', 'fragile' – but it all comes to much the same thing. Liminal clients need therapists who can both validate their experience, and help them to learn ways of coping better, and, of course, believing that one's experience is valid – more normal than what passes for 'normal', in fact – is itself a profound help in coping.

Again, what liminal clients – the liminal parts of all of us – do *not* need is for a therapist to tell us that what we are experiencing is really 'just' about our childhood. Certainly that part of us was traumatised in childhood, as the reality of the adult world impacted us, and often that impact will have been extreme – experiences of abuse often sensitise people to liminal reality, as we discussed in Chapter 4 (Bernstein, 2005). But the experiences we have in the here and now cannot be reduced to the effects of childhood; generally they are reflections of current reality, though sometimes this may take a bizarre form – liminal individuals have often sought out means of explaining their experiences, and sometimes they have found them far outside the mainstream.

I am very much including among liminal experiences those generally labelled 'paranormal': telepathy, clairvoyance, synchronicity and so on. As a leading expert on the paranormal in psychotherapy has written:

> Those of us who have taken a public position espousing the reality of psi events are aware of a lost battalion of people who have telepathic dreams [and, I would add, many other such experiences] ... which left them confused and concerned often to the point where they questioned their own sanity. To share it with others would risk rebuff. ... One hopes that greater knowledge and a deeper understanding on the part of the therapist ... will someday save these individuals from the pain and distress of a frustrated search for help.
>
> (Ullman, 2003: 43–4)

Liminal information – messages from the Web – consists not only of messages of danger and disaster. People in touch with this level of experience often bring great hope and beauty into the world. Therapy can support them in what they perceive, help them protect themselves from the toxic aspects of their psychic environment, and defend the reality and value of their perceptions against sceptical and cynical attack. An important book in this area is Elaine Aron's *The Highly Sensitive Person* (Aron, 1999), which in a very common-sense and matter-of-fact way validates and indeed gives a positive value to sensitivity. Speaking to the highly sensitive, Aron summarises:

> You pick up on the subtleties that others miss and so naturally you arrive quickly at the level of arousal past which you are no

> longer comfortable. The first fact about you could not be true without the second being true as well. It's a package deal, and a very good package.
>
> (Aron, 1999: 20)

I frequently lend this book to clients, as a starting point for learning to value qualities in themselves that have been attacked by those around them.

Clinical aspect

Clients with strong liminal awareness are often very afraid to disclose this in therapy. They have learnt to be cautious, especially with people in authority, which is how therapists are often seen. Before they will share their experience with us, they have to learn to trust us, and an important condition for this to happen is that we are honest with them about what is going on for us. Very often they will know about it anyway, though they may or may not be confident in this knowledge, but it generally appears in therapy in indirect form, for example as reports of dreams. I have many times had clients tell me a dream which reveals something about my current life situation, and I have learnt that it is important for me to validate this information – not necessarily by explaining what is going on for me, but more often by saying something like 'Actually, that's not too far off the mark,' and then going on to look at other associations with the dream.

In other areas this validation needs to go a lot further. As I said above, when people express their pain about the state of the world, the last thing they need is a tortuous explanation in terms of their personal history. The world *is* in a catastrophic state; other-than-human life, as well as human life, *is* suffering dreadfully. If we don't acknowledge this, how can we expect to work successfully with someone who feels it in their gut as an immediate reality?

The example that comes to mind is from quite a long time ago: during the first Gulf War, a client expressed the belief that the massive tonnage of bombs being dropped in Iraq was affecting her and other people's sleep in this country, and perhaps affecting the earth's axis. My first impulse, as an annoyingly rational white Western man, was to explain how that couldn't possibly be so. Luckily, I interrupted this habitual reflex, and said something like 'Yes, it *should* disturb our sleep'. Hearing my words, I connected much more deeply with my own horror about what was going on. Liminally aware clients are our teachers.

EMBODIMENT

At the same time as holding a clear connection with liminality – with the 'psychic' and 'spiritual' – wild therapy balances this with grounding in our embodiment. Liminally sensitive people have often been shocked out of their bodies, and may have difficulty tolerating a fully embodied awareness – it feels traumatic to them. Just as wild therapy leads over-grounded, 'hard-headed' people to explore liminal states of being, so it leads under-grounded people to explore earthy, fleshly states of being.

In parallel to this, at the same time as holding a clear sense of the otherness of other-than-human creatures, wild therapy also holds the awareness that we too are animals – and all the paradoxes and complexities of 'same' and 'other' that this implies (see Chapter 7). But one clear truth is that as animals, we have bodies – in fact, we *are* bodies; something that therapy has not always been eager to acknowledge. Working therapeutically in full awareness that there are two bodies in the room can be extremely challenging: those two bodies can have all sorts of powerful feelings about each other – can want to do all sorts of things to each other – and it would often be easier to keep a distance of dissociation around them. Easier, but less useful.

The slight *double entendre* of the previous paragraph was intentional: some of the things that bodies in therapy want to do to each other are indeed sexual. But the *idea* of sexual feelings is a good deal more prevalent than their actuality: in fantasy – often the fantasy of other people rather than the two participants – it can take over from all the many other impulses that will arise – to fight, to run away, to push and pull, to kick, to shake, to hold gently, to dance with, to tickle! Embodiment, sad to say, is often wholly identified with sexuality; this is one of the most stultifying aspects of our contemporary culture, and can make embodied therapy very difficult.

However it also gives therapy the task of opening out people's sense of bodily relationship to include more than sexuality: reminding them of the infinite sensuousness of embodied existence, the continuous relationship we build with the world through smell, taste, touch, sight and hearing, along with other more subtle sensory pathways like kinesthesia and proprioception. Embodied therapy invites clients to play with their bodily experience, to flirt with the sensory universe. Again with the *double entendre*! – because we can't open our bodily senses without addressing the sexual framing of bodily experience which stands in the way.

This sexualisation of the senses is equivalent to what Ferenczi (1933/1999b) called the 'confusion of tongues' between child and adult ways of being in the world. It is possible to have what we can call an erotic relationship with being alive, a constant renewal of joy and pleasure in existence, which in some ways is founded very literally on the physical act of breathing:

> A deep and enduring feeling of well-being and strength, a feeling of which one can become aware each time one directs attention to it, even when struggling with difficulties or when feeling bodily pain ... some of this feeling can be traced to the feelings of *pleasure in the genitals during expiration*.
>
> (Raknes, 1971: 166–7, original italics)

Many children live wholly or partly in this state of erotic aliveness; it flows into what Richard Sorensen calls 'sociosensuality'. As we grow up in Western culture, this erotic quality tends to become increasingly restricted to sexuality, and genital sexuality at that: our genitals are a sort of reservation where the erotic charge that is taboo elsewhere in life is allowed to make its home. Therapy which supports clients in exploring their embodied experience is bound to connect both with the taboo pleasure of embodied aliveness, and with the pain of loss that attaches to it. This is particularly intense when the focus is on embodied *relationship.*

When we start to connect more deeply with our embodiment, we discover there the inscriptions of culture: all the manifold ways in which our bodies have been shaped and trained, hurt and maimed, by domestication. As Mary Douglas says:

> The social body constrains the way the physical body is perceived. The physical experience of the body, always modified by the social categories through which it is known, sustains a particular view of society. There is a continual exchange of meanings between the two kinds of bodily experience so that each reinforces the categories of the other.
>
> (Douglas, 1973: 93)

Michel Foucault explores 'how the relations of power are able to pass materially into the very density of bodies without even having to be relayed by the representations of subjects' (Foucault, 1979: 69).The body we encounter in the therapy room is not some sort of primally free organismic entity: it is profoundly conditioned by domestication, and at the same time profoundly creative in its ways of relating to domestication (Totton, 2010). All of this complexity begins to unfold when we bring our awareness to bodily process.

Mary-Jayne Rust writes powerfully about how one dimension of embodied being, our relationship with eating, connects outward into ecological dimensions through the wider senses of consumption (see also Riebel, 2001), and about how embodied relating helps bring this into awareness:

> When we eat too much, or when we get caught in the grip of consumerism, we are longing for emotional nourishment. Therapy helps us to move from food to human relationship. But we need to move beyond this, to recognise our profound need to relate with the rest of nature; we are all hungry for a relationship with land, with place, with our bodies. This is nature hunger.
>
> ... If we are able to re-conceive the self as interconnected with body, soul and land, we might just be giving ourselves and clients the tools to recreate a life where self, nature and culture are reconnected, and where we can begin to live more lightly on the earth.
>
> (Rust, 2008b: 75)

Clinical aspect

Embodied relating is by far the most interesting and challenging aspect of embodied therapy. Useful and important as it is to help clients explore their internally focused bodily experience, there comes a point sooner or later when the energy flows into impulses that relate to the *other* – specifically, the therapist. They begin to feel an embodied urge to do something to *us.* As soon as this urge starts to flicker into existence, I try to support it and respond to it, gently enough that I don't scare it away. Often the first impulses are to fend me off, just as on a verbal and fantasy level the first transference feelings are usually resistance: the client wants to push me away, to turn aside from me, to jostle me and tussle with me. As we physically explore these interactions, they may develop into a scenario of defiance and standing one's ground; once the client has experienced their own power to say No to me, the desire and capacity for a more interactive physicality may develop, an exploration of how our bodies can cooperate and play with each other.

In traditional terms, what I have just described is embodied work on the Oedipal terrain. With some clients, like 'Angela' whom I discussed above, the work is initially pre-Oedipal, exploring the possibility of being held and nurtured, but this too can develop in a more reciprocal direction. In the work which Angela and I did together, there came a point when her experience of my touch was no longer wholly in the register of infancy; she began, and *needed* to begin, to have specifically sexual feelings in response to our physical contact. Not surprisingly, some of this was mirrored in me; the quality of my erotic countertransference also shifted. This was frightening for both of us.

Interestingly, though, it was precisely the depth and solidity of our touch-relationship which enabled us to weather the crisis and actually to *explore* our feelings, on a level of sensation and fantasy, without at any point crossing the boundaries which the situation needed. We moved, in other words, from enacting mother–infant dynamics to enacting father–daughter dynamics; just as Angela had been able to nourish and heal herself on the infant level, she was able to heal the absence in her life of a father who could appreciate and respond to her sexuality without exploiting it (Samuels, 1993: 152–3). This work was far deeper – and, of course, far scarier – when channelled through the medium of touch.

SPONTANEITY

> The hunter does not look tranquilly in one determined direction, sure beforehand that the game will pass in front of him [masculine *sic* throughout]. The hunter knows that he does not know what is going to happen ... thus he needs to prepare an attention which does not consist in riveting itself on the presumed but consists precisely in not presuming anything and in avoiding inattentiveness. It is a 'universal' attention, which does not inscribe itself on any point and tries to be on all points.
>
> (Ortega y Gasset, 1943/1995: 138)

This splendid quotation is a very close parallel with Freud's concept of the therapist's 'evenly suspended attention', which seems to me an essential aspect of wild therapy:

> The technique ... consists simply in not directing one's notice to anything in particular and in maintaining the same 'evenly-suspended attention' (as I have called it) in the face of all that one hears. ... as soon as anyone deliberately concentrates his attention to a certain degree, he begins to select from the material before him; one point will be fixed in his mind with particular clearness and some other will be correspondingly disregarded, and in making this selection he will be following his expectations or inclinations. This, however, is precisely what must not be done.
>
> (Freud, 1912: 111–12)

It is also reminiscent of Carlos Castaneda's (or Don Juan's) discussion of 'stalking': 'The first principles of stalking is that a warrior stalks himself, with ruthlessness, cunning, patience and sweetness' (Castaneda, 1987: 101). And: 'For a warrior there is no end to the mystery of being, whether being means being a pebble, or an ant or oneself. That is a warrior's humbleness. One is equal to everything' (Castaneda, 1972: 8). Each of these passages from Ortega y Gasset, Freud and Castaneda has a very different tone and mood, but I think that each is telling us about the importance of relaxed spontaneity, of being alert, open and responsive to whatever happens with as little preconception as possible.

Like most significant therapy skills, spontaneity is both an important part of being able to relate *with* the client, and also something that we are in effect modelling *for* the client: lack of spontaneity is often something that leads people to seek therapy, since without it their life lacks savour and richness. Also like most significant therapy skills, however, it is not something that one can directly learn! It is what Amy Mindell (2003) calls a 'metaskill', a life attitude which informs technique but is itself beyond technique. The two sides of spontaneity are being *receptive* to what is, and being *responsive* to what is – finding the authentic gesture, the authentic heartfelt act, and committing to it.

Many clients will reserve their trust, reserve themselves, unless and until they experience this authenticity in us. Much useful work can of course take place without it – work on their *mis*trust, if you like, on all their previous experiences of missing authentic encounter. Without authenticity we can explore the wound, and the client can learn how to manage their woundedness better, but we will never reach the sort of contact that facilitates deep change. And for the therapist to respond spontaneously, without monitoring herself, is one way to guarantee authenticity.

Clinical aspect

A commitment to spontaneity means that once in a while one may do something that is momentarily shocking even to oneself. At times this seems the only way to break through an impasse in the work: some clients' emotional fields are able to create a deeply stuck place that draws the therapist in completely, crippling our ability to think creatively. So it is necessary *not* to think in order to jump out of the system (Kurtz, 1985: 15/4–15/6).

One client succeeded in having this effect on me, which was obviously deeply frustrating for him too. All his attempts – often very creative – to break us out of the impasse were simultaneously effective in immobilising me even further: for example, he told me that he couldn't tolerate my silences, so I found myself trying to fill every space with words, which simply made me too self-conscious to do anything authentic. He continued to goad me in ways which I now see expressed his own wish for authentic relationship – although at the same time he found this unbearably invasive. One day he was getting at me in a nitpicking way – I can no longer remember what about – and without thought, I exclaimed, 'Fuck off!'

My own immediate response to this was horror and shame – I was deeply invested in being helpful to this wounded person, and now I had done an unforgiveable thing. The client's response, though, was unequivocal and embodied: for several minutes he laughed and laughed! Much of the tension of the previous months of sitting together in stuckness was released in this deep laughter, and although our relational problems were not resolved, they were considerably eased. I would say that the client was enabled to trust me more by seeing that I trusted him, and myself, enough to be spontaneous.

Had I planned this, of course, it would certainly have misfired severely. It was not a laborious example of 'paradoxical injunction', but an effortless moment of non-thinking, though one anchored in many years of thinking about and doing therapy. We cannot plan to be spontaneous; it is a matter of throwing ourselves into the unknown. So I will not be starting the 'Fuck off' school of psychotherapy – though I think many therapeutic innovations have come out of moments like this.

UNDEFENSIVE PRACTICE: BOUNDLESSNESS

> The inability to tolerate empty space limits the amount of space available.
>
> (Bion, 1992: 304)

The 'Fuck off' vignette above is, I believe, a good example of undefensive practice – as are many spontaneous responses. In Chapter 6, I explored and critiqued the concept of 'therapeutic boundaries', arguing that while some clients at some moments need firm boundaries, other clients, or the same clients at a different point, have a much more important need for authenticity, even when this means certain boundaries are crossed. I suggested that an overriding emphasis on boundaries inevitably creates a posture of 'defensive practice' which makes trust and liking – in *either* direction – very difficult to achieve.

What is the opposite of being boundaried? One answer is 'unboundaried'; another is 'boundless'. Undefensive practice, I suggest, draws on a sense of boundlessness – a sense of abundance, of space, of attention, of care. This is therapy as a 'giving environment' (Bird-David, 1990), in the way that indigenous cultures experience the world as a giving environment, 'a benign spiritual home' (Barker, 2006: 58). However difficult the experiences of therapy may be, boundlessness and undefensiveness create a ground of safety and trust.

As I have suggested above, every therapeutic relationship needs to be a *relationship*: a place where two subjectivities meet, with all the difficulty and painfulness this implies, but also with a developing willingness and capacity to tolerate the other person's otherness. For a therapist to hold careful boundaries because they believe they *must*, or because they are afraid of the uncontrollability of closeness, cripples the potential for relatedness, but for a therapist to hold such boundaries as an honouring of the client's woundedness is itself relational. The only valid generalisation about relationships is that they are each unique, and therapists are artisans of relationship, co-creating one-off works with their clients.

To sum up: a practitioner who cannot offer her clients boundaries is dangerous. But a practitioner who cannot offer her clients boundlessness is useless.

Clinical aspect

It isn't easy to find ways to illustrate a theme which is so subtle yet so fundamental. I think the most useful thing is for me to say something about how my approach to these issues has developed and where I am now about them. When I started my therapy practice, like most new therapists – although I was trained in a relatively 'wild' and unorthodox style – I was very serious about the parameters of time, money, cancellations and so on: they were my safety net, or my comfort blanket, in this intensely scary new world. At the same time, though, I came into therapy from a background of libertarian political activism, which predisposed me to take the client's views seriously, and to try to adapt to their needs if I could.

Looking back, this meant that I combined a shallow rigidity with a shallow permissiveness! At times I painted myself into all sorts of unnecessary corners, similar to the way that inexperienced parents do – drawing a line in the sand about things that really didn't matter very much, then suddenly crumbling and agreeing to change arrangements without thinking the implications through, often ending up in difficulties as a result. As a young man it was also too easy for me to blur the line between exploring bodily erotic feeling and flirting.

Realising that I was in a dangerous situation, I found myself a psychoanalytically oriented supervisor. It was enormously useful for me to have a firm, coherent, rigorous schema against which to test any variations I felt drawn to make. I was also extremely lucky to have a supervisor who, although herself pretty orthodox in her boundaries, told me 'You can do an awful lot of things in therapy *so long as you are able to talk about it*' – to talk through the effects and implications both with the client and in supervision.

It has become clear to me over the years that my own insecurity was what caused most of my problems: on the whole, difficulties arose not so much from *what* I did, as from the underlying anxiety behind it. As I have become more secure and more relaxed as a therapist, I have become more able to experiment without anxiety. So now my default position is to be open to anything a client suggests about frequency, timing, venue and so on: whatever is practically possible for me I am willing to try, because I trust that I will be aware of its effects on both myself and the client, and able to find ways to talk about it. Similarly with money, I will agree to what the client feels they can afford so long as I can afford it too, especially if their circumstances change while we are already working together. My only stipulation is that if the client suggests something I have never thought about before, I want to sleep on it before I make a decision!

What I am trying to say is that rigid systems are very useful indeed in soothing the natural anxiety that one feels as an inexperienced therapist. And, of course, they will also often soothe anxiety in an inexperienced client; some clients are much more comfortable with a conventional and predictable structure. Recently I asked a fairly new client whether we could rearrange our appointment for the next week because I had a problem about being there at the usual time. They agreed willingly enough – but forgot to turn up at the agreed new time, had to check back with me twice about the time of the subsequent appointment, and took another couple of weeks before they settled down again. I apologised for disrupting our work, and made a note not to do it again.

Many clients, however, feel very differently – they are uncomfortably restricted by rigid arrangements, which they see as being for the benefit of the therapist (as indeed they often are). And now that I no longer feel a personal need for this sort of structure so as to avoid boundarilessness, I can increasingly come from the place of boundlessness, of generosity and humanity. Resting in boundlessness, my state of being has the effect of drawing my client's being into resonance, so that at our best moments we can move away from domesticated reality and explore the wild open spaces together.

As I said at the start of this chapter, wild therapy is an attitude of mind, rather than a bag of tricks. Hopefully I have managed to give some sense of what I mean by this attitude of mind, and of its implications for practice. As I also said at the start, many of these things are already being done, perhaps by you who are reading this book, and many of them I have learnt about from other practitioners. Wild therapy is already a reality – which may benefit from having a name.

10

Living Wild

> It is, perhaps, the darkest pain of the contemporary human that we are losing everything of true worth from this world. In all the four directions, the animals are leaving. Through our failed humanity they are vanishing.
>
> (Hogan, 1998: 15)

Of all the quotations I have gathered in the process of writing this book, the one above from Linda Hogan speaks most powerfully to my own feelings of grief and shame about what is happening to the world. This sense of the loss of 'everything of true worth' is the context for what I have written, and the ultimate reason for wanting to write it. In the face of such loss, and in the knowledge that it cannot now be averted, we have to ask ourselves: What is still important? What is worth doing?

A part of my own answer is that it is worth bearing witness. But beyond that, no matter what is lost, something will almost certainly remain; which gives us a responsibility to preserve and pass on what we can to that future world. It seems to me that we can expect one of two negative likelihoods: social collapse in parallel with ecosystem collapse, or a hi-tech dystopia which maintains some human life in a planetary wasteland. I am not despairing: there is still a possibility of positive change in time to rescue some – not all – of the abundance we were born into. And the planet will survive. But for both those futures which seem to me most probable, though they are very different from each other the work required of us is much the same: to enable the survival not only of humans and other beings, but of *attitudes* and *ideas*: to establish a tradition of right living which can survive physical and/or psychological hardship and privation, and seed a new and better culture in the future. It seems to me that such a culture would be based on an ethic of non-interference, deriving from the experience of wild mind.

As Kim Stanley Robinson says:

> We are in the process of rethinking the future, of inventing a new consensus vision of what it might be. This is happening all across contemporary culture, in a great variety of forms, with names like the environmental movement, green political parties, deep ecology, the land ethic, landscape restoration, sociobiology, sustainable agriculture, ecofeminism, social ecology, bioregionalism, animal liberation, steady-state economics. All these movements contain efforts to reimagine a sustainable human society.
>
> (Robinson, 1994: 10)

I believe that a certain kind of psychotherapy, which in this book I call wild therapy, can contribute powerfully to the new culture which is trying to be born out of the wreckage. I don't think therapy is the only, or even the most important, aspect of the new culture; it just happens to be the one I know most about, the one to which I have devoted a lot of my life and energy, and the one which hopefully I can influence to develop in a certain direction.

HIGH DREAMING

The two possible worlds outlined above are what Arnold Mindell calls my 'low dreams' of our collective future. They need to be balanced by a 'high dream' (Mindell, 1995: 199–201): what does the future that I *want* look like, the sustainable human society where we live from wild mind? Luckily I don't need to envision this from scratch: it is closely similar to the society described in Ursula Le Guin's magnificent novel, *Always Coming Home* (Le Guin, 1988). Le Guin describes a wild human culture (part of a network of small-scale wild human cultures) with a crucial difference from existing indigenous societies: it comes *after*, rather than *before*, industrial-technological civilisation.

The specific group Le Guin imagines, the Kesh, refer to domesticated society as *tavkach*, 'the City of Man':

> This word may be translated as civilisation, or as history.
>
> The historical period, the era of human existence that followed the Neolithic era for some thousands of years in various parts of the earth, and from which prehistory and 'primitive cultures' are specifically excluded, appears to be what is referred to by the Kesh phrases, 'the time outside', 'when they lived outside the world,', and 'the City of Man'. ...This period in which we live, our civilisation, Civilisation as we know it, appeared in Valley thought as a remote region, set apart from the community and continuity of human/animal/earthly existence – a sort of peninsula

> sticking out from the mainland, very thickly built upon, very heavily populated, very obscure, and very far away.
>
> (Le Guin, 1988: 152–3)

Le Guin's Kesh people exist 'inside the world', free from the alienation of domesticated civilisation. Although they forage, they also use agriculture and live in permanent settlements: as I suggested in Chapters 4 and 5 agriculture and settlement do not necessarily, although they usually do historically, imply the loss of wildness and living 'outside the world'. The Kesh have a rich and complex culture, resting on a simple but efficient and sustainable technological base; they also have access if they want it to the whole information trove of humanity, the 'City of Mind'. At the same time, they exist in both practical and symbolic community with the other-than-human and the more-than-human.

THERAPY FOR THE WORLD

This sounds impossibly ideal; but in another sense we are not so far away from it. The biggest material obstacle is our over-population, which can be brought down given time (if it is not brought down suddenly through disaster). We have the ability to live sustainably, given the will, and an appropriate economic system which does not depend on continual expansion (Booth, 1998). All that it will really take to come back inside the world – all, I say, as if this were easy! – is a change of heart.

Changes of heart are what therapy specialises in; and ever since it began, therapy has been trying to help the human world change its heart, by offering it collective as well as individual therapy. As Andrew Samuels says, this is 'inflated, even oracular stuff' – but he balances this by arguing that 'it is also imaginative, creative, and ... in tune with the world's desire to be treated' (Samuels, 1993: 29). The only problem, he points out, is that like many individual clients who at first seem enthusiastic, the world doesn't turn up for therapy.

> So – here are the depth psychologists. Ready, willing and able to treat the world. ... They are pretty sure that the world has asked for therapy or analysis. But ... the world has not shown up for its first session. The world is ambivalent about its therapy, suspicious of its political therapists, reluctant to be a patient ....
>
> (Samuels, 1993: 30)

We have seen more than sufficient explanation for this reluctance in previous chapters. Most human beings are deeply traumatised, acutely or sub-critically, personally and/or by inheritance, and living in a society which as a whole is also traumatised; and trauma gives rise to dissociation and denial together with addiction to substitute satisfactions. In Chapter 5 I traced this trauma to its origins, mythical or otherwise, in what I have called the Neolithic bargain, when we exchanged freedom and wellbeing for safety and increasingly damaged attachment. The structures of domination which were thus created now reach very deeply into our psyches and bodies; in viral fashion, they seek to take over and reshape every new social formation that arises. 'Authority is never abolished but constantly reinscribes itself in new places. ... Every new path to freedom creates new, sometimes even more intractable, obstacles to freedom' (Bernstein, 2002: 7).

The most crucial step we could potentially take towards wildness would be to move towards social justice and genuine democracy. Besides being a huge gain in its own right, this would support gradual population reduction (people have less children when they feel more secure), release the spontaneous flow of creative social energy, and begin the process of healing individual and societal trauma, thus liberating attention for the other-than-human and more-than-human. If resources are distributed equitably, we will all have to live simply and cheaply: according to the internet, global income averages out at perhaps $7,000 each – roughly the per capita income in Mexico, Chile or Latvia (*Boston Globe*, 2007). This gives an extremely rough measure (since some of that income is unsustainable) of what we have available: not much, but enough, so long as social capital is devoted to supporting all individuals equally.

The cultural gain from social justice, however, would be immeasurable, and would begin to free our attention to deal with the environmental crises we face. In advanced capitalist culture, nearly all of us are on the edge of being unable to cope, unable to do what we have to do and process what we have to process while also handling our internal emotional states. And a further level of this is cultural overwhelm, the result of many generations of damage through war, famine, disease, and abuse. We are all deeply distressed and struggling to cope; and we bring this distress to environmental issues just as we do to everything else.

Individuals seek to protect a fragile bubble of personal reality which makes their life bearable. Some key elements of this are fun, freedom, status-based identity, and, most fundamentally, relaxation. People like me who talk about environmental catastrophe appear to threaten all of these elements, which in many of their most common forms – consumption, travel, entertainment – require high carbon levels. And most crucially, such information seems to threaten *relaxation*: the human need for downtime, empty mental space, periods when we are not anxious and planning for survival. Even if we can only obtain relaxation through getting drunk and watching TV, it is still deeply precious, and we will protect it at all costs.

Hence for large numbers of people it is not climate change itself which appears as a danger, but rather *news* of climate change, which might break into their fragile bubble of emotional survival. They respond to this news as mammals respond to any threat to survival: with the well-known triad of fight/flight/freeze (Levine, 1997: 95ff; Ogden et al, 2006). In particular, many people *freeze*: they use the response reserved for desperate situations where we are completely helpless, and our best option is to turn off, go into trance and hope to be overlooked.

This is closely related to *dissociation* (Levine, 1997: 136–41; Ogden et al, 2006: 36ff): an important part of the mammalian repertoire, but one which gets drastically overused in modern urban environments, where we often need it just to get through the morning rush hour. In some contexts it is a healthy, pro-survival talent, an ability to enter dreaming and insulate ourselves from stressful input; but unfortunately this doesn't help with the situation we are currently facing. In some ways climate change *deniers* are a better prospect for environmentalists than climate change *ignorers*: at least they are mobilised enough around the issue to fight the information rather than freeze or run away. (Activists, of course, are also using a 'fight' strategy to cope with overwhelm – which makes them vulnerable to collapse and burnout.)

Until people are willing and able to tolerate the feelings which information about environmental crisis sets off in them – feelings like fear, grief, rage, despair – it will be very difficult for them to absorb that information, and therefore to act on it. So how can we help them (and ourselves) to come out of overwhelm? The first thing to do when faced with overwhelm in a therapeutic situation is to point out to the person that this is what is going on: 'It's all a bit much, isn't it?' 'It's hard for you to take things in just now.' Just on its own, this helps people contact reality and find some solid ground. Then we need to build a sense of safety which will allow them to access their embodied emotions.

This approach could be applied to collective overwhelm around climate change and other environmental disaster. If people feel threatened by the *news* of danger, then redoubling our efforts to spread the news will actually be counterproductive. As 'therapists to the world', we need to find ways of helping people become aware that they are in overwhelm, under the bedclothes with their fingers in their ears. We also need a parallel strategy of helping people reconnect with their innate love and awe for the other-than-human and more-than-human, so that they start to feel revulsion against their mistreatment.

These strategies are supportive rather than aggressive; tuning in to the human capacity for wild mind, rather than driving it underground. However, they are hard to apply in a situation which screams 'EMERGENCY' as soon as we let it into our consciousness. My experience is that even at conferences and workshops specifically intended to provide a safe space for our emotional reactions to environmental crisis, many participants are to some extent sleepwalking, using the event as an opportunity to work out personal issues. Full-time activists may tend either to burn out or to become numb and hard-bitten, in a similar way to hospital staff or fire brigade workers.

And, of course, change is not only a matter of individual or even collective consciousness. There are huge structures of power and money which necessarily oppose the wilding of the world, because any such process will destroy them. We may despise political leaders for their inaction around climate change, but few of them are fools: they know that capitalism can only survive through constant expansion, and that the consequences if capitalism abruptly fails will be disastrous – for humans – on a level similar to the consequences of climate change. At the height of the recent banking crisis, there were apocalyptic newspaper headlines talking about how it was 'wrecking the world': partly, perhaps, a displacement of anxiety around climate change, but also a not inaccurate recognition of how completely we are now dependent on the capitalist system. Only those of us deeply committed to the other-than-human could easily choose the collapse of capitalism over the collapse of the ecosphere.

Knowing all this, it is very hard to map an effective way forward. Luckily, though, we also know that *things will happen of their own accord*, as newly emergent features of the complex web of being, not following any intention or plan. This may not be enough; but we can relax in the knowledge that it will be as good as it is possible for it to be. To repeat my favourite passages from the *Tao Te Ching* (which I think are my favourites because I need a lot of reminding):

> Do you think you can take over the universe and improve it?
> I do not believe it can be done.
> ...
> The world is ruled by letting things take their course.
> It cannot be ruled by interfering.
> (Feng & English, 1972: Sections 29 and 48)

This is both a frustrating reality, and an enormous relief. If we accept the truth of it, it comforts us, stops us wasting our time trying to control the future, and at the same time shows us our path, which is to *envision* and *live* the future we desire.

BACK TO THE FUTURE

> Despite the constant threat of violence and war, despite the sickness of the planet and its political systems, never before has the restlessness for freedom and democracy been so widespread throughout the world. ... This world of rage and love is the real foundation on which the constituent power of the multitude rests.
> (Hardt & Negri, 2006: 353)

Let's return, then, to the question of what this desirable future is like and how we might begin to live it now. How complex can a culture be and still be sustainable? This seems like an appropriate question, but I suggest that it actually isn't: the wild world is far more complex than any human culture. The problem has been that culture is an *over-simplification* of the world, just as a garden is an over-simplification of wildness. A better question, therefore is: Can we humans build a culture which lives up to and expresses the complexity of the world we inhabit?

Such a culture would have to give up hierarchy and control as its structure and goal (see Bookchin, 1982/2005). As we saw in Chapter 6, top-down hierarchy distorts reality and blocks authentic communication. Similarly, the attempt to control reality by clearing away its more recalcitrant aspects tends to damage the reality one is trying to control (one example is the over-use of antibiotics and disinfectants, creating resistant bacteria and weak or hypervigilant immune systems). Giving up hierarchy and control, which has been our primary cultural mode since the Neolithic, would be an epochal shift for humanity, and it is hard to see this happening as a deliberate choice.

However there are aspects of spontaneous cultural evolution which give grounds for hope. Michael Hardt and Antonio Negri describe how the processes set in train by globalisation and its resistance are creating a situation which exposes the hollowness of sovereignty and rule:

> Suddenly, with our new perspective, it appears that not only is it not necessary for the one to rule, but in fact that the one never rules! ... Instead of an external authority imposing order on society from above, the various elements present in society are able collaboratively to organize society themselves.
> (Hardt & Negri, 2006: 337)

It is always the ruled, the people who do the necessary jobs, who have made society function; the real trick of rulership is to obscure this reality (even from the rulers themselves). But the veil is perhaps beginning to slip.

As Hardt and Negri recognise, information technology is a demonstration case of how 'unitary control is not necessary for innovation and ... on the contrary, innovation requires common resources, open access, and free interaction' (Hardt & Negri, 2006: 337). The internet has given rise to the potential for a complex, autonomous network of wild information ('Information wants to be free', as the slogan goes), allowing negotiating, decision-making and exchange transactions which are clean of compulsion and exploitation (some initial references on this complex area, from a variety of ideological perspectives, are Veneris, 1990; Bousquet & Wills, 2002; Buchanan, 2003; Rheingold, 2003; Downes, 2009; Shirky, 2009). As always, this innovation is double-edged, creating new opportunities for control at the same time as new opportunities for freedom.

Freedom from control, in our current situation, goes beyond the traditional anarchist focus on the oppressive *other*: we need to recognise the message of ecological systems, that we ourselves as individuals are not and cannot be 'in control', but that it is the complexity of the collective and its multifold interactions which generates change. Hardt and Negri use the image of:

> an orchestra with no conductor – an orchestra that through constant communication determines its own beat and would be thrown off and silenced only by the imposition of a conductor's central authority. ... We produce and innovate together only in networks. If there is an act of genius, it is the genius of the multitude.
>
> (Hardt & Negri, 2006: 338)

As we saw in Chapter 2, Wolf Singer (2005) uses the same image of an orchestra without a conductor to describe the brain.

This is the basis for an ecological society, founded on ecological consciousness. And, paradoxically, there is little that we as individuals can do to create it deliberately! If it is going to come into existence, then it must be already brewing, already cooking in many thousands of places around the planet; slowly assembling itself out of millions of local acts of creativity and resistance. As Ursula Le Guin has one of her characters say:

> You cannot buy the Revolution. You cannot make the Revolution. You can only be the Revolution. It is in your spirit, or it is nowhere.
>
> (Le Guin, 1975: 250)

SOMETIMES LIKE FALLING SNOW

> The great Creator told us, I'm going to teach you these songs, but before I teach you these songs, I'm going to break your heart.
>
> (Larry Eddy, Chemehuevi Paiute Salt Singer, quoted in Hebner & Plyler, 2010: 17)

In Chapter 4, I quoted extensively from the work of Darrell Posey, an anthropologist who worked for many years with the Kayapó people of the Upper Amazon. In his published work, Posey makes great efforts to stay within the accepted academic paradigm as he describes Kayapó culture and his relationship with it. After Posey's death, however, his colleague Michael Balick wrote of how Posey, in England, had previously sensed the death of his Kayapó teacher, Beptopoop, when 'as he put it, Betopoop's spirit flew over the pond' at Posey's house in Oxford. '"I felt he was there,"' Posey said. '"I felt he was with me and I knew he had come to impart his last teachings and say goodbye"' (Balick, 2006: xvi).

This is a very different sort of relationship between wild and domesticated humans from the accepted mainstream one, where we are the experts who study indigenous culture from the outside. It is clear that Posey was *changed* by his contact with Beptopoop and his people; as, no doubt, they were changed by their contact with him (Posey helped them gain a political voice on the future of the Amazon region). As a result of this experience of Beptopoop's spirit flying over the pond, Posey said, '"during these past few years I have begun to understand this next level of his knowledge"' (Balick, 2006: xvi). Whether through contact with indigenous peoples, or with the other-than-human and more-than-human, or simply with our own wild mind, we in the Western mainstream urgently need to understand 'this next level', which we might for example call spirit, and which draws us into a different relationship with the world.

Several years ago I wrote this poem (see Totton, 1984/2004: 157, where it is incorporated into a longer work):

> *Song of the Nomads*
> Don't settle
> for less
> than love
> (and love keeps moving on)

In some ways this book, and my life as a therapist and as a human being, have been an exploration of the poem's implications. Wild therapy is un-settling, for both therapist and client: it moves us out of settlement, makes us leave our comfortable home and wander, following love. Wild foragers need to keep moving so as to find food, but their need for movement surely cannot be reduced to economics. Wild humans need to keep moving in order to find love, in all its many forms – most fundamentally, the love of existence, our love for it and its love for us.

Let me end, then, with a simple and profound message that sums up everything we and our descendants need to know: a statement I have already quoted in Chapter 8, in which the Inuit shaman Najagneq describes what he learnt on his initiatory vision quest, while fasting out on the ice (Osterman, 1927: 128):

> I heard the voice of nature itself speak to me, and it spoke with the voice of a gentle motherly solicitude and affection. Or it sounded sometimes like children's voices, or sometimes like falling snow, and what it said was, 'Do not be afraid of the universe'.

References

Abram, D (1997) *The Spell of the Sensuous: Perception and language in a more-than-human world.* New York: Vintage Books.

Anderson, K (1997) A walk on the wild side: A critical geography of domestication. *Progress in Human Geography, 21*(4), 463–85.

Andrews, R (1992) Western science learns from native culture. *The Scientist, 6*(6), 6. Online at http://www.the-scientist.com/article/display/11264/#ixzz0w6YNcV71

Angell, J (1994) An empowering growth experience for women. *Women & Therapy, 15*(3 & 4), 85–99.

Apffel-Marglin, F (1990) Smallpox in two systems of knowledge. In F Apffel-Marglin & SA Marglin (Eds) *Dominating Knowledge: Development, culture and resistance* (pp. 102–43). Oxford: Clarendon Press.

Apffel-Marglin, F & Rivera, VJ (1995) *Regeneration in the Andes*. Quebec: Intercultura; Institute of Montreal.

Ardener, E (1989) Belief and the problem of women. In *The Voice of Prophecy and Other Essays* (pp. 72–85). Oxford: Blackwell. (Original work published 1977)

Armstrong, J (1995) Keepers of the earth. In T Roszak, ME Gomes & AD Kanner (Eds) *Ecopsychology: Restoring the earth, healing the mind* (pp. 316–24). San Francisco: Sierra Club Books.

Arneach, L (2008) The first fire. In *Long-Ago Stories of the Eastern Cherokee* (pp. 34–7). Charleston, SC: History Press.

Aron, EN (1999) *The Highly Sensitive Person: How to thrive when the world overwhelms you*. London: Thorsons.

Bagemihl, B (1999) *Biological Exuberance: Animal homosexuality and natural diversity*. New York: St Martin's Press.

Balick, M (2006) Co-editor's note. In DA Posey & MJ Balick (Eds) *Human Impacts on Amazonia: The role of traditional ecological knowledge in conservation and development* (pp. xv–xvi). New York: Columbia University Press.

Banuri, T (1990) Modernization and its discontents: A cultural perspective on the theories of development. In F Apffel-Marglin & SA Marglin (Eds) *Dominating Knowledge: Development, culture and resistance* (pp. 73–101). Oxford: Clarendon Press.

Barad, K (2003) Posthumanist performativity: Toward an understanding of how matter comes to matter. *Signs: Journal of Women in Culture and Society, 28*(3), 801–31.

Barker, G (2006) *The Agricultural Revolution in Prehistory: Why did foragers become farmers?* Oxford: Oxford University Press.

Barnard, J (2000) Oregon's monster mushroom is world's biggest living thing. *The Independent on Sunday*, August 6th. Online at http://www.independent.co.uk/news/science/oregons-monster-mushroom-is-worlds-biggest-living-thing-710278.html
Baron, D (2004) *The Beast in the Garden: A modern parable of man and nature*. New York: WW Norton.
Bates, WH (2008) *Better Eyesight Without Glasses*. New Delhi: Orient Books. (Original work published 1920)
Bateson, G (1973) *Steps to an Ecology of Mind*. London: Paladin.
Bateson, G (1980) *Mind and Nature: A necessary unity*. London: Fontana/Collins.
Bauman, Z (1991) *Modernity and Ambivalence*. Ithaca, NY: Cornell University Press.
Bauman, Z (1992, November 13) The solution as problem. *Times Higher Education Supplement, 1045*, 25.
Bekoff, M (2009) Animal emotions, wild justice and why they matter: Grieving magpies, a pissy baboon, and empathic elephants. *Emotion, Space and Society, 2*(2), 1–4.
Bekoff, M & Pearce, J (2010) *Wild Justice: The moral lives of animals.* Chicago: Chicago University Press.
Benjamin, J (1998) *Shadow of the Other: Intersubjectivity and gender in psychoanalysis*. London: Routledge.
Berger, J (1980) Why look at animals? In *About Looking* (pp. 1–28). New York: Pantheon.
Beringer, A & Martin, P (2003) On adventure therapy and the natural worlds: Respecting nature's healing. *Journal of Adventure Education and Outdoor Learning, 3*(1), 29–40.
Berman, E (2007) Call of the wild. *American Journal of Psychoanalysis, 67*, 211–20.
Berne, E (1968) *Games People Play*. Harmondsworth: Penguin.
Bernheimer, R (1952) *Wild Men in the Middle Ages: A study in art, sentiment and demonology.* Cambridge, MA: Harvard University Press.
Bernstein, C (2002) Electronic pies in the poetry skies. In M Bousquet & K Wills (Eds) *The Politics of Information: The electronic mediation of social change* (pp. 7–11). Alt-X Press. Online at http://www.altx.com/ebooks/download.cfm/infopol.pdf
Bernstein, J (2005) *Living in the Borderland*. London: Routledge.
Besserman, P & Steger, M (1991) *Crazy Clouds: Zen radicals, rebels and reformers*. Boston: Shambhala.
Bettelheim, B (1982) *Freud and Man's Soul*. New York: Alfred Knopf.
Bion, WR (1992) *Cogitations*. London: Karnac.
Bion, WR (1997) *Taming Wild Thoughts* (F Bion, Ed). London: Karnac Books.
Bion, WR (2000) *Clinical Seminars and Other Works*. London: Karnac.
Bird-David, N (1990) The giving environment. Another perspective on the economic system of hunter-gatherers. *Current Anthropology, 31*, 183–96.
Bird-David, N (1993) Tribal metaphorisation of human-nature relatedness: A comparative analysis. In K Milton (Ed) *Environmentalism: The view from anthropology* (pp. 111–24). London: Routledge.
Bisson, T (1994) Bears discover fire. In KS Robinson (Ed) *Future Primitive:*

The new ecotopias (pp. 17–28). New York: Tor.

Bly, RW (1977) *The Kabir Book: Forty-four versions of the ecstatic poems of Kabir*. Boston: Beacon Press.

Bly, RW (1992) *Iron John*. New York: Vintage Books.

Boniface, MR (2000) Towards an understanding of flow and other positive experience phenomena within outdoor and adventurous activities. *Journal of Adventure Education and Outdoor Learning, 1*(1), 55–68.

Bookchin, M (2005) *The Ecology of Freedom: The emergence and dissolution of hierarchy.* Oakland, CA: KA Press. (Original work published 1982)

Booth, D (1998) *The Environmental Consequences of Growth: Steady-state economics as an alternative to economic decline*. London: Routledge.

Boston Globe (2007, October 7) The Globalist Quiz: Average earnings worldwide. Online at http://www.boston.com/news/world/articles/2007/10/07/average_earnings_worldwide/

Bousquet, M & Wills, K (2002) *The Politics of Information: The electronic mediation of social change*. Alt-X Press. Online at http://www.altx.com/ebooks/download.cfm/infopol.pdf

Bradshaw, GA, Capaldo, T, Lindner, L & Grow, G (2009) Developmental context effects on bicultural posttrauma self repair in chimpanzees. *Developmental Psychology, 45*(5), 1376–88.

Brannon, EM & Terrace, HS (2000) Representation of the numerosities 1–9 by Rhesus Macaques *(Macaca mulatto)*. *Journal of Experimental Psychology: Animal Behaviour Processes, 26*(1), 31–49.

Brook, I (1998) Goethean science as a way to read landscape. *Landscape Research, 23*(1), 51–69.

Brosnan, SF & de Waal, FBM (2003) Monkeys reject unequal pay. *Nature, 425*, 297–9.

Brown, NO (1968) *Life against Death: The psychoanalytic meaning of history*. London: Sphere. (Original work published 1959)

Bruges, J (2009) *The Biochar Debate: Charcoal's potential to reverse climate change and build soil fertility*. Totnes: Green Books.

Buchan, J (2001) *The Three Hostages*. Kelly Bray, Cornwall: House of Stratus. (Original work published 1924)

Buchanan, M (2003) *Small World: Uncovering nature's hidden networks*. London: Phoenix.

Budiansky, S (1997) *The Covenant of the Wild: Why animals chose domestication*. London: Phoenix.

Buhner, SH (2002) *The Lost Language of Plants*. White River Junction, VT: Chelsea Green Publishing.

Buhner, SH (2004) *The Secret Teaching of Plants*. Rochester, VT: Bear & Company.

Burroughs, W (1968) *The Naked Lunch*. London: Corgi. (Original work published 1959)

Buzzell, L & Chalquist, C (Eds) (2009) *Ecotherapy: Healing with nature in mind*. San Francisco: Sierra Club Books.

Cameron, G (1997) *Spiritual Crisis in Early Irish Literature and Later Folk Life*. MSc dissertation, Edinburgh University. Online at http://www.celticshamanism.com/alt_thesis.html#aithed

Castaneda, C (1972) *Journey to Ixtlan.* New York: Simon & Schuster.

Castaneda, C (1987) *The Power of Silence*. New York: Prentice-Hall.

Caswell, K (2007) Hunger on the mountain. *Janus Head, 9*(2), 605–24.
Cavalli-Sforza, LL (2000) *Genes, Peoples and Languages*. London: Allen Lane, The Penguin Press.
Chatwin, B (1990) *What Am I Doing Here?* London: Picador.
Clark, N (2000) 'Botanizing on the asphalt'? The complex life of cosmopolitan bodies. *Body and Society, 6*, 12–33.
Clement, CR (2006) Demand for two classes of traditional agroecological knowledge in modern Amazonia. In DA Posey & MJ Balick (Eds) *Human Impacts on Amazonia: The role of traditional ecological knowledge in conservation and development* (pp. 33–50). New York: Columbia University Press.
Cohen, S (1972) *Folk Devils and Moral Panics*. London: Routledge.
Conner, M (2007) *The use of force and restraint in Wilderness Therapy Treatment Programs: Issues.* Online at http://www.wildernesstherapy.org/Wilderness/ForceRestraint.htm
Cook, FH (1977) *Hua-Yen Buddhism: The Jewel Net of Indra*. University Park, PA: Penn State University Press.
Cooper, N (2001) The state of mind we're in: Social anxiety, governance and the audit society. *Psychoanalytic Studies, 3*(3–4), 349–62.
Coppinger, RP & Smith, CK (1983) The domestication of evolution. *Environmental Conservation, 10*(4), 283–92.
Cox, M & Theilgard, A (1987) *Mutative Metaphors in Psychotherapy: The Aeolian mode*. London: Tavistock.
Cronon, W (1996) The trouble with wilderness: Or, getting back to the wrong nature. *Environmental History, 1*(1), 7–28.
Crowley, A (1972) *Moonchild*. London: Sphere. (Original work published 1929)
Csikszentmihalyi, M (1990) *Flow: The psychology of optimal experience*. New York: Harper & Row.
Currie, CR, Scott, JA, Summerbell, RC & Malloch, D (1999) Fungus-growing ants use antibiotic-producing bacteria to control garden parasites. *Nature, 398*, 701–4.
Damasio, A (1994) *Descartes' Error: Emotion, reason and the human brain*. London: Papermac.
Damasio, A (2000) *The Feeling of What Happens: Body, emotion and the making of consciousness*. London: Heinemann.
Dames, M (2002) *Merlin and Wales: A magician's landscape*. London: Thames & Hudson.
Dangerous Pages (2009) Banned, censored, challenged: Bury My Heart at Wounded Knee. Blog at http://dangerouspages.blogspot.com/2009/06/banned-book-bury-my-heart-at-wounded.html [A number of web sources repeat this story without substantiation, so it is possibly an internet myth; but the details are so specific that it seems likely to be true.]
Davies, JM (2004) Whose bad objects are we anyway? Repetition and our elusive love affair with evil. *Psychoanalytic Dialogues, 14*(6), 711–32.
Davis, M (1998) *Ecology of Fear: Los Angeles and the imagination of disaster*. New York: Metropolitan Books.
Dawkins, R (1989) *The Selfish Gene* (2nd ed). Oxford: Oxford University Press.
Dawkins, R (1993) Gaps in the mind. In P Cavalieri & P Singer (Eds) *The*

Great Ape Project (pp. 80–7). New York: St Martin's Press.
De Landa, M (2000) *A Thousand Years of Nonlinear History*. New York: Swerve Editions.
Del Tredici, P (2006) Brave new ecology. *Landscape Architecture, February*, 46–52.
Del Tredici, P (2010) *Wild Urban Plants of the Northeast: A field guide*. Ithaca, NY: Comstock Publishing Associates.
Del Tredici, P, Broder, L, Francis, K, Pierce-McManamon, A & Lomarow, S (2010) *E*vue: Emergent Vegetation of the Urban Ecosystem.* Website. Online at http://www.gsd.harvard.edu/loeb_library/information_systems/projects/E_vue/
Derrida, J (1998) *Of Grammatology* (G Spivak, Trans). Baltimore, MD: Johns Hopkins University Press.
De Waal, FBM & Brosnan, SF (2006) Simple and complex reciprocity in primates. In PM Kappeler & CP van Schaik (Eds) *Cooperation in Primates and Humans: Mechanisms and evolution* (pp. 85–105). Berlin: Springer.
Diamond, J (2002) Evolution, consequences and future of plant and animal domestication. *Nature, 418*, 700–7.
Diehl, ERM (2009) Gardens that heal. In L Buzzell & C Chalquist (Eds) *Ecotherapy: Healing with nature in mind* (pp. 166–73). San Francisco: Sierra Club Books.
Dixon, N (1981) *Preconscious Processing*. Chichester: John Wiley and Sons.
Dorko, BL (nd) *Without volition: The presence and purpose of ideomotor movement.* Online at: http://www.barrettdorko.com/articles/ideomotor.htm
Douglas, M (1970) *Purity and Danger: An analysis of concepts of pollution and taboo*. Harmondsworth: Penguin.
Douglas, M (1973) *Natural Symbols.* New York: Vintage.
Downes, L (2009) *The Laws of Disruption: Harnessing the new forces that govern life and business in the digital age*. New York: Basic Books.
Draper, RJ, Gerber, GJ & Layng, EM (1990) Defining the role of pet animals in psychotherapy. *Psychiatric Journal of the University of Ottawa, 15*(3), 169–72.
Dunn, JR (1999) At home in the suburbs. *PERC Reports, 17*(4), 2–4.
Dunsany, Lord (1982) *The King of Elfland's Daughter*. London: Unwin. (Original work published 1924)
Eisenberg, E (1998) *The Ecology of Eden: Humans, nature and human nature*. London: Picador.
Eisler, R (1996) *Sacred Pleasure: Sex, myth, and the politics of the body. New paths to power and love*. Shaftesbury, Dorset: Element.
Eliot, TS (1932) *Sweeney Agonistes*. London: Faber & Faber.
Epstein, RS & Simon, RI (1990) The exploitation index: An early warning indicator of boundary violations in psychotherapy. *Bulletin of the Menninger Clinic, 54*, 450–65.
Feng, G-F & English, J (1972) *Tao Te Ching*. Aldershot: Wildwood House.
Ferenczi, S (1999a) The principle of relaxation and neocatharsis. In J Barossa (Ed) *Selected Writings of Sandor Ferenczi* (pp. 275–92). London: Penguin. (Original work published 1929)
Ferenczi, S (1999b) Confusion of tongues between adults and the child (the language of tenderness and of passion). In J Barossa (Ed), *Selected*

Writings of Sandor Ferenczi (pp. 293–303). London: Penguin. (Original work published 1933)

Fisher, A (2002) *Radical Ecopsychology: Psychology in the service of life*. Albany, NY: State University of New York Press.

Fortune, C (2002) *The Sandor Ferenczi–Georg Groddeck Correspondence, 1921–1933*. London: Open Gate Press.

Foster, S & Little, M (1988) *The Book of the Vision Quest*. New York: Prentice Hall.

Foster, S & Little, M (1989) *The Roaring of the Sacred River*. New York: Prentice Hall.

Foucault, M (1979) *Michel Foucault: Power, truth, strategy* (M Morris & P Patton, Eds). Sydney: Feral Publications.

Frayssinet, F (2007, May 23) *Indigenous Resistance Movement Defends Traditional Beliefs*. Online at http://ipsnews.net/news.asp?idnews=37862

Freud, E & Meng, H (Eds) (1963) *Psychoanalysis and Faith: The letters of Sigmund Freud and Oskar Pfister*. London: Chatto & Windus.

Freud, S (1900) *The Interpretation of Dreams.* Standard Edition Vols IV & V (2nd ed). London: Hogarth Press (1953).

Freud, S (1908) *Creative Writers and Day-Dreaming*. Standard Edition Vol IX (pp. 141–54). London: Hogarth Press (1959).

Freud, S (1910) On 'Wild' Psychoanalysis. In *Wild Analysis* (A Bance, Trans, with an introduction by A Phillips, pp. 1–9). London: Penguin (2002).

Freud, S (1912) *Recommendations to Physicians Practising Psycho-Analysis*. Standard Edition Vol XII (pp. 109–20). London: Hogarth Press (1958).

Freud, S (1913) On Beginning the Treatment *(Further Recommendations on the Technique of Psycho-Analysis, I)*. Standard Edition Vol XII (pp. 121–44). London: Hogarth Press (1958).

Freud, S (1914) Remembering, Repeating and Working Through *(Further Recommendations on the Technique of Psycho-Analysis, II)*. Standard Edition Vol XII (pp. 145–56). London: Hogarth Press (1958).

Freud, S (1915a) *The Unconscious*. Standard Edition Vol XIV (pp. 159–215). London: Hogarth Press (1957).

Freud, S (1915b) Observations on Transference-Love *(Further Recommendations on the Technique of Psycho-Analysis, III)*. Standard Edition Vol XII (pp. 157–71). London: Hogarth Press (1959).

Freud, S (1916–17) *Introductory Lectures on Psycho-analysis*. Standard Edition Vol XV (pp. 1–440). London: Hogarth Press (1963).

Freud, S (1917) Letter from Sigmund Freud to Georg Groddeck, June 5, 1917. In EL Freud (Ed) *Letters of Sigmund Freud 1873–1939* (pp. 316–18). London: Hogarth Press (1961).

Freud, S (1919) *The Uncanny.* Standard Edition Vol XVII (pp. 217–56). London: Hogarth Press (1955).

Freud, S (1920) *Beyond the Pleasure Principle*. Standard Edition Vol XVIII (pp. 1–64). London: Hogarth Press (1955).

Freud, S (1923) *The Ego and the Id*. Standard Edition Vol XIX (pp. 1–66). London: Hogarth Press (1955).

Freud, S (1926) *The Question of Lay Analysis*. Standard Edition Vol XX (pp. 177–258). London: Hogarth Press (1959).

Freud, S (1927) *The Future of an Illusion*. Standard Edition Vol XXI (pp. 1–

56). London: Hogarth Press (1961).
Freud, S (1933) *New Introductory Lectures on Psycho-Analysis*. Standard Edition Vol XXII (pp. 1–182). London: Hogarth Press (1964).
Freud, S & Jung, CG (1974) *The Freud/Jung Letters: The correspondence between Sigmund Freud and CG Jung* (W McGuire, Ed). Princeton, NJ: Princeton University Press.
Friese, G, Hendee, JC & Kinziger, M (1998) The wilderness experience program industry in the United States: Characteristics and dynamics. *Journal of Experiential Education, 21*(1), 40–5.
Frohoff, T (1998) Beyond species. In L Hogan, D Metzger & B Peterson (Eds) *Intimate Nature: The bond between women and animals* (pp. 78–84). New York: Fawcett Columbine.
Fromm, E (1973) *The Crisis of Psychoanalysis*. Harmondsworth: Penguin.
Fromm, E (1980) *The Fear of Freedom*. London: Routledge & Kegan Paul.
Frost, R (1995) *Collected Poems, Prose and Plays* (M Richardson & R Poirier, Eds). New York: Library of America.
Fry, DP (2007) *Beyond War: The human potential for peace.* New York: Oxford Press.
Fuchs, T (2002) Mind, meaning, and the brain. *Philosophy, Psychiatry, & Psychology, 9*(3), 261–4.
Gass, MA (Ed) (1993) *Adventure Therapy: Therapeutic applications of adventure programming*. Dubuque, IA: Kendall/Hunt.
Gatenby, D & Breazeal, C (2005) *Robot Birds: Enabling socializing opportunities through human-robot interaction.* Online at http://gray10b.com/sinbrew/BirdRobotPaper03.pdf
Gay, P (1995) *Freud: A life for our time*. London: Papermac.
Geertz, C (1973) Thick description: Toward an interpretive theory of culture. In *The Interpretation of Cultures: Selected essays* (pp. 3–30). New York: Basic Books.
Geertz, C (1983) *Local Knowledge: Further essays in interpretive anthropology*. New York: Basic Books.
Gerdes, HH & Negrão Carvalho, R (2008) Intercellular transfer mediated by tunneling nanotubes. *Current Opinion in Cell Biology, 20*, 470–5.
Gibson, EJ (1969) *Principles of Perceptual Learning and Development*. New York: Appleton-Century-Crofts.
Gibson, JJ (1979) *The Ecological Approach to Visual Perception*. Boston: Houghton Mifflin.
Gibson, JJ (1982) *Reasons for Realism: Selected essays*. Hillsdale, NJ: Lawrence Erlbaum.
Gibson, W (2010) *Zero History*. London: Viking.
Gill, N & Anderson, K (2005) Improvement in the inland: Culture and nature in the Australian rangelands. *Australian Humanities Review, 34*. Online at http://www.australianhumanitiesreview.org/archive/Issue-Jan-2005/gill.html
Gillis, HL & Ringer, M (1999) Adventure as therapy. In JC Miles & S Priest (Eds) *Adventure Programming* (pp. 29–37). State College, PA: Venture Publishing.
Glass, C (2009) Belts gleaming. *London Review of Books, 31*(11), 15–16.
Glaser, B (2007) Prehistorically modified soils of central Amazonia: A model for sustainable agriculture in the twenty-first century. *Philosophical*

Transactions of the Royal Society B, 362, 187–96.
Glendinning, S (2000) From animal life to city life. *Angelaki: Journal of the Theoretical Humanities, 5*, 19–30.
Goethe, JW (2003) *Faust, Part II, Act V* (AC Kline, Trans). (Original work published 1838) Online at http://www.poetryintranslation.com/PITBR/German/FaustIIActV.htm
Goodrich, PH (2003) *Merlin: A casebook*. London: Routledge.
Grandin, G (2009) Fordlandia: The rise and fall of Henry Ford's forgotten jungle city. New York: Metropolitan.
Gray, J (1993) *Men Are from Mars, Women Are from Venus: A practical guide for improving communication and getting what you want in your relationships*. Shaftesbury, Dorset: Element Books.
Gray, J (2007) Are we born moral? *New York Review of Books, 54*(8), 26–8.
Greenway, R (1995) The wilderness effect and ecopsychology. In T Roszak, ME Gomes & AD Kanner (Eds) *Ecopsychology: Restoring the earth, healing the mind* (pp. 122–35). San Francisco: Sierra Club Books.
Greenway, R (2009) The wilderness experience as therapy: We've been here before. In L Buzzell & C Chalquist (Eds) *Ecotherapy: Healing with nature in mind* (pp. 132–9). San Francisco: Sierra Club Books.
Griffin, S (1984) *Woman and Nature: The roaring inside her*. London: The Women's Press.
Groddeck, G (1977) *The Meaning of Illness* (L Schacht, Ed). London: Maresfield Library.
Grossman, CM & Grossman, S (1967) *The Wild Analyst*. New York: Dell.
Groves, CP (1999) The advantages and disadvantages of being domesticated. *Perspectives in Human Biology, 4*, 1–12.
Guardian (2007, May 21) Gay flamingos adopt abandoned chick. Online at http://www.guardian.co.uk/environment/2007/may/21/conservationandendangeredspecies.climatechange
Gutheil, TG & Gabbard, GO (1993) The concept of boundaries in clinical practice: Theoretical and risk-management dimensions. *American Journal of Psychiatry, 150,* 188–96.
Halpin, M & Ames, M (1980) *The Tsimshian Monkey Masks and Sasquatch*. Vancouver: University of British Columbia Press.
Hamilton, LS (1990) Restoration of degraded tropical forests. In JJ Berger (Ed) *Environmental Restoration: Science and strategies for restoring the earth* (pp. 113–22). Washington, DC: Island Press.
Hannah, B (2005) *The Archetypal Symbolism of Animals*. New York: Chiron Publications.
Hardin, G (1968) The tragedy of the commons. *Science, 162*(3859), 1243–8.
Hardin, G (1998) Extensions of 'the tragedy of the commons'. *Science, 280*(5364), 682–3.
Hardt, M & Negri, A (2006) *Multitude*. London: Penguin.
Harper, S (1995) The way of wilderness. In T Roszak, ME Gomes & AD Kanner (Eds) *Ecopsychology: Restoring the earth, healing the mind* (pp. 183–200). San Francisco: Sierra Club Books.
Harries-Jones, P (1995) *A Recursive Vision: Ecological understanding and Gregory Bateson*. Toronto: University of Toronto Press.
Hazen-Hammond, S (1999) *Spider Woman's Web: Traditional Native Ameri-*

can tales about women's power. New York: Perigee Books.
HD [Hilda Doolittle] (1985) *Tribute to Freud*. Manchester: Carcanet.
Hebner, L & Plyler, ML (2010) *Southern Paiute: A portrait*. Logan, UT: Utah State University Press. Online at http://issuu.com/usupress/docs/southern_paiute
Hecht, SB & Posey, DA (1989) Preliminary results on soil management techniques of the Kayapó Indians. In DA Posey & W Balee (Eds) *Resource Management in Amazonia: Indigenous and folk strategies. Advances in Economic Botany, 7* (pp. 174–88). New York: New York Botanical Garden.
Heckenberger, MJ, Kuikuro, A, Kuikuro, UT, Russell, JC, Schmidt, M, Fausto, C & Franchetto, B (2003) Amazonia 1492: Pristine forest or cultural parkland? *Science, 301*, 1710–14.
Heckenberger, MJ, Russell, JC, Fausto, C, Toney, JR, Schmidt, MJ, Pereira, E, Franchetto, B & Kuikuro, A (2008) Anthropogenic landscapes, and the future of the Amazon. *Science, 321*, 1214–17.
Hemming, J (2006) Romance and reality: The first European vision of Brazilian Indians. In DA Posey & MJ Balick (Eds) *Human Impacts on Amazonia: The role of traditional ecological knowledge in conservation and development* (pp. 5–16). New York: Columbia University Press.
Highpine, G (1992) Attitudes towards Bigfoot in many North American cultures. *The Track Record, 18*. Online at http://www.bigfootencounters.com/legends/highpine.htm
Hill, MO (1997) CG Jung in the heart of darkness. *Spring: Journal of Archetype and Culture, 61*, 25–33.
Hill, MO & Kandemwa, MA (1997) *Twin from Another Tribe: The story of two shamanic healers from Africa and North America*. Wheaton, IL: Quest Books.
Hillman, J (1979) *The Dream and the Underworld.* New York: Harper & Row.
Hillman, J & McLean, M (1997) *Dream Animals*. San Francisco: Chronicle Books.
Hitchcock, RF (1996) Prisoner of the Sás: The Brazil and Portugal years of Anthony Knyvett of Westminster's Journal, 1593–1601. *Portuguese Studies, 12*, 40–54.
Hoban, R (1993) *The Mouse and His Child*. London: Puffin.
Hodder, I (1990) *The Domestication of Europe: Structure and contingency in Neolithic societies*. Oxford: Blackwell.
Hodder, I (1993) The narrative and rhetoric of material culture sequences. *World Archaeology, 25*, 2, 268–82.
Hogan, L (1998) First people. In L Hogan, D Metzger & B Peterson (Eds) *Intimate Nature: The bond between women and animals* (pp. 6–19). New York: Fawcett Columbine.
Hopkins, DR (1983) *Princes and Peasants: Smallpox in history*. Chicago: University of Chicago Press.
Hrdy, SB (2009) *Mothers and Others: The evolutionary origins of mutual understanding*. London: Belknap.
Humphries, C (2010, May 23) This is not a weed. *The Boston Globe*. Online at http://www.boston.com/bostonglobe/ideas/articles/2010/05/23/this_is_not_a_weed/?page=1
Hurtig, J, Chiu, DT & Onfelt, B (2010) Intercellular nanotubes: Insights from

imaging studies and beyond. *Wiley Interdisciplinary Reviews: Nanomedicine and Nanobiotechnology, 2*(3), 260–76.

Husband, T (1980) *The Wild Man: Medieval myth and symbolism*. New York: Metropolitan Museum of Art.

Huxley, A (1954) *The Doors of Perception*. London: Chatto & Windus. Online at http://www.psychedelic-library.org/doors.htm

Huxley, TH (1893) On the hypothesis that animals are automata, and its history. In *Collected Essays, Vol I* (pp. 199–250). London: Macmillan. (Original work published 1874). Online at http://aleph0.clarku.edu/huxley/CE1/AnAuto.html

Irie-Sugimoto, N, Kobayashi, T, Sato, T & Hasegawa, T (2009) Relative quantity judgment by Asian elephants (*Elephas maximus*). *Animal Cognition, 12*, 193–9.

Jackson, DL & Jackson, LL (Eds) (2002) *The Farm as Natural Habitat: Reconnecting food systems with ecosystems*. Washington, DC: Island Press.

Jacoby, M (1986) Getting in touch and touching. In N Schwarz-Salant & M Stein (Eds) *The Body in Analysis* (pp. 109–26). Wilmette, IL: Chiron.

James, W (2003) Does 'consciousness' exist? In *Essays in Radical Empiricism* (pp. 1–20). New York: Dover Publications. (Original work published 1904)

Janik, VM, Sayigh, LS & Wells, RS (2006) Signature whistle shape conveys identity information to bottlenose dolphins. *Proceedings of the National Academy of Sciences, 103*(21), 8293–7.

Janzen, HH (2009) Long-term ecological sites: Musings on the future, as seen (dimly) from the past. *Global Change Biology, 15, 2770–8.*

Johnson, DH (1997) *Groundworks: Narratives of embodiment*. Berkeley, CA: North Atlantic Books.

Johnson, M (1992) *Lore: Capturing traditional environmental knowledge*. Ottawa, Canada: IDRC.

Johnston, SH & Farber, BA (1996) The maintenance of boundaries in psychotherapeutic practice. *Psychotherapy, 33*, 391–402.

Jones, O (2000) (Un)ethical geographies of human–non-human relations: Encounters, collectives and spaces. In C Philo & C Wilbert (Eds) *Animal Spaces, Beastly Places: New geographies of human–animal relations* (pp. 268–91). London: Routledge.

Jorgensen, A & Tylecote, M (2007) Ambivalent landscapes: Wilderness in the urban interstices. *Landscape Research, 32*(4), 443–62.

Jung, CG (1963) *Memories, Dreams, Reflections*. London: Collins and Routledge & Kegan Paul.

Jung, CG (1964) *Man and His Symbols*. New York: Doubleday.

Jung, CG (1966) *Two Essays on Analytical Psychology.* Collected Works Vol 7. Princeton, NJ: Princeton University Press. (Original work published 1917, 1928)

Jung, CG (1969) *The Structure and Dynamics of the Psyche*. Collected Works Vol 8. Princeton, NJ: Princeton University Press. (Original work published 1938)

Jung, CG (1970a) *Woman in Europe*. Collected Works Vol 10 (pp. 113–33). Princeton, NJ: Princeton University Press. (Original work published 1927)

Jung, CG (1970b) *The Complications of American Psychology*. Collected Works Vol 10 (pp. 502–14). Princeton, NJ: Princeton University Press. (Original work published 1930)

Jung, CG (1970c) *Archaic Man*. Collected Works Vol 10 (pp. 50–73). Princeton, NJ: Princeton University Press. (Original work published 1930)

Jung, CG (1970d) *What India Can Teach Us*. Collected Works Vol 10 (pp. 525–30). Princeton, NJ: Princeton University Press. (Original work published 1939)

Jung, CG (1970e) *The Meaning of Psychology for Modern Man*. Collected Works Vol 10 (pp. 134–56). Princeton, NJ: Princeton University Press. (Original work published 1933–1934)

Jung, CG (1971) *Psychological Types*. Collected Works Vol. 6. Princeton, NJ: Princeton University Press. (Original work published 1921)

Jung, CG (1976a) *The Tavistock Lectures: On the theory and practice of analytical psychology*. *Lecture II*. Collected Works Vol. 18 (pp. 36–69). Princeton, NJ: Princeton University Press. (Original work published 1935)

Jung, CG (1976b) *Letters, Vol II*: *1951–1961* (G Adler, Ed). London: Routledge & Kegan Paul.

Jung, CG (1992). *Letters, Vol I: 1906–1950* (G Adler & A Jaffe, Eds) Princeton, NJ: Princeton University Press.

Jung, CG (1998) *Visions: Notes of the seminar given in 1930–1934* (C Douglas, Ed). London: Routledge.

Kaplan, R & Kaplan, S (1989) *Experience of Nature*. New York: Cambridge University Press.

Kaplan, S (1995) The restorative benefits of nature: Towards an integrative framework. *Journal of Environmental Psychology, 16*, 169–82.

Karol, J (2007) Applying a traditional individual psychotherapy model to equine-facilitated psychotherapy (EFP): Theory and method. *Clinical Child Psychology and Psychiatry 12*, 77–91.

Kauffman, SA (1995) *At Home in the Universe: The search for the laws of self-organization and complexity*. Oxford: Oxford University Press.

Kauffman, SA (2000) *Investigations*. Oxford: Oxford University Press.

Keams, G (1992) Grandmother Spider Brings the Sun: A Cherokee story. New York: Rising Moon.

Keeley, L (1996) *War Before Civilization: The myth of the peaceful savage*. Oxford: Oxford University Press.

Kelly, C (2010) One stock and nation. *London Review of Books, 32*(3), 15–16.

Kelly, RL (1995) *The Foraging Spectrum: Diversity in hunter-gatherer lifeways*. Washington, DC: Smithsonian Institution Press.

Kerr, M & Key, D (2010) The ecology of the unconscious. Submitted to the *European Journal of Ecopsychology*.

Key, D (2003) *The Ecology of Adventure*. MSc thesis, Centre for Human Ecology, Edinburgh. unpublished.

Kohanov, L (2001) *The Tao of Equus*. Novato, CA: New World Library.

Koole, SL & Van den Berg, AE (2005) Lost in the wilderness: Terror management, action orientation, and nature evaluation. *Journal of Personality and Social Psychology, 88*(6), 1014–28.

Korten, DC (2007) *The Great Turning: From empire to earth community*. San Francisco: Berrett-Koehler.

Kristeva, J (1982) *Powers of Horror: An essay on abjection*. New York: Columbia University Press.

Kurtz, R (1985) *Hakomi Therapy* (2nd ed). Boulder, CO: Hakomi Institute.

Lafferty, RA (1994) Boomer flats. In KS Robinson (Ed) *Future Primitive: The new ecotopias* (pp. 53–71). New York: Tor. (Boomer Flats first published 1974)

Layton, R (1999) The human evolutionary timescale and the transition between hunting and gathering, and farming. In J Bintliff (Ed) *Structure and Contingency: Evolutionary processes in life and human society* (pp. 102–17). London: Leicester University Press.

Lazarus, AA (1994) How certain boundaries and ethics diminish therapeutic effectiveness. *Ethics and Behavior, 4*(3), 255–61.

LeBlanc, S (2003) *Constant Battles: Why we fight*. New York: St Martin's Griffin.

Le Goff, J (1988) *The Medieval Imagination*. Chicago and London: University of Chicago Press.

Leach, HM (2003) Human domestication reconsidered. *Current Anthropology, 44*(3), 349–60.

Lee, RB & DeVore, I (Eds) (1968) *Man the Hunter*. Hawthorne, NY: Aldine De Gruyter.

Le Guin, UK (1975) *The Dispossessed.* London: Panther.

Le Guin, UK (1988) *Always Coming Home*. London: Grafton Books.

Le Guin, UK (1989) Women/wilderness. In *Dancing at the Edge of the World: Thoughts on words, women, places* (pp. 161–4). London: Gollancz.

Le Guin, UK (1996) The Shobies' story. In *A Fisherman of the Inland Sea* (pp. 75–105). London: Gollancz.

Le Guin, UK (2000) *The Telling*. London: Gollancz.

Lehman, J, Kern, DC, Glaser, B & Woods, WI (2003) *Amazonian Dark Earths: Origins, properties, management*. Dordrecht, Netherlands: Kluwer Academic.

Lessing, D (1981) *Shikasta*. London: Granada.

Levi-Strauss, C (1963) *Structural Anthropology*. New York: Basic Books.

Levi-Strauss, C (1966) *The Savage Mind*. London: Weidenfeld & Nicolson.

Levine, P (1997) *Waking the Tiger: Healing trauma – The innate capacity to transform overwhelming experiences*. Berkeley, CA: North Atlantic Books.

Levinson, BM (1996) *Pet-Oriented Child Psychotherapy* (Revised and updated by GP Mallon). Springfield, IL: Charles C Thomas.

Libet, BJ (1985) Unconscious cerebral initiative and the role of conscious will in voluntary action. *The Behavioral and Brain Sciences, 8*, 529–39.

Libet, BJ (2003) Can conscious experience affect brain activity? *Journal of Consciousness Studies, 10*(12), 24–8.

Linden, S & Grut, J (2002) *The Healing Fields: Working with psychotherapy and nature to rebuild shattered lives*. London: Frances Lincoln.

Lindqvist, S (2008) *Terra Nullius: A journey through no one's land*. London: Granta Books.

Little, M (1990) *Psychotic Anxieties and Containment: A personal record of an analysis with Winnicott*. Northvale, NJ: Jason Aronson.

Lohser, B & Newton, PM (1996) *Unorthodox Freud: The view from the couch*. London: Guilford Press.

Lomas, P (1994) *True and False Experience: The human element in psychotherapy.* Piscataway, NJ: Transaction Publishers. (Original work published 1974)

Luniak, M (2004) Synurbization – adaptation of animal wildlife to urban development. In WW Shaw, LK Harris & L Vandruff (Eds) *Proceedings of the 4th International Urban Wildlife Symposium* (pp. 50–5). Tucson, AZ: College of Agriculture and Life Sciences, University of Tucson. Online at http://cals.arizona.edu/pubs/adjunct/snr0704/snr07041f.pdf

Lynch, D (1990) *Wild at Heart* [feature film]. Polygram.

Mabey, R (1993, November 14) Close to the earth. *Independent on Sunday*. Online at http://www.independent.co.uk/

Macfarlane, R (2007) *The Wild Places*. London: Granta Books.

Macy, J (1991) *World as Lover, World as Self*. Berkeley, CA: Parallax Press.

Macy, J (1995) *Mutual Causality in Buddhism and General Systems Theory: The dharma of natural systems*. Columbia, MO: South Asia Books.

Macy, J & Brown, MY (1998) *Coming Back to Life: Practices to reconnect our lives, our world*. Gabriola Island, BC, Canada: New Society.

Mainland, LG (1927) *Secrets of the Zoo*. London: Partridge.

Maiteny, P (2005) Linking(thinking) everyday life to natural systems and resource use. Unit 4 of *LinkingThinking: New perspectives on thinking and learning for sustainability*. Aberfeldy: Worldwide Fund for Nature Scotland. Online at http://www.eauc.org.uk/file_uploads/linkingthinking-302.pdf

Maiteny, P (2008) The importance of psychotherapy as an eco-systemic activity. *The Psychotherapist, 40*, 31–3.

Mallon, GA (1994) Some of our best therapists are dogs. *Child and Youth Care Forum, 23*(2), 89–101.

Mann, CC (2002) The real dirt on rainforest fertility. *Science, 297*, 920–3.

Marcuse, H (1966) *Eros and Civilisation*. Boston: Beacon Press. (Original work published 1955)

Marglin, SA (1990a) Towards the decolonization of the mind. In F Apffel-Marglin & SA Marglin (Eds) *Dominating Knowledge: Development, culture and resistance* (pp. 1–28). Oxford: Clarendon Press.

Marglin, SA (1990b) Losing touch: The cultural conditions of worker accommodation and resistance. In F Apffel-Marglin & SA Marglin (Eds) *Dominating Knowledge: Development, culture and resistance* (pp. 217–82). Oxford: Clarendon Press.

Marquis, JM (1972) An expedient model for behavior therapy. In AA Lazarus (Ed) *Clinical Behavior Therapy* (pp. 41–72). New York: Brunner-Mazel.

Martin, CL (1993) *In the Spirit of the Earth*. Baltimore: Johns Hopkins University Press.

Martinez-Alier, J (1995) Political ecology, distributional conflicts, and economic incommensurability. *New Left Review, 1*(211), 70–88.

Maslow, A (1971) *The Farther Reaches of Human Nature*. New York: Viking.

Mason, H (Trans) (1970) *Gilgamesh: A verse epic*. New York: New American Library.

Masson, J (Ed) (1985) *The Complete Letters of Sigmund Freud to Wilhelm Fliess.* Harvard: Belknap.

Matthiessen, P (1991) *In the Spirit of Crazy Horse*. New York: Viking Penguin.

McClellan, JE & Dorn, H (2006) *Science and Technology in World History*. Baltimore, MD: Johns Hopkins University Press.

Merleau-Ponty, M (1968) *The Visible and the Invisible*. Evanston, IL: Northwestern University Press.

Metzger, D (2009) *Speaking with Elephants*. Online document at http://www.deenametzger.com/animals/animals_long1.html

Metzinger, T (2003) *Being No One: The self-model theory of subjectivity*. Cambridge, MA: MIT Press.

Metzinger, T (2009) *The Ego Tunnel: The science of the mind and the myth of the self*. New York: Basic Books.

Meyer, SM (2006) *The End of the Wild*. Cambridge MA: MIT Press.

Mindell, A (1993) *The Shaman's Body*. San Francisco: Harper San Francisco.

Mindell, A (1995) *Sitting in the Fire: Large group transformation using conflict and diversity*. Portland, OR: Lao Tse Press.

Mindell, A (2003) *Metaskills: The spiritual art of therapy*. Portland, OR: Lao Tse Press.

Minton, A (2009) *Ground Control: Fear and happiness in the 21st-century city.* London: Penguin.

Mooney, J (1996) *Myths of the Cherokee*. Mineola, NY: Dover. (Original work published 1900) Online at http://www.sacred-texts.com/nam/cher/motc/

Naddair, K (1987) *Keltic Folk and Faerie Tales: Their hidden meaning explored*. London: Century Rider.

Naess, A (1995) Self-realization: An ecological approach to being in the world. In AR Drengson & Y Inoue (Eds) *The Deep Ecology Movement: An introductory anthology* (pp. 13–30). Berkeley, CA: North Atlantic Books.

Nashe, R (1967) *Wilderness and the American Mind*. New Haven, CT: Yale University Press.

Neves, E, Barreto, C & McEwan, C (2001) Introduction. In C McEwan, C Barreto & E Neves (Eds) *Unknown Amazon* (pp. 14–19). London: British Museum Press.

Newman, M (2010, January 28) Stark facts exposed about anti-regulation therapist. *Times Higher Education Supplement*. Online together with readers' responses at http://www.timeshighereducation.co.uk/story.asp?storycode=410179

Nørretranders, T (1999) *The User Illusion: Cutting consciousness down to size*. London: Penguin.

O'Brien, F (1967) *At Swim-Two-Birds*. London: Penguin. (Original work published 1939)

O'Connor, TP (1997) Working at relationships: Another look at animal domestication. *Antiquity, 71,* 149–56.

Ó Cuiv, B (Ed) (1952–1954) The Romance of Mis and Dubh Ruis. *Celtica, 2,* 325–33.

Odling-Smee FJ, Laland KN & Feldman MW (2003) Niche construction: The neglected process in evolution. *Monographs in Population Biology, 37*. Princeton, NJ: Princeton University Press.

Ogden, P, Minton, K & Pain, C (2006) *Trauma and the Body: A sensorimotor approach to psychotherapy*. New York: WW Norton.

O'Keeffe, JG (Ed & Trans) (1904) *Buile Shuibhne (The Frenzy of Suibhne)*. London: Irish Texts Society. Online at http://www.ucc.ie/celt/published/T302018/index.html

Oliver, M (1992) *New and Selected Poems*. Boston: Beacon Press.

Ortega y Gasset, J (1995) *Meditations on Hunting*. Belgrade, MT: Wilderness Adventures Press. (Original work published 1943)

Osterman, H (1927) *The Alaskan Eskimos as Described in the Posthumous Notes of Dr Knud Rasmussen. The report of the fifth Thule expedition 1921–4, X*(3). Copenhagen: Nordisk Verlag.

Panter-Brick, C, Layton, RH & Rowley-Conwy, P (2001) *Hunter-Gatherers: An inter-disciplinary perspective*. Cambridge: Cambridge University Press.

Parry, D (1989) *Warriors of the Heart*. Cooperstown, NY: Sunstone Publications.

Parry, JJ (Trans) (2008) *Vita Merlini – The Life of Merlin by Geoffrey of Monmouth*. Charleston, SC: Forgotten Books. (Original work published 1925) Online at http://www.forgottenbooks.org/info/9781605064833

PBS (2006) *Chimpanzees: An unnatural history*. Blog comments. http://www.pbs.org/wnet/nature/episodes/chimpanzees-an-unnatural-history/introduction/2493/#comments

Peerbolte, ML (2003) Parapsychology and psychoanalysis. In N Totton (Ed) *Psychoanalysis and the Paranormal: Lands of darkness* (pp. 47–72). London: Karnac.

Perls, F, Hefferline, RF & Goodman, P (1973) *Gestalt Therapy: Excitement and growth in the human personality*. Harmondsworth: Penguin. (Original work published 1951)

Petersen, JB, Neves, E & Heckenberger, MJ (2001) Gift from the past: Terra preta and prehistoric Amerindian occupation in Amazonia. In C McEwan, C Barreto & E Neves (Eds) *Unknown Amazon* (pp. 86–105). London: British Museum Press.

Pew Commission on Industrial Farm Animal Production (2008) *Putting Meat on the Table: Industrial farm animal production in America*. The Johns Hopkins Bloomberg School of Public Health. Online at http://www.ncifap.org/reports/

Pfister, SF (2009) *The Big Book about Nothing: If not now ... when?* Tucson, AZ: Wheatmark, Inc.

Phillip, A (1988) *The Voyage of Governor Phillip to Botany Bay*. Facsimile Edition. Melbourne: Hutchinson. (Original work published 1789)

Phillips, A (2002) Introduction. In S Freud, *Wild Analysis* (A Bance, Trans, pp. vii–xxv). London: Penguin.

Philo, C (1995) Animals, geography and the city: Notes on inclusions and exclusions. *Environment and Planning D: Society and Space, 13*(6), 655–81.

Philo, C, & Wilbert, C (2000) Animals spaces, beastly places: An introduction. In C Philo & C Wilbert (Eds) *Animal Spaces, Beastly Places: New geographies of human-animal relations* (pp. 1–34). London: Routledge.

Piers, C (2007) Emergence: When a difference in degree becomes a difference in kind. In C Piers, JP Muller & J Brent (Eds), *Self-Organizing Complexity in Psychological Systems* (pp. 83–110). Lanham, MD: Jason Aronson.

Piers, C, Muller, JP & Brent, J (Eds) (2007) *Self-Organizing Complexity in Psychological Systems*. Lanham, MD: Jason Aronson.

Pieterse, J (1992) *White on Black: Images of Africa and Blacks in Western popular culture*. London: Yale.

Pinkola Estes, C (1992) *Women who Run with the Wolves: Contacting the power of the wild woman*. London: Rider.

Planning Pool (2009). *In New York City: Abandoned elevated rail becomes a new urban park*. Online at http://planningpool.com/2009/07/land-use/in-new-york-city-abandoned-elevated-rail-becomes-a-new-urban-park/

Plenderleith, K (1999) Traditional agriculture and soil management. In D Posey (Ed) *Cultural and Spiritual Values of Biodiversity* (pp. 285–323). London: Intermediate Technology Publications.

Plotnik, JM, de Waal, FBM & Reiss, D (2006) Self-recognition in an Asian elephant. *Proceedings of the National Academy of Sciences, 103*(45), 17053–7.

Pollan, M (2003) *Second Nature: A gardener's education*. New York: Grove Press.

Polster, E & Polster, M (1974) *Gestalt Therapy Integrated: Contours of theory and practice*. New York: Vintage.

Popper, K (1974) *The Poverty of Historicism*. London: Routledge & Kegan Paul.

Posey, DA (2002) *Kayapó Ethnoecology and Culture* (K Plenderleith, Ed). London: Routledge.

Postle, D (2007) *Regulating the Psychological Therapies: From taxonomy to taxidermy*. Ross-on-Wye: PCCS Books.

Powell, S (1999) *Almost a Whisper: A holistic approach to working with your horse*. Loveland, CO: Alpine Publications.

Power, S (2008) The Democrats and national security. *New York Review of Books, 55*(15), 66–72.

Pratt, C (2007) *The Encyclopaedia of Shamanism, Vol I*. New York: Rosen Publishing Group.

Prescott, J (1975) Body pleasure and the origins of violence. *Bulletin of Atomic Scientists,* November, pp. 10–20. Online at http://www.scireview.de/prescott/article.html

Price, EO (1999) Behavioral development in animals undergoing domestication. *Applied Animal Behaviour Science, 65*, 245–71.

Prince Constantijn of the Netherlands (2005, December 7) Speech, Amsterdam. Online at http://www.koninklijkhuis.nl/english/News/Speeches_archive/2005/Speech_by_Prince_Constantijn_Amsterdam_7_december_2005.html

Prior, H, Schwarz, A & Güntürkün, O (2008) Mirror-induced behavior in the magpie (*Pica pica*): Evidence of self-recognition. *PLoS Biology, 6*(8), 1642–50.

Project R&R (2006) Billy Jo – the chimpanzee who won everyone's heart – dies February 14, 2006 at Fauna. Interview with Gloria Grow. Online at http://www.releasechimps.org/chimpanzees/their-stories/billy-jo/

Pruetz, JD & Bertolani, P (2007) Savanna chimpanzees, *Pan troglodytes verus*, hunt with tools. *Current Biology, 17*, 412–17.

Quammen, D (1998, October) Planet of weeds. *Harpers Magazine, 297*, 57–69. Online at http://www.harpers.org/archive/1998/10/0059715

Raknes, O (1971) *Wilhelm Reich and Orgonomy*. Baltimore, MD: Pelican Books.

Range, F, Horn, L, Viranyi, Z & Huber, L (2009) The absence of reward induces inequity aversion in dogs. *Proceedings of the National Academic of Science 106*, 340–45.

Rangell, L (1979) Contemporary issues in the theory of therapy. *Journal of the American Psychoanalytic Association, 27S*, 81–112.

Ratcliffe, F (1947) *Flying Fox and Drifting Sand*. Sydney: Angus & Robertson.

Reich, W (1972) *Character Analysis*. New York: Farrar, Straus & Giroux. (Original work published 1933)

Reich, W (1975) *The Mass Psychology of Fascism.* Harmondsworth: Penguin. (Original work published 1946)

Reich, W (1983) *The Function of the Orgasm*. London: Souvenir Press. (Original work published 1942)

Reuters (2008, November 17) Britons think children are 'animals'. Nov 17. Online at http://uk.reuters.com/article/idUKTRE4AG2L220081117

Rheingold, H (2003) *Smart Mobs: The next social revolution*. Jackson, TN: Perseus Books.

Ridley, M (2004) *Nature via Nurture: Genes, experience and what makes us human*. New York: Harper Perennial.

Riebel, L (2001) Consuming the Earth: Eating disorders and ecopsychology. *Journal of Humanistic Psychology, 41*, 38–58.

Roazen, P (1976) *Freud and His Followers*. Harmondsworth: Penguin.

Robinson, KS (1994) Introduction. In KS Robinson (Ed) *Future Primitive: The new ecotopias* (pp. 9–11). New York: Tor.

Rogers, CR (1978) *Carl Rogers on Personal Power: Inner strength and its revolutionary impact*. London: Constable.

Rogers, CR (1980) Some new challenges to the helping professions. In *A Way of Being* (pp. 235–59). Boston: Houghton Mifflin. (Original work published 1973)

Rogers, P (1998) The human heart in conflict with itself. In L Hogan, D Metzger & B Peterson (Eds) *Intimate Nature: The bond between women and animals* (pp. xvii–xxi). New York: Fawcett Columbine.

Rose, DB (1988) Exploring an aboriginal land ethic. *Meanjin, 47*, 378–87.

Rose, DB (1995) *Land Management Issues: Attitudes and perceptions amongst Aboriginal people of Central Australia*. Alice Springs: Central Land Council.

Roszak, T, Gomes, ME & Kanner, AD (Eds) (1996) *Ecopsychology: Restoring the earth, healing the mind*. San Francisco: Sierra Club Books.

Roughgarden, J (2004) *Evolution's Rainbow: Diversity, gender and sexuality in nature and people*. Berkeley, CA: University of California Press.

Rudnytsky, PL (2002) *Reading Psychoanalysis: Freud, Rank, Ferenczi, Groddeck*. Ithaca, NY: Cornell University Press.

Rumi, J (1999) *The Essential Rumi* (C Barks, Trans and Ed). London: Arkana.

Russell, B (1995) *An Outline of Philosophy*. London: Routledge.

Russell, KC & Farnum, J (2004) A concurrent model of the wilderness therapy process. *Journal of Adventure Education & Outdoor Learning, 4*(1), 39–55.

Rust, M-J (2008a) Climate on the couch: Unconscious processes in relation to the environmental crisis. *Psychotherapy and Politics International, 6*(3), 157–70.

Rust, M-J (2008b) Nature hunger: Eating problems and consuming the Earth. *Counselling Psychology Review, 23*(2), 70–8.

Rust, M-J (2009a) The myths by which we live – or die? The psychological dimensions of our environmental crisis. *Transformations*, Spring, pp. 8–14. Online at http://pcsr.org.uk/doc/Transformations_Spring_09_copy_.pdf

Rust, M-J (2009b) Why and how do therapists become ecotherapists? In L Buzzell & C Chalquist (Eds) *Ecotherapy: Healing with nature in mind* (pp. 37–45). San Francisco: Sierra Club Books.

Rust, M-J & Key, D (2007) Ecotherapy: Working with the healing power of wild places. Course flyer. Online at http://www.mjrust.net/downloads/Ecotherapy%20course%20Oct%2007.pdf.

Ryle, G (2002) *The Concept of Mind*. Chicago: University of Chicago Press. (Original work published 1949)

Ryle, G (2009) *Collected Papers: Collected essays 1929–1968, Vol 2*. London: Routledge.

Sabini, M (Ed) (2002) *The Earth Has a Soul: CG Jung's writings on nature, technology and modern life*. Berkeley, CA: North Atlantic Books.

Sachar, L (2000) *Holes*. London: Bloomsbury.

Samuels, A (1993) *The Political Psyche*. London: Routledge.

Sandler, J (1983) Reflections on some relations between psychoanalytic concepts and psychoanalytic practice. *International Journal of Psycho-Analysis, 64*, 35–45.

Sassaman, KE (2004) Complex hunter-gatherers in evolution and history: A North American perspective. *Journal of Archaeological Research, 12*(3), 227–80.

Schacht, L (1977) Introduction. In G Groddeck, *The Meaning of Illness* (L Schacht, Ed, pp. 1–30). London: Karnac.

Schama, S (1995) *Landscape and Memory*. New York: Vintage Books.

Scher, SJ & McNeeley, JA (Eds) (2007) *Farming with Nature: The science and practice of ecoagriculture*. Washington, DC: Island Press.

Schweitzer, PP, Biesele, M, & Hitchcock, RK (Eds) (2000) *Hunters and Gatherers in the Modern World: Conflict, resistance, and self-determination*. Oxford: Berghahn.

Scott, JC (1998) *Seeing like a State: How certain schemes to improve the human condition have failed*. New Haven, CT: Yale University Press.

Scott, JC (2009) Duas cervejas. *London Review of Books, 31*(19), 31–3.

Scull, J (2009) Tailoring nature therapy to the client. In L Buzzell & C Chalquist (Eds) *Ecotherapy: Healing with nature in mind* (pp. 140–8). San Francisco: Sierra Club Books.

Searles, H (1960) *The Non-Human Environment in Normal Development and in Schizophrenia*. New York: International Universities Press.

Segal, H (1988) Silence is the real crime. In HB Levine, D Jacobs & LJ Rubin (Eds) *Psychoanalysis and the Nuclear Threat: Clinical and theoretical studies* (pp. 35–58). Hillsdale, NJ: Analytic Press.

Sewall, L (1999) *Sight and Sensibility: The ecopsychology of perception*. New York: Tarcher/Putnam.

Shamdasani, S (2003) *Jung and the Making of Modern Psychology: The dream of a science*. Cambridge: Cambridge University Press.

Shapiro, S (1995) *Talking with Patients*. Northvale, NJ: Jason Aronson.

Sharaf, M (1984) *Fury on Earth: A biography of Wilhelm Reich*. London: Hutchinson.

Shepard, P (1996) *The Others: How animals made us human*. Washington, DC: Island Press.

Shirky, C (2009) *Here Comes Everybody: How change happens when people come together*. London: Penguin.

Showalter, E (1981) Feminist criticism in the wilderness. *Critical Inquiry, 8*(2), 179–205.

Shrestha, A & Clements, D (Eds) (2004) *New Dimensions in Agroecology*. London: CRC Press.

Shultis, J (1999) The duality of wilderness: Comparing popular and political conceptions of wilderness in New Zealand. *Society & Natural Resources, 12,* 389–404.

Sibley, D (1995) *Geographies of Exclusion: Society and difference in the West*. London: Routledge.

Simmons, IG (1979) *Biogeography: Natural and cultural*. London: Hodder & Stoughton.

Simon, RI (1989) Sexual exploitation of patients: How it begins before it happens. *Psychiatric Annals, 19*, 104–22.

Singer, W (2005) The brain – An orchestra without a conductor. *Max Planck Research, 3*, 15–18. Online at http://www.mpg.de/988983/W004_Culture-Society_014_018.pdf

Slikkerveer, LJ (1999) Ethnoscience, 'tek' and its application to conservation. In D Posey (Ed) *Cultural and Spiritual Values of Biodiversity* (pp. 167–259). London: Intermediate Technology Publications.

Smith, DL (1999) Maintaining boundaries in psychotherapy: A view from evolutionary psychoanalysis. In C Feltham (Ed) *Controversies in Psychotherapy and Counselling* (pp. 132–41). London: Sage.

Smith, M & Davidson, J (2006) 'It makes my skin crawl ...': The embodiment of disgust in phobias of 'Nature'. *Body and Society, 12*, 43–67.

Snyder, G (1990) *The Practice of the Wild.* Washington, DC: Shoemaker & Hoard.

Somé, M (1994) Rights of passage. *Utne Reader, 64*, 67–8.

Soper, K (1995) *What Is Nature?* Oxford: Blackwell.

Sorenson, ER (1997) Sensuality and consciousness V: Emergence of the 'savage savage'. The study of child behavior and human development in cultural isolates. *Anthropology of Consciousness, 8*(1), 1–9.

Sorenson, ER (1998) Preconquest consciousness. In H Wautischer (Ed) *Tribal Epistemologies: Essays in the philosophy of anthropology* (pp. 79–113). Aldershot: Ashgate Publishing. Available online at http://rewild.info/anthropik/vault/sorenson-preconquest/index.html

Sorenson, ER (2006) *Some types of society foster liminal consciousness, others shatter it: The study of child behavior and human development in cultural isolates.* Online document at http://www.learningmethods.com/downloads/pdf/sorenson—liminal.consciousness.pdf

Spector, L, Klein, J, Perry, C & Feinstein, M (2003) Emergence of collective behavior in evolving populations of flying agents. In *Proceedings of the Genetic and Evolutionary Computation Conference (GECCO-2003)* (pp. 61–73). Berlin: Springer-Verlag.

Spiegelman, JM (2003) Developments in the concept of synchronicity in the analytic relationship and in theory. In N Totton (Ed) *Psychoanalysis and the Paranormal: Lands of darkness* (pp. 143–60). London: Karnac.

Spirn, AW (1984) *The Granite Garden: Urban nature and human design*. New York: Basic Books.

Spitz, H (1997) *Nonconscious Movements: From mystical messages to facilitated communication.* Mahwah, NJ: Lawrence Erlbaum.

Spriggs, M (1996) Early agriculture and what went before in Island Melanesia: Continuity or intrusion? In DR Harris (Ed) *The Origins and Spread of Agriculture and Pastoralism in Eurasia* (pp. 524–37). London: UCL Press.

Steckel, RH & Wallis, J (2007) *Stones, Bones, and States: A new approach to the Neolithic revolution*. Available online at http://www.nber.org/~confer/2007/daes07/steckel.pdf

Steeves, HP (2002) The familiar other and feral selves: Life at the human/animal boundary. In ANH Creager & WC Jordan (Eds) *The Animal/Human Boundary: Historical perspectives* (pp. 228–64). Rochester, NY: University of Rochester Press.

Stein, S (1993) *Noah's Garden: Restoring the ecology of our own backyards*. New York: Houghton Mifflin.

Steiner, C (1981) *The Other Side of Power*. New York: Grove Press.

Stern, N (2006) *The Economics of Climate Change: The Stern Review*. Cambridge: Cambridge University Press.

Stevens, B (1977) Body work. In JO Stevens (Ed) *Gestalt Is* (pp. 160–91). New York: Bantam Books.

Straw, D (2000) What animals teach me about forgiveness. *Planet Vermont Quarterly, 8*(4). http://planetvermont.com/pvq/v8n4/animals.html

Stross, C (2006) *Accelerando.* London: Orbit.

Suzuki, R, Buck, JR & Tyack, PL (2006) Information entropy of humpback whale songs. *Journal of the Acoustical Society of America, 119*(3), 1849–66.

Swan, JA (1991) *The Power of Place and Human Environments*. Wheaton, IL: Quest Books.

Syse, KVL (2010) Expert systems, local knowledge and power in Argyll, Scotland. *Landscape Research, 35*(4), 469–84.

Taylor, AH, Hunt, GR, Medina, FS & Gray, RD (*2009)* Do New Caledonian crows solve physical problems through causal reasoning? *Proceedings of the Royal Society, Biological Sciences, 276*(1655), 247–54.

Taylor, FW (1967) *The Principles of Scientific Management*. New York: Norton. (Original work published 1911)

Taylor Parker, S, Mitchell, RW & Boccia, ML (Eds) (2006) *Self-Awareness in Animals and Humans: Developmental perspectives*. Cambridge: Cambridge University Press.

Thompson, S (2008) Out of puff. *London Review of Books*, 19 June, 26–7.

Thoreau, HD (1856, August 30) *Journal entry.* Online at http://www.library.ucsb.edu/thoreau/writings_journals_pdfs/J11f1-f3.pdf

Thoreau, HD (1862) *Walking,* Part II. Online at http://thoreau.eserver.org/walking2.html

Thoreau, HD (1864) The Maine woods: *Ktaadn*, Part 6. Online at http://thoreau.eserver.org/ktaadn06.html

Thorne, BJ (1987) Beyond the core conditions. In W Dryden (Ed) *Key Cases in Psychotherapy* (pp. 48–77). London: Croom Helm.

Totton, N (1998) *The Water in the Glass: Body and mind in psychoanalysis*. London: Rebus Press.

Totton, N (2000) *Psychotherapy and Politics*. London: Sage.

Totton, N (2003a) *Body Psychotherapy: An introduction*. Maidenhead: Open University Press.

Totton, N (2003b) Introduction. In N Totton (Ed) *Psychoanalysis and the Paranormal: Lands of darkness* (pp. 1–14). London: Karnac.

Totton, N (2003c) 'Each single ego': Telepathy and psychoanalysis. In N Totton (Ed) *Psychoanalysis and the Paranormal: Lands of darkness* (pp. 197–208). London: Karnac.

Totton, N (2004) You can't get there from here. In *Press When Illuminated: New and selected poems* (pp. 141–57). Cambridge: Salt Publishing. (Original work published 1984)

Totton, N (2005) Can therapy help make a better future? *Psychotherapy and Politics, 3*(2), 83–95.

Totton, N (2006) A body psychotherapist's approach to touch. In G Galton (Ed) *Touch Papers: Dialogues on touch in the psychoanalytic space* (pp. 145–61). London: Karnac.

Totton, N (2007) Funny you should say that: Paranormality, at the margins and the centre of psychotherapy. *European Journal of Psychotherapy and Counselling, 9*(4), 389–401.

Totton, N (2008) In and out of the mainstream: Therapy in its social and political context. In S Haugh & S Paul (Eds) *The Therapeutic Relationship: Perspectives and themes* (pp. 145–55). Ross-on-Wye: PCCS Books.

Totton, N (2009) Body psychotherapy and social theory. *Body, Movement and Dance in Psychotherapy, 4*(3), 187–200.

Totton, N (2010) Being, having and becoming bodies. *Body, Movement and Dance in Psychotherapy, 5*(1), 21–30.

Totton, N (in press) Not a tame lion: Psychotherapy in a safety-obsessed culture. In L Bondi, D Carr, C Clark & C Clegg (Eds) *Towards Professional Wisdom*. Aldershot: Ashgate.

Tovey, A (2009a) Course journal for Msc in Human Ecology, University of Strathclyde. Unpublished.

Tovey, A (2009b) *Wild Mind: Exploring the experiential interface of Self and wild places, its role in the lives of environmental educators, and its wider relevance to society*. MSc dissertation, Centre for Human Ecology, University of Strathclyde. Unpublished.

Trut, LN (1999) Early canid domestication: The farm-fox experiment. *American Scientist, 87*, 160–169.

Tuan, Y-F (1974) *Topophilia: A study of environmental perception, attitudes, and values*. Englewood Cliffs, NJ: Prentice-Hall.

Turnbull, CM (1976) *Wayward Servants: The two worlds of the African pygmies*. Westport, CT: Greenwood Press.

Turnbull, CM (1980) *The Mountain People*. London: Macmillan.

Turner, JS (2000) *The Extended Organism: The physiology of animal-built structures*. Cambridge, MA: Harvard University Press.

Ullman, M (2003) Dream telepathy: Experimental and clinical findings. In N

Totton (Ed) *Psychoanalysis and the Paranormal: Lands of darkness* (pp. 15–46). London: Karnac.

US Department of Agriculture (2006a) *Poultry slaughter: 2005 annual summary.* Online at http://usda.mannlib.cornell.edu/usda/nass/PoulSlauSu//2000s/2006/PoulSlauSu-02-28-2006.pdf

US Department of Agriculture (2006b) *Livestock slaughter: 2005 summary.* Online at http://usda.mannlib.cornell.edu/usda/nass/LiveSlauSu//2000s/2006/LiveSlauSu-03-06-2006_revision.pdf

Van der Ploeg, JD (1993) Potatoes and knowledge. In M Hobart (Ed) *An Anthropological Critique of Development: The growth of ignorance* (pp. 209–27). London: Routledge.

Vasconcelos, AT, Tiddy, DR, Westby, A & Reilly, PJA, (1990) Detoxification of cassava during gari preparation. *International Journal of Food Science and Technology, 25*(2), 198–203.

Veneris, Y (1990) Modelling the transition from the industrial to the informational revolution. *Environment and Planning A, 22,* 399–416.

Wada, K, Shibata, T, Saito, T, Sakamoto, K & Tanie, K (2005) Psychological and social effects of one-year robot-assisted activity on elderly people at a health service facility for the aged. *Robotics and Automation. Proceedings of the 2005 IEEE International Conference*, pp. 2785–90.

Wadley, G & Martin, A (2000) The origins of agriculture: A biological perspective and a new hypothesis. *Journal of the Australasian College of Nutritional & Environmental Medicine, 19*(1), 3–12.

Walker, A (2005) Everything is a human being. In *Living by the Word* (pp. 139–52). London: Phoenix. (Original work published 1983)

Watts, A (1979) *Tao: The watercourse way*. Harmondsworth: Penguin.

Watts, A (1999) *Buddhism: The religion of no-religion*. North Clarendon, VT: Tuttle Publishing.

Wegner, D (2002) *The Illusion of Conscious Will*. Boston: MIT Press.

Weisman, A (2007) *The World Without Us*. London: Virgin Books.

Wells, ES, Rosen, LW & Walshaw, S (1997) Use of feral cats in psychotherapy. *Anthrozoos, 10*(2/3), 125–30.

West, R (2007) *Out of the Shadow: Ecopsychology, story and encounters with the land.* Charlottesville, VA: University of Virginia Press.

Weston, A (Ed) (1999) *An Invitation to Environmental Philosophy*. Oxford: Oxford University Press.

Whitt, LA (1999) Metaphor and power in indigenous and Western knowledge systems. In DA Posey (Ed) *Cultural and Spiritual Values of Biodiversity* (pp. 69–72). London: Intermediate Technology Publications.

Whitt, LA, Roberts, M, Waerete, N & Grieves, V (2003) Indigenous perspectives. In D Jamieson (Ed) *A Companion to Environmental Philosophy* (pp. 3–20). Oxford: Blackwell.

Wilden, A (1972) *System and Structure*. London: Tavistock.

Wilden, A (1987a) *Man and Woman, War and Peace*. London: Routledge & Kegan Paul.

Wilden, A (1987b) *The Rules Are No Game: The strategy of communication*. London: Routledge & Kegan Paul.

Williams, G (1997) *Internal Landscapes and Foreign Bodies: Eating disorders and other pathologies*. London: Duckworth.

Williams, RJ, Berlow, EL, Dunne, JA, Barabasi, A-L, & Martinez, ND (2002)

Two degrees of separation in complex food webs. *Proceedings of the National Academy of Sciences, 99*(20), 12913–16. Online at: http://www.barabasilab.com/pubs/CCNR-ALB_Publications/200210-01_PNAS-TwoDegrees/200210-01_PNAS-TwoDegrees.pdf

Willis, AJ (1997) The ecosystem: An evolving concept viewed historically. Functional Ecology, *11*(2), 268–71.

Wilson, EO (1990) *Biophilia*. Cambridge, MA: Harvard University Press.

Wilson, PJ (1988) *The Domestication of the Human Species*. New Haven, CT: Yale University Press.

Wilson, PJ (2007) Agriculture or architecture? The beginnings of domestication. In R Cassidy & MH Mullin (Eds) *Where the Wild Things Are Now: Domestication reconsidered* (pp. 101–21). Oxford: Berg.

Winkler, R (2003) *Going Wild: Adventures with birds in the suburban wilderness.* Washington, DC: National Geographic Books.

Wong, D (1997) *Taoism*. Boston: Shambhala.

Worsley, P (1997) *Knowledges: What different peoples make of the world.* London: Profile Books.

Wyckoff, H (Ed) (1976) *Love, Therapy and Politics*. New York: Grove Press.

Wynne, B (1995) May the sheep safely graze? A reflexive view of the expert-lay knowledge divide. In S Lash, B Szerzynzki & B Wynne (Eds) *Risk, Environment and Modernity: Towards a new ecology* (pp. 44–83). London: Sage.

Yamamoto, D (2000) *The Boundaries of the Human in Medieval English Literature*. Oxford: Oxford University Press.

Zur, O (2004) To cross or not to cross: Do boundaries in therapy protect or harm. *Psychotherapy Bulletin, 39*(3), 27–32.

Index

REICHIAN GROWTH WORK

Melting the blocks to life and love

NICK TOTTON &
EM EDMONDSON

978 1 906254 12 4, £12.99

This is an updated second edition of the still sought-after classic. Nick Totton and Em Edmondson set out to convey the essential features of Reichian therapy in concrete and easily understandable language at a time when embodiment and body therapy is enjoying renewed recognition and interest. This edition contains new material on the concepts of *attachment* and *trauma* and outlines how new discoveries in neuroscience have confirmed many of body psychotherapists' strongest beliefs.

Maybe capitalism's latest crisis will force people to re-read Reich as the relevant theorist of alternative ways to organise our world. If that thought interests you, start here ...
Andrew Samuels, Professor of Analytical Psychology, University of Essex

CONTENTS